Mother

from Shannus.

Christmas 1987

THE COAST
OF SOUTHERN AFRICA

AUTHOR'S DEDICATION

To my father, James Edward Kench

PHOTOGRAPHER'S DEDICATION

To the arrival of our little Kate, and those dear to me

THE COAST OF SOUTHERN AFRICA

TEXT BY
John Kench

PHOTOGRAPHS BY
Ken Gerhardt

CONSULTANT
Professor George Branch

C. Struik Publishers, Cape Town

AUTHOR'S
ACKNOWLEDGEMENTS

The act of writing this book brought the mysterious world of the seashore and its creatures alive for me as never before. For this adventure of the imagination, I owe a central debt to my consultant on the work, George Branch, Associate Professor of Zoology at the University of Cape Town. One of the most respected researchers in the field of southern African marine biology, Professor Branch has also gained wide renown with his superb general study of the local marine life, *The Living Shores of Southern Africa*. Not only his wisdom and experience but his abiding passion for his subject were irresistibly contagious and a constant source of inspiration. He was never too busy to track down a perplexing detail, to unravel the intricacies of a marine life cycle or food web, or to discuss the larger issues of conservation and the ecological clash of man and nature. Every page of this book bears witness to the integrity of his vision, and I would like to record my sincere gratitude for his help and friendship.

As well as following every stage of the work in detail as it evolved, Professor Branch also directed me to many other informed sources. Many of the scientists concerned are on the staff of the University of Cape Town, primarily in the Department of Zoology. Professor Gideon Louw, for example, provided the fascinating background material on the ecology of the plants and animals of the Namib desert shore. Professor Alec Brown, a leading sandy beach investigator in South Africa, very kindly supplied both general material on sandy beach ecology and his own research papers on the *Bullia* species, as well as checking part of the text. I am also grateful to Professor Roy Siegfried, of the Percy FitzPatrick Institute of African Ornithology, for his analysis, based on personal research, of the thermoregulatory effect of the colour schemes of Xhosa huts, described in the Transkei chapter.

A number of experts in other departments of the University generously lent both time and expertise to the project. I am particularly indebted to Professor Arthur O. Fuller, of the Department of Geology, for explaining the complexities of the geologic evolution of the Cape Peninsula, described in Chapter Three. Eric Axelson, Emeritus Professor of History and the country's leading exponent of Portuguese maritime history, very kindly read the text and corrected many details on the progress of the early Portuguese navigators. John Grindley, Associate Professor at the School of Environmental Studies, supplied material based on his own extensive researches into the threatened ecology of the Knysna estuary. Barrie Gasson, of the Department of Urban and Regional Planning, provided a useful review of the conditions in the False Bay ecology. Many others elucidated specific points, including Rudy van der Elst, of the Oceanographic Research Institute in Durban; Dr Peter Best, who very kindly supplied information and photographs of whales, including the stunning shot of a breaching whale; and Dr Susan Nicolson, entomologist in the UCT Department of Zoology, who identified the beetle *Calosis amabilis*. Dr J.M.

Bremner of the Department of Geology at UCT and marine archaeologist Jim Jobling gave assistance with the maps.

A word must be put in here for a further source, that of the excellent publication of the Wildlife Society of Southern Africa, *African Wildlife*. Three issues in particular were of great value, since they reviewed important matters in a single issue, those devoted to De Hoop Vlei, the fate of the Knysna elephants, and the flora and fauna of Maputaland. To the many well-known scientists whose work formed the basis for these articles I would like to record my appreciation.

The form of the book as it emerged was the responsibility of the team of editors and designers with whom it has been my pleasure and privilege to work at Struik Publishers. I would particularly like to single out the contribution of editor Leni Martin. Her work in both shaping and polishing the text was a model of creative editing at its best. Her enthusiasm and dedication to the task were shared by designer Walther Votteler, responsible for a lucid balance of text and pictures throughout, while the fine maps and drawings of artist Anne Westoby give an appropriate finishing touch to the book. Pieter Struik, Executive Director, carried the project through an efficient and streamlined production process. I would also like to record my thanks to Peter Borchert, Editorial Director of Struik Publishers, who first suggested the idea for the book, for many helpful suggestions and for continued interest and support.

Finally, I would like to add a very large thank you to my wife, Ekin, and my children, Paul and Nicola, who helped to keep me cheerfully afloat through a highly aquatic year.
JOHN KENCH, CAPE TOWN 1984

PHOTOGRAPHER'S
ACKNOWLEDGEMENTS

A number of people have helped me both to gain access to places I wanted to photograph and in giving freely of information and advice. I would like to thank the Secretary for the Interior, KwaZulu Government Services; Professor Arthur Dye of the University of Transkei; Rudy and Blythe Loutit, and the staff of the Department of Agriculture and Nature Conservation of South-West Africa; Gwillym and Kathy Rees for making Ichaboe possible; Dr J. Vincent and the friendly staff of the Natal Parks Board; Commander D.J. Visser of the South African Navy in Simon's Town; Gerald Wright of the Cape Point Nature Reserve; Doug, Sue and their friends for introducing me to the Wild Coast, and Ian and Lynn for their luxurious hospitality at Mngazi; and Jack and Vossie of the Knysna Oyster Company. I am particularly indebted to Professor Alfredo Guillet for his inspiration and company, to old friends and new ones made along the way, and to Gavin, whose companionship and enthusiasm were so encouraging. Finally, my sincere thanks go to Professor George Branch, who behind the scenes made it all possible.
KEN GERHARDT, CAPE TOWN 1984

1. (Opposite title page) *In a relatively tranquil mood, the incoming tide laps the beaches of Dassen Island, off the west coast.* 2. (Overleaf) *A glimpse of the elemental power of a south Atlantic gale as it drives six-metre waves over 'Darwin's Rocks' in the Cape Peninsula.*
3. (Page 8) *On the beach near Swakopmund, two pelicans gaze towards the cold, fish-laden waters of the Benguela Current.*

CONTENTS

INTRODUCTION
COAST OF MANY LEGENDS

The first recorded exploration of the southern African coast took place over two and a half thousand years ago. In about 600 BC the Egyptian pharoah Neco sent a crew of Phoenicians, the finest sailors in the ancient world, to circumnavigate the landmass of 'Libya', then believed to be no more than a large island.

Their voyage was described by Herodotus, the 'father of history', who related how they sailed south from the Red Sea into the 'Southern Ocean', today's Indian Ocean. With the onset of autumn, they put ashore to sow a patch of land with grain, waiting to gather the harvest before taking to sea again the following year. Borne along by the powerful winds and currents that sweep this long, hot shore, they must have seen many marvels. One phenomenon in particular amazed them. As they turned with the coast south and then west, the sun appeared to desert its usual place in the heavens and swing around to the north, 'on their right hand'. After two years they reached the 'Pillars of Heracles', the Straits of Gibraltar, and entered the Mediterranean, arriving back in Egypt in the third year of their voyage. There they told their story, which to some, including Herodotus, appeared somewhat tall. The shift in the sun's position particularly aroused the historian's scepticism, and although others may have believed it, he remained unconvinced. Ironically, this single detail, impossible to predict for those crossing the equator for the first time, provides the strongest evidence in support of the Phoenicians' claim.

Thus was born the first legend on a coast of many legends. Since the days of Neco's expedition many others have braved the coast of 'Libya', driven by a variety of motives. Like the Phoenicians, they found that this was far from being an island. It was a vast and mysterious 'dark continent', inhabited by strange people, teeming with wild animals, and bounded by a coastline of surpassing grandeur. But if magnificent, this coast could also be treacherous, and nowhere more so than in its southern reaches. From the 'Skeleton Coast' to the 'Cape of Storms' and to the 'Wild Coast', these are among the most dangerous waters in the world. Their mood can change with little warning from mirrored tranquillity to elemental fury, as many have learned to their cost. Upwards of three thousand ships have foundered here, from early Portuguese vessels such as *São Bento* and *Nossa Senhora dos Milagros*, to famous nineteenth-century ones such as *Arniston* and *Birkenhead*. Nor are modern ships immune from the wrath of the southern seas, as is witnessed by the fate of the liner *Waratah*, lost without trace off the south-east coast in 1909, and that of the 93 000-tonne tanker *Malmöhus*, whose bows were swept away by huge waves in 1966.

The hazards of exploration were followed by the long toil of settlement. From the advent of the Dutch East India Company in the mid-Seventeenth Century, the rich coastal land was cleared and tilled. Towns and villages grew up in sheltered bays, beside estuaries, on the banks of lagoons and coastal rivers. The gifts of sea and shore were gathered, from fish and shellfish to seabirds' eggs, from guano to sealskins and whalebone. The mineral wealth of the coast, of gold and diamonds, brought many thousands of prospectors in the late Nineteenth Century, and a new kind of community appeared in places such as Kolmanskop, on the Namib coast, and Millwood, deep in the Knysna forest. In the present century, with rapid population growth, cities such as Cape Town and Durban expanded to provide harbour facilities for the increased agricultural and industrial produce of the hinterland.

Notwithstanding these developments, the works of man remain largely dwarfed by those of nature. The southern coastline is the setting for an astounding variety of plants and animals in many different habitats, such as the windswept dunes of the Namib, the underwater forests of kelp along the Cape west coast, the dense forests of Knysna and Tsitsikamma, the mangrove forests and swamps of Natal, and the richly coloured but highly competitive environment of the coral reefs of Maputaland. In the offshore waters are many islands, the home of tightly packed colonies of seabirds and seals, while the shore itself is dotted with lakes and lagoons. These range from Langebaan and De Hoop Vlei to the subtropical Lake St Lucia and the complex of lakes at Kosi Bay. Each is vastly different from the next, and inhabited by a myriad animals large and small, from the tiny tenebrionid beetles of the Namib to the three metre-long leatherback turtle of subtropical waters, from mussels and whelks to whales, from fiddler crabs to fish eagles, from sea-slugs to that awesome ruler of the sea, the shark.

The distribution of all these species is influenced by many factors. Among the most important are the currents, of which two dominate the southern African shores. On the west coast is the cold Benguela Current, which arises in the south as part of a huge stream of water circulating anti-clockwise around the south Atlantic and bringing cold water up the coast. Its counterpart on the east coast is the warm Agulhas stream, one of the world's fastest and most powerful currents. Part of the anti-clockwise gyre of the Indian Ocean, it derives from the Mozambique Current further north. It descends from north to south, a great ocean river flowing down the east coast and then veering away in the south to travel eastward and rejoin the circulation around the Indian Ocean. Whereas the Benguela carries a memory of the icy south in its chill waters, the Agulhas brings warm-water conditions, together with many subtropical species, into southern African waters. Along the south coast it loses momentum, eventually encountering cold water from the West Wind Drift south of the Cape Peninsula, a collision responsible for the often turbulent conditions in this region.

The currents and the waves have a direct physical effect on the shoreline, constantly adding or removing sand from the beaches, carving out bays or building up promontories. In exposed areas such as that of the Namib shore, the Benguela Current shifts millions of tonnes of sand annually along hundreds of kilometres. The life cycles of many marine species are synchronized with the cycle of the currents. Animals such as the turtles depend on the gyre of the Indian Ocean to bring them back to their nesting grounds, and larval forms of intertidal species are distributed to new areas of settlement. In particular, the Benguela Current hosts highly important stocks of fish and seafood which owe their existence to a phenomenon known to scientists as 'upwelling'.

Upwelling is found in other parts of the world, but nowhere on the scale experienced on the west coast of southern Africa. Decaying animal and plant life in the Atlantic Ocean sinks to the bottom of the sea and there accumulates in great concentration. The process of decay yields very large quantities of organic nutrients, and a number of physical forces then act upon this rich potential food source. The power of the Benguela Current itself distributes the nutrients northwards along the coast from the Cape to Namibia and beyond. Equally important are the strong prevailing south-easterly winds which cut obliquely across the coast on their way to the north Atlantic. Coupled with these is the effect of the 'Coriolis force', the turning moment of the earth as it exerts a tug on the sea.

Between them, these forces have the effect of pushing the coastal surface water offshore. As this happens, the heavily nutrient-rich waters from below are 'upwelled', that is, drawn upward to the surface. When the concentrated nutrients come within reach of the sun's rays in the

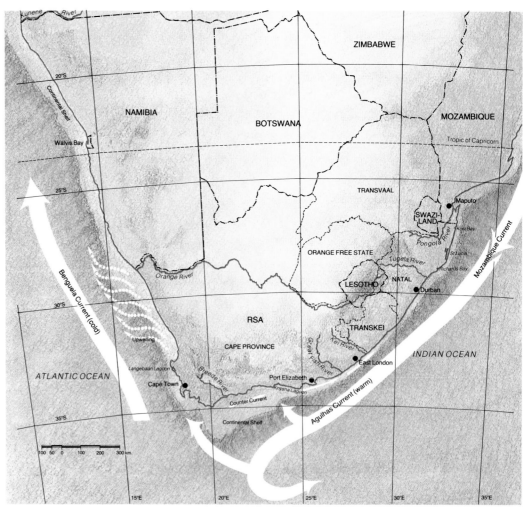

euphotic zone, or upper 'skin' of the sea, vast quantities of phytoplankton, minute floating plant life, make use of it and breed prolifically. In turn, the phytoplankton supports zooplankton, the floating animal forms which, like their plant counterparts, come in an almost infinite variety of microscopic shapes and sizes, and include the larvae of many larger animals, drifting at this stage of their lives with the current. Among the earliest forms of life to evolve, the plankton multiply in mind-boggling quantities, despite their small size. Indeed, it has been estimated that together the phytoplankton and zooplankton make up about 90 per cent of all plant and animal life on earth!

The major food source of the sea, plankton is the foundation of the great food web which embraces all animals, from the deep sea to the intertidal zone, from sandy beaches to rocky shores, estuaries and lagoons, and includes many of the animals on shore as well. On the west coast, planktonic 'blooms' generated by upwelling support enormous shoals of fish, of sardines and pilchards, as well as large beds of mussels which form the main food of rock lobsters (popularly known as 'crayfish'). All these in turn are the basis of the country's fishing industry.

There are many fishing towns and villages scattered around the coast, but the main centres are on the west, in the swarming harbours of St Helena Bay and Saldanha Bay, and at Walvis Bay, a South African enclave in the long coast of Namibia. Between them, these fisheries net some R50 million in fish every year, the rock lobster catch alone being worth about R20 million.

Man is thus a part, if indirectly, of the food web of the ocean, one of its many beneficiaries. Like everything else in nature, this is not a static relationship, but is constantly changing and evolving, growing and dying. It is as old as the life of man on the shore, but its recorded beginning on the coast of southern Africa is signalled by the arrival of the first Portuguese navigators, five hundred years ago.

A Portuguese poet once wrote of his countrymen that their own small country was their cradle, but the whole world was their grave. The initial inspiration for their startling expansion was that of Prince Henry the Navigator, in the mid-Fifteenth Century. While he had no idea how to navigate a ship himself, Henry was convinced of the necessity of it in others. His one over-riding idea was to find a sea route around Africa to the riches of the

Orient which had long been known to the men of Europe. Since the days of Marco Polo, the overland spice trade with the east had made fat profits for princes and merchants. Unhappily, though, the route lay through the lands of the Saracens, the sworn enemies of Christendom. Henry was determined that his people should be the first to find an alternative route. First, however, he had to persuade them to go. To the south lay the great brooding Atlantic, the ominous 'Green Sea of Darkness'. The limits of Portuguese exploration in the 1450s were the laconically named Cabo Nam – 'Cape No' in Portuguese – and Cabo Bojador, on the north African shore opposite the Canary Islands. No man could sail past Bojador, the 'Outreacher', and return alive, Henry's navigators told him. He refused to listen. Instead, he equipped them, stocked their carracks, supplied them with carved stone *padrão* crosses to mark their way, and thrust them forth into the unknown.

Henry himself had been dead for seventeen years before his dream was fulfilled. By then many navigators had set out, each voyage overlapping the one before. In 1484 Diogo Cão reached the coast of today's Namibia. At what is now Cape Cross, north of Swakopmund, he erected a limestone cross on a stark and barren shore peopled only by seals and seabirds. Three years later his achievement was capped by that of a young man named Bartolomeu Dias. Like all the others, he set out from Lisbon in ships which by modern standards were puny. His squadron was composed of his flagship *S. Cristovão*, a second caravel and a smaller supply ship, captained by

his brother, Diogo Dias. They followed the route mapped by Cão to its limit, then sailed on, tacking against the powerful current, until they reached the area of today's Lambert's Bay. From here they swung out to sea in a wide arc, to be caught for five weeks in a storm that drove them to the east. When they eventually made a landfall, near the mouth of the Gouritz River, Dias calculated his bearings and to his joy realized that he had rounded the unseen cape. With India ever in his mind, he pushed on eastwards, to Mossel Bay and then Algoa Bay. Here, however, his weary crew rebelled. Dias cajoled them a few kilometres further, to the mouth of the Keiskamma River, but the renewed threat of mutiny finally persuaded him to turn back.

On 12 March 1488 they erected a last cross, in the name of St Gregory, on the promontory now called Kwaaihoek at the eastern end of Algoa Bay. On the return voyage around the south coast in fair weather they made the acquaintance of the low headland later to be known as Cape Agulhas. Further on they came to a more dramatic landmark, a jagged outcrop of granite and sandstone projecting south into the ocean. Remembering the weather he had encountered in this area on the outward journey, Dias named it 'Cabo Tormentoso', the 'Cape of Storms', although the Portuguese king was later to give it the more heartening title 'Cabo da Boa Esperança', the 'Cape of Good Hope'.

It was a hope soon to be fulfilled. Dias' epic voyage marked the start of a spate of further exploration. Within a few years Vasco da Gama had scratched another line on the parchment map of the world, from

Africa to India. A sea route between Europe and Asia was established, to continue a major highway of trade down to the present – the bulk of the world's crude oil, for example, is carried around these shores.

During the long years of establishing their trade route the Portuguese were not alone. They were watched from the shore, sometimes with curiosity, sometimes hostility, by the local inhabitants. These small, yellow-skinned people, today known collectively as the Khoisan, fell into two main groups: Bushmen, or San, and Hottentots, or Khoikhoi, hunters and herders respectively. They had long lived here, for the remains of their ancestors have been found in many midden and cave sites around the coast – among them the cave at Baboon Point near Elands Bay, Peers Cave in the Cape Peninsula, and the caves of the Robberg Peninsula which contain some of the richest finds of their kind. These peoples' lives were based on a pattern of seasonal migration. They spent the summer months inland when game was plentiful, but wintered in the coastal caves. The deposits of shells, bones, tools and artefacts they left behind sometimes reach amazing depths.

By the time of the first Europeans' arrival, however, their hold on the land had begun to be challenged, and not only by the strangely clothed men in their 'floating houses'. From the north on both the western and the eastern sides of the continent had come large, dark-skinned

4. *At the end of a long day's fishing, the crew relax alongside their small open boat on the beach at Jeffrey's Bay.*

intruders, the Bantu-speaking Nguni peoples. They were a loosely organized society of many clans, and hunting and pastoralism formed the basis of their lives. By the Fifteenth Century they were well settled as far south as the region known today as the Transkei, and it is believed that contact with the Portuguese had an influence on their social and military organization, as well as on their methods of manufacturing weapons.

The major Portuguese bases in southern Africa were in Angola and Mozambique. In general, they shunned the bleaker shores further south, coming ashore only to barter copper and iron trinkets for the Hottentots' cattle and to fill their barrels with fresh water. The lure was the wealth of India, not that of Africa. For a hundred and fifty years the 'dark continent' remained simply an enormous obstacle to the real goal. Only in the mid-Seventeenth Century did permanent settlement begin, stimulated by shifts in the European balance of power. By now the Portuguese overseas empire had collapsed under its own weight, and others were beginning to jostle for position in the sea lanes to the east. Among these were the men of the Dutch East India Company, shipping home the annual fortunes in spices from their possessions in the East Indies. Deteriorating relations between Catholic and Protestant countries, for commercial as well as religious reasons, led to the closure of the port of Lisbon to Dutch shipping which had traditionally stopped there for water and provisions before heading south. Now, perforce, the journey had to be direct from Holland to Batavia. In 1651 the directors of the Company, the Council of Seventeen, mooted a permanent watering and provisioning depôt on the southern African coast. It would operate as a halfway house for the fleet, where the sick could be put ashore to recuperate, where running repairs on ships could be carried out, and where water, meat and crops could be supplied.

A number of possible situations were discussed before the Cape of Good Hope was chosen. It was, of course, already well known to the Dutch. Only the year before the crew of the stranded vessel *Haerlem* had spent several months there before being rescued. Among the rescuers was a young man named Jan van Riebeeck who had taken the opportunity to explore 'Tafel Baay' and its environs. Back in Amsterdam, the Council of Seventeen called him in to ask for an account of the area and its potential for settlement. On the strength of his recommendations, the Cape was accepted as the place for the new outpost, and Van Riebeeck himself

was given the job of setting it up. At the end of 1651 a fleet of three ships under his command set sail from Texel, arriving in Table Bay in April 1652.

The difference between a brief visit and a permanent stay was soon brought home to the new Commander, his family, and the men under him – about a hundred people all told. Barbarically magnificent, the land thronged with game. Van Riebeeck himself described a Zeekoevlei crowded with hippo and trumpeting elephants, its banks browsed by rhino. The mountains behind the tiny settlement were the domain of the massive black-maned Cape lion, the very terror it inspired dooming it to early extinction. In summer a violent south-easterly wind swept through the colony, uprooting the crops. And if the place was hot and windswept in summer, in winter it could be almost as cold as Holland. The winter rains were torrential, tumbling in flood down the valley, and on stormy nights the bay where their ships lay at anchor erupted into a churning maelstrom.

But the 'Hon. Company', as Van Riebeeck referred to his employers, was well satisfied with the work he accomplished in his ten-year 'tour of duty' at the Cape. He settled the people and oversaw the planting of crops in the Company's gardens and the building of a wood and mud-brick fort near the loading jetty at the water's edge. From this starting point the colony quickly spread. After a few years Van Riebeeck released a number of men from the Company's service to work their own land. These 'Free Burgher' farmers were the first of many settlers who were to open up the interior to agriculture, and in doing so increasingly leave the sea behind. The expansion of this land-based Protestant community soon brought it into conflict with the Khoisan, who were either driven out or absorbed into a growing population of imported slaves. By the middle of the Eighteenth Century the colony's borders had expanded along the south coast to Algoa Bay and beyond.

This border was perpetually unsettled, an ongoing headache for a succession of Dutch East India Company governors. The problem was inherited by the British when they took over the Cape at the end of the century, first with the Battle of Muizenberg in 1795, and then, after a break during which the colony was handed back to the Dutch, with the Battle of Blaauwberg in 1806. Numerically a minority, the newcomers set about trying to establish peace, particularly in the east where the Dutch farmers were being increasingly harried by the Xhosa. In the

hope of securing this part of the border, the British government encouraged immigration to the eastern Cape. With the promise of land as their spur, some 4 000 people, subsequently given the collective name of the '1820 Settlers', left Britain to forge a new life in the distant wilderness. Forced to fight for their survival against heavy odds, these pioneers gave rise to a community which played an important rôle in the cultural development of the country.

Throughout the Nineteenth Century more settlements were founded, in the East London area, at the 'Bay of Natal', now Durban, and in South-West Africa, where British and German immigrants jostled for control, the British being centred at Walvis Bay while the German settlers occupied most of the surrounding territory, a vast plateau of grassland rimmed by the coastal desert of the Namib. Once the settlements along the coast had been established, pioneers gradually moved inland. The principal migration took place in the 1830s, when the Dutch community at the Cape, in reaction to the emancipation of their slaves by the British as well as many other grievances, trekked north to found the two Boer republics of the Orange Free State and the Transvaal.

While the past three centuries have seen the establishment of man in the subcontinent, they have also witnessed the steady displacement of wildlife. The larger animals, whether dangerous or not, were the first to go. By the end of the Nineteenth Century the blue antelope, the Cape lion and the quagga were all gone from the western Cape, doomed to extinction. Animals not destroyed, such as the elephant, buffalo and hippo, were forced into retreat. Some found temporary refuge. Many of the elephants, for example, moved into the protection of the forests of Knysna or the dense thorn scrub of Addo. The development of the modern rifle in the Nineteenth Century, however, made even these sanctuaries unsafe. This was the heyday of the hunter, before the decimation he caused deprived him of anything more to hunt. By the turn of the present century, the real danger of a mass extinction of southern African wildlife had become apparent.

In the same period an equally relentless plunder of the sea took place. Sealing and egg-collecting – particularly the eggs of the jackass penguin – took a heavy toll. These depredations paled, however, beside the fate of the whales. Though the Norse and Eskimo peoples had long depended upon whaling, only in the Eighteenth Century did it become a serious large-scale operation. Norwegian, English, and above all, New England whalers ventured around the world in search of their prey. Of their courage there was no doubt. They took their lives in their hands, harpooning the animals by hand from open boats roped together in convoy. They made fortunes for the raw, tough fleet owners back home in Nantucket and Sag Harbour, as the whales supplied many profitable luxuries, from oil for lamps to bone for corsets and umbrellas.

Among the places on which they descended was the west coast of southern Africa. In voyages of up to three years they plundered the cold Atlantic coast, notwithstanding first Dutch and later British attempts to limit their activities. By the mid-Nineteenth Century the whale stocks had fallen to the extent that the balance between effort and returns had begun to tip, and there was a lull. But the respite was short-lived, as technology soon swung the balance back, with the invention of the explosive-tipped mechanical harpoon capable of both killing the whale and securing it with steel barbs at 50 metres. This was followed by the development of factory ships with tryworks for processing the blubber into oil on board. The result was a hunt on an unprecedented scale, one which within a few decades brought several larger species such as the right, the bowhead and the blue whales to the brink of extinction. Two things saved them. One was further advances in technology, which found substitutes for the whale products, and the other was public opinion, slowly awakening to awareness of the slaughter taking place at sea. The last two South African whaling stations, at Donkergat, near Saldanha, and Durban were closed down in 1967 and 1975 respectively. Since then these huge marine mammals have returned in increasing numbers to mate and calve in local waters.

While whale products have become dispensable, fish remain an important source of protein. For many generations local shoals were exploited on a small scale, for the needs of the early community at the Cape were humble. Coloured and Malay fishermen worked from open boats in Table Bay, a cheerful and easy-going community which even managed to build up a small export trade in salted snoek to the Dutch possession

5. *One of the innumerable wrecks which litter the storm-battered northern reaches of Namibia's Skeleton Coast.*

of Mauritius. Rock lobster, too, were abundant, living in dense colonies in knee-deep water near the shore, to be had for the picking. In fact, they were so common they were looked down on, and sold to the poor for less than a penny each.

Steady population increase and the innovations of the Industrial Revolution changed all this. The steam trawler did away with the old open-boat method. The first cannery, with its crude but effective canning machines, was set up in Table Bay. After the discovery of gold and diamonds in the Transvaal and northern Cape, the first 'fish trains' left Cape Town docks for the mining towns. Throughout the upheavals of the Anglo-Boer War and the two World Wars the catch increased steadily. At this time the bulk of the haul was of demersal or bottom-dwelling fish, caught in trawl nets pulled along the sea-bed. These included species such as kabeljou, sole, Cape hake or stockfish, and kingklip. From the 1940s, however, the netting of pelagic fish began to take precedence. The surface-dwelling pelagic fish are caught in purse-seine nets which are supported from the surface by floats, and they include pilchard, anchovy and maasbanker. This harvest of silver was to make the fishermen's fortunes in the years to come. Their main target was the pilchard, *Sardinops ocellata,* which in those days gathered in enormous shoals on the edge of the great plankton blooms of the upwelling. Lurking in deeper waters by day, they surfaced at night to feed, and to be captured in their millions by the purse-seine fishermen of Saldanha Bay and Walvis Bay. With increased investments came a refinement and sophistication of the techniques of pelagic fishing. Factory ships able to work outside the then twelve-mile territorial limit, spotter planes, and advanced depth-sounding and fish-detecting systems all combined to draw a sharp upward line on the graph of fishing company profits.

The result was the wonderful west coast 'fish boom' of the post-war years. For the fishermen, after generations of struggle, it was a time of crazy plenty. Much wild roistering and spending of profits took place. Young men flocked from around the country to join in the scramble, working long nights on heaving decks and spending their few spare hours in breaking up the coastal bars. But if the night before was magnificent in its lurid abandon, the morning after turned out cold and grey. Suddenly, as is the way of boom times, it all came to an end. Having paid for a million drinks, the fisherman's friend, the humble pilchard, gave up the unequal struggle for survival. The

recuperative powers of the shoals had been taxed beyond their limits. Fishing had become over-fishing, and the glorious fish boom turned into an inglorious crash.

The fisheries of the South African west coast were the first to go. From a peak reached in the early 1960s the catches gradually declined to an all-time low of 16 000 tonnes in 1974. The collapse of the Namibian fishing industry occurred later but was more precipitate, as catches slumped by 73 per cent from the 1968 peak of 1,4 million tonnes. Increases in the quotas simply doubled the strain on the fish, and a total ban on pilchard fishing in Namibian waters is now in force. Mesh sizes of the nets have been reduced to capture the smaller anchovy instead, but there are signs that this species, too, is now under stress from over-fishing.

Government decisions on 'maximum sustainable yield', on quotas, legal net sizes, and on the timing of the fishing seasons, are based on a number of factors. These include the size and strength of the fish stocks, the ages of the animals, whether they are juveniles or adults, and the spawning period each year, a question much debated. Research in these areas is carried out by a number of government bodies, the most important being the Sea

Fisheries Research Institute whose task it is to investigate all aspects, physical, chemical and biological, relating to resources of the western and southern coastal waters. A number of other organizations carry out associated studies. Practical research on fishing methods and technology, for example, is the field of the Fisheries Development Corporation, while the Fishing Industry Research Institute concentrates on research pertaining to the processing of fish and other marine products.

An important part in this debate is played by the universities, many of which have courses related to marine matters. The University of Cape Town has departments of Oceanography and Zoology, the latter including courses in Marine Biology. The university's Department of Environmental Studies, too, has as a major concern the protection of marine habitats. The University of Port Elizabeth, Rhodes University, and the University of Natal also include marine studies in their programmes. The South African Museum in Cape Town, the Port Elizabeth Museum and Oceanarium, and the Oceanographic Research Institute in Durban carry out important work, focussing on specific features and problems of their coastal regions. The Durban body, for example, has done pioneer studies on sharks. Other disciplines in South African universities, from history to palaeontology, from geology to meteorology, also have a bearing on the corpus of marine knowledge.

Over the past half century local scientists have built up a dynamic and very complex image of the shore which encompasses not only the marine flora and fauna of today, but their precursors in the past. These in turn are studied in the context of the evolution of the earth itself, from the moment of its separation from the sun as a molten mass approximately 4 600 million years ago. As the newly formed planet cooled, water vapour condensed to form the oceans, and it was in this primordial sea that life began. Single-celled organisms were the first to develop. Dominated by bacteria and blue-green algal mats, the seas gradually filled with living matter. Then, 600 million years ago, at the beginning of the Cambrian period of geological evolution, the bulk of the marine invertebrate classes

6. *Granite and sandstone meet in the precipitate cliffs of Chapman's Peak in the Cape Peninsula.* **7.** *(Overleaf)* '*Hole in the Wall', in the Transkei, is one of the east coast's most spectacular rock formations.*

of life emerged within the short space of about 10 million years. Primitive fishes followed, and from these came the ancestor of the land animals, the lungfish. About 225 million years ago a major event disturbed the seas, the so-called 'Permian extinction', in which, for no clear reason, about half the known marine species, including an entire class, the Trilobita, were wiped out.

By this time many creatures had found their way onto the land. The world they inhabited, however, was very different from that of today. Two hundred million years ago the bulk of the world's land-mass was concentrated in the southern hemisphere as an enormous continent, posthumously named 'Gondwanaland' by scientists. Between 200 and 180 million years ago this continent began to break up and its component parts to separate in a phenomenon known as 'Continental Drift'. Over many millions of years the continents of Africa, Antarctica, South America and Australia were thus formed. Africa, as we know it today, emerged as a high plateau encompassed by mountain ranges separated from the sea by a coastal 'terrace'. This extends into the sea as a 'continental shelf'. Relatively narrow around most of the coastline, it reaches its broadest on the south coast, where the Agulhas Bank extends several hundred kilometres out to sea.

At the time when Gondwanaland was breaking up, the earth was ruled by the great reptiles, the saurischian and ornithischian dinosaurs, fossils of which have been found in many places in southern Africa. By about 75 million years ago, however, these awesome creatures had died out, their demise hastened by the onset of a series of massive ice ages which held the earth in their grip almost down to the present, for the last ice age tailed away a mere 10 000 years ago. These glacial periods had a profound effect on the coastal topography. With the lowering of the temperature, much of the world's water was frozen into the polar ice-caps, resulting in a drop in the sea-level and an extension of the continental coastlines. On the southern African coast, a fall in sea-level of up to 100 metres resulted in a shore 80 kilometres further out than at present. During the glacial periods, the African climate was cool and moist, supporting thick vegetation. In the interglacial periods, however, the temperature on occasion rose above its present level, resulting in a retreat of the ice-caps and a sea-level many metres higher than that of today. Evidence for these changes is found in wave-cut ledges and fossil shells high on coastal cliffs.

With the extinction of the reptiles, a new group of animals became dominant. These were the mammals, warm-blooded creatures able to survive extremes of heat and cold. For the next 70 million years, before the coming of man, they had the earth to themselves. During the glacial period many of them inhabited the broad, fertile coastal strip, and large numbers of their fossil remains have been found at two important west coast sites: at Langebaanweg, a few kilometres inland from Saldanha, and at Arrisdrift, in the northern Cape. The remains range from those of small animals such as the tiny herbivorous pika and the *Prohyrax*, an ancestor of the dassie, to the giant buffalo, with a horn span of up to three metres, the four-tusked, elephant-like *Anancus* and, most impressive of all, the giant cave bear, *Agriotherium africanum*, a Miocene carnivore which stood three metres high and weighed up to a tonne.

With changing circumstances most of these animals died out or evolved new forms. Africa became the hot, dry continent of today, and the Miocene food web crumbled as the lush coastal vegetation receded. In its place, new flora and fauna developed within a variety of habitats along the coast, ranging from the deep sea to rocky shores and sandy beaches, from estuaries and lagoons to kelp beds, coral reefs and sand dunes. Each has its own characteristic species, and its own complex laws of survival.

The least known is the deep sea. If man has conquered much of the land and the shore, the region of the sea below the influence of the sun's rays remains a vast and mysterious realm, though the bathysphere has enabled man to catch a tantalizing glimpse of a strange suite of fishes adapted to living under conditions of extreme pressure on the ocean bed. Their gaping mouths armed with needle-sharp teeth, these fishes are often also equipped with luminous cells which may attract their prey. The mid-ocean region above them is equally lightless and barren, though it is inhabited by giant squids, the prey of sperm whales which dive hundreds of metres to do violent life-and-death battle in the inky darkness.

The upper or euphotic level of the sea, within reach of the sun, is the domain of the plankton and of the bulk of the open-sea species, including the pelagic fishes. Even here, though, the majority tend to live within reach of the continental shelf, where food is most abundant.

It is the inshore waters, however, particularly along the rocky shores, that have the greatest concentration and variety of marine flora and fauna. Here

food is abundant, particularly in the areas of upwelling. On the debit side, however, there are a number of physical stresses, especially in the area between the low- and high-tide marks. The availability of food across this narrow intertidal region, together with the accompanying physical stresses, has resulted in a phenomenon studied closely by marine scientists, that of zonation of the rocky shore species. Though it varies from one sector of the coast to another, in general this zonation is remarkably consistent.

Low down on the shore is the infratidal zone. Here the food supply is at its greatest, either imported from the open sea by the waves or home-grown in the form of thick beds of seaweed. These algae form the basic diet of a number of herbivorous animals, such as winkles, limpets and chitons, which in turn are eaten by the carnivores. But while food is abundant at this level, competition for space is intense. In addition, wave action is fierce, washing away all but the most tenacious, and the animals are exposed to roving carnivores from the open sea.

Above the infratidal zone, the mid-shore area comprises another two zones, the lower Balanoid and upper Balanoid, named after the barnacles which are dominant at this level. It is here that the bulk of intertidal species occurs. The food supply is good, for many algae flourish here and wave action is generally weaker. On the other hand, because of the ebb and flow of the tide, conditions are more variable. Twice a day the animals are either submerged in cold water and subjected to wave action, or exposed to sun and air. These contingencies have drawn from them a remarkable number of structural and behavioural adaptations, allowing for survival under a wide range of conditions.

The upper region of the shore is the Littorina level, named after the small snail which has made a speciality of surviving here. This is a harsh, dry environment, and while it is little affected by tidal or wave action, it offers scant supplies of food and an almost constant exposure to the sun, with a high risk of desiccation.

While these four main zones are found on most of the rocky shores around the southern coastline, there are regional differences between the west, south and east coasts. On the west coast, for example, between the infratidal and the lower Balanoid levels, is a further zone, the Cochlear/Argenvillei zone, dominated by two species of limpet, *Patella cochlear* and *P. argenvillei*, the latter found mainly to the north. On the south coast a similar zone is inhabited predominantly by

Patella cochlear, which occurs here in very high densities. The east coast lacks a corresponding Cochlear zone, but features instead an oyster belt higher on the shore, with colonies of the Natal rock oyster, *Saccostrea cuccullata,* between the upper Balanoid and the Littorina levels. While only one *Littorina* species, the hardy *L. africana,* is found on the west and south coasts, three species of this gastropod occur on the high shore of the east coast.

There is a marked contrast between life on the rocky shores and that on sandy beaches. Relatively few animals are adapted to the latter environment. There is no firm substratum on which sessile, or rock-clinging, animals such as mussels and limpets can hold. For the same reason the algae, the food web's primary producer on rocky shores, are lacking here. Food must therefore be imported to the beach, either in the form of dead or dying animals washed up by the sea, or in the organically rich spume which is left by the filtering action of the sand after the retreat of the tide. A number of animals depend on these sources of nutrition, including particle feeders such as the white mussel and the sea louse. The most characteristic and important of the sandy beach animals, however, are plough snails of the *Bullia* genus, scavengers which live on carrion cast up on the beach. Since this is an unpredictable food source, the plough snail is adapted to spending over 90 per cent of its life buried under the sand on the low shore. When the tide comes in, and food is available, it emerges at the surface of the sand. Turning on its back and spreading out its large, flat foot as a kind of underwater sail, it 'surfs' up onto the beach. In a crowd, the snails converge with uncanny accuracy on any stranded animal, exploring it with long proboscides through which they suck up soft tissue. Once the incoming tide threatens to carry them up to the high shore where they could be stranded, the plough snails bury themselves in the mid-shore sand and emerge only when the ebbing tide will carry them back to their original positions. There they dig in and wait until hunger or the scent of another meal stirs them again to action.

Estuaries, with the lagoons and wetlands which often accompany them, support a wealth of animals of many kinds. Conditions are unpredictable, however, with floods bringing down fresh water and silt from the river catchment area, and the sea contributing salt water and tidal action. There is thus specific stress for many species in the 'gradient of salinity' along the estuary, from salt water at the mouth to fresh water at the head.

These drawbacks are easily outweighed by the advantages of a highly productive environment. The calm, shallow waters allow the development of rich growths of salt-marsh vegetation such as the eelgrass *Zostera,* which die and decay to make food for bacteria. These support the estuarine invertebrates, the food of fish and wading birds. Besides a host of invertebrates such as mud-prawns and bloodworms, juveniles of about 80 species of marine fish use estuaries as 'nursery areas'. The spawning, egg and larval stages of development take place at sea, but when the young fish reach about 15 millimetres in length they migrate to the nearby estuary, and there remain until they are large enough to return and complete their cycle at sea.

Besides these general habitats, there are a number of others which, while important, are more localized. On the west coast where the upwelling occurs, for example, are found dense underwater kelp forests. Their framework is the large *Ecklonia maxima,* with its familiar floating bulbs and fronds, which provides a food base for many species in the form of fragments of the fronds broken off by wave action.

On the subtropical reaches of the Transkei and Natal coasts many mangrove forests grow around the estuaries. They are adapted to colonizing the mudbanks, and their leaves provide food for a variety of endemic species, including a number of mud-dwelling crabs. Off the coast of northern Natal are undersea coral reefs, supporting a dazzling array of creatures, among them most of the 1 500 southern African fish species. Competition for food is intense and, not surprisingly, some of the more venomous animals, from stonefish to rabbitfish, are found here.

Struggle for survival of another kind is seen in the sand dunes. Found all around the coast, they reach their apotheosis in the 'Gobaba', the great dunes of the Namib shore. Water and nutrition here are of the scantest, the only moisture coming from the cold mist which blows in from the sea and the only food source being wind-blown detritus from inland. Yet, even in these uncompromising conditions, a group of small creatures demonstrate nature's inexhaustible ability to adapt.

Among all the pressures to which the coastal wildlife is subject, that of man himself is becoming increasingly critical. From being a rare bird of passage five centuries ago, he has become a major force. Ironically, those areas most amenable to the animals are often also equally attractive to man. Seals and seabirds share the fish catch with the

8. *A lonely Xhosa hut typifies the Transkeian landscape near Presley Bay.* **9.** (Overleaf) *A creaming wave catches a flicker of wintry light as a trio of fishing boats ride at anchor in the offshore waters near Elands Bay.*

purse-seine fishermen. Estuaries and wetlands, the haunt of so many important species, also attract holidaymakers. Reclamation of estuarine wetlands for agriculture and housing effectively destroys them as ecological entities, as has occurred in many estuaries in Natal, where sugar farming has made heavy inroads on river banks and increased the siltation of mangrove forests. Harbour facilities have grown to keep pace with the expansion of mining and industry. Saldanha Bay and Richards Bay are the scene of modern harbour installations which have brought pressure on the local wildlife. Coastal rail and road bridges reduce normal tidal exchange and inhibit the passage of floodwaters down estuaries.

A further hazard of human activity on the shore is that of pollution. It takes many forms, from sewage and chemical effluent to the thermal pollution of power stations. A newcomer is radioactive pollution, as yet something of an unknown quantity. Perhaps the most publicized form, though, is oil pollution. Some 600 million tonnes of crude oil are carried annually around the coast from the Middle East to Europe and the Americas. Despite precautions, many accidents have taken place, the most recent being in August 1983 when, following a fire on the Spanish supertanker *Castillo de Bellver*, over a quarter of a million tonnes of oil were

released into the sea off Saldanha – though on this occasion the south-easter came to the rescue and blew the slick offshore. Oil in the sea soon ceases to be toxic, since most of the poisonous constituents quickly evaporate. But the residual tar, thick and heavy, is washed to shore, more often than not with fatal results. It affects almost every kind of marine animal, but none more so than the seabirds, particularly the jackass penguins, whose natural skin oils are dissolved by the oil, so that their feathers lose their waterproofing quality and the birds die of exposure.

With the rapid increase in population, the general encroachment of human society on the traditional domain of the animals will become more difficult to contain. Protection of the wildlife at present is provided by a system of parks and reserves. Under the aegis of provincial authorities as well as the National Parks Board, there are a number of these on the southern African coastline, including the proposed Langebaan Coastal National Park, the Cape Point Nature Reserve, the De Hoop Nature Reserve, the Tsitsikamma Coastal National Park with its adjacent Tsitsikamma Forest National Park, the Dwesa Nature Reserve in the Transkei, and the reserves and sanctuaries of northern Natal, at Richards Bay, Lake St Lucia and Sodwana Bay. A distinction

must be made between the status of national parks and reserves. Parks are constitutionally protected and therefore may not be reallocated for any human use that is not connected with conservation. Reserves, on the other hand, do not enjoy this guarantee, as was made abundantly clear with the recent decision to use a large area of the De Hoop Nature Reserve on the south coast for a military rocket-testing range. One omission in the list of adequately protected habitats, that of estuaries, particularly troubles ecologists. At present, few estuaries enjoy any real protection, yet they are the most sensitive and most threatened of marine habitats.

The future of the coast thus hangs in the balance of man and nature. Herein lies a paradox. Man is a unique animal, the 'thinking ape'. His knowledge has given him unprecedented control over the world around him, but it has also revealed to him his smallness in the scheme of things, not least on the seashore. From the Kunene River to Kosi Bay, the coast of southern Africa runs in a great arc for 4 600 kilometres. Its dimensions in time are equally grand, for it goes back countless millions of years. On this ancient shore man is a newcomer, a child with a bucket and spade. He has built much, learned much, and has even on occasion given back a little of what he has taken. But his works remain castles of sand beside the creations of nature.

NAMIBIA
THE DESERT SHORE

In a near-desert area at the mouth of the Kuiseb River, a few kilometres from Walvis Bay on the Namibian coast, lives a small group of about 450 people. Known as the Topnaar Hottentots, they are one of the few remaining clans of the once populous Khoisan peoples of southern Africa. In the name of survival they have learned to wrest a livelihood from one of the world's harshest landscapes.

The main group is divided into two

smaller groups. The 'Kuisenin', or 'Kuiseb people', live inland along the river, only paying seasonal visits to the coast. They keep cattle, but also depend on the nara melon which grows along the river.

The other group, of about 200, are the 'Hurinen', the 'Sea people', who live near the river mouth. Like the Kuiseb people, they keep cattle, but it is the sea which provides the main source of food, as it has done for many generations. They are expert fishermen, with a deep knowledge of the ways of the sea. This ancient bond is remembered in a praise-poem handed down from their Khoisan forebears:

> 'Sea, oh sea, you great water
> Water of our Aoni people
> Praise the sea, you Aoni children
> Through him we have raised
> Stingrays and steenbras
> And galjoen
> From him we have eaten
> You great sea, oh great water
> Water of our Aoni children
> Flow, you black precipice
> Feeder of our children
> Please give me the stingray
> Give me the barbel
> Give me the whale
> Give me the sand shark
> Give me the steenbras
> Give me the stockfish
> Flow, oh fat
> Flow, you fleshrich water!'

This 'fleshrich water' bounds the vast and awesome land of Namibia. The Benguela Current sweeps northward along the full 1 400-kilometre length of the shore, from

10. *The cold Benguela Current is a major source of life on the harsh desert shore of the Namib, generating the thick mist seen here near Sandwich Bay and providing moisture in an area almost devoid of rainfall.*

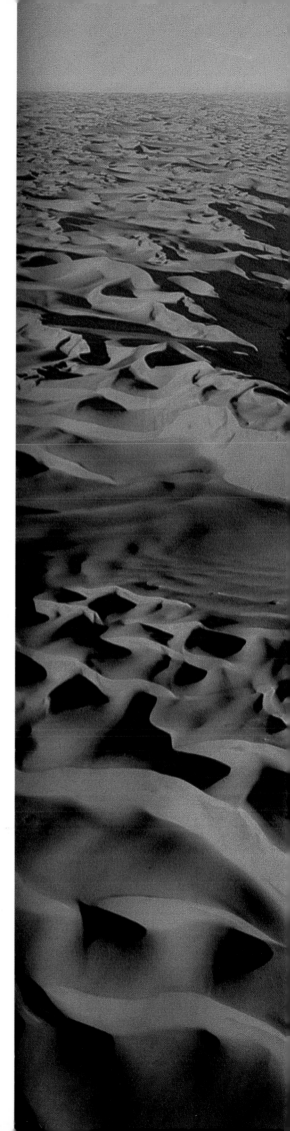

11. *Now corroded by wind and salt water, the old jetty at Swakopmund was built in 1911 to handle produce from the interior. Today it is a favourite haunt of anglers.*

the border with South Africa at the Orange River in the south to the Kunene River in the north. A high central plateau of grassland is fringed by mountain escarpments on its western side. Between the escarpments and the sea lies the Namib Desert.

The Namib and the Benguela Current go hand in hand. The burning Namibian sun heats the land to such a temperature that cloud cover can rarely form and what little rain there is comes across the mountains from the east. The result is one of the world's unforgettable places, a wilderness of grey gravel plains, of stunted trees, of outcrops of rock carved in fantastic shapes by wind and sand. Across these desert regions stretch watercourses such as that of the Kuiseb River which rarely fill with running water, and when they do, only with 'flash floods' brought down from the highlands of the interior.

All this is climaxed by the 'Gobaba', the 'dune sea' of the central Namib. From the area of Lüderitz in the south it reaches 400 kilometres northward to the abrupt boundary of the Kuiseb River, and extends up to 100 kilometres inland. Tinged orange and yellow by iron oxide, these dunes are higher than those of the Sahara, and can be seen from the moon.

Ever moving, ever changing in outline, their mutability enhanced by shifts of light, they have an inhuman beauty, and an overwhelming power to awe. A nineteenth-century Swedish traveller, Charles Andersson, described his dismay at his first sight of them: 'A place fitter to represent the infernal regions could scarcely, in searching the world around, be found. A shudder, amounting almost to fear, came over me when its frightful desolation first broke upon my view. Death, I exclaimed, would be preferable to banishment in such a country.'

If the Gobaba has a rival in desolation, it is in the Skeleton Coast, the almost uninhabited northern coast which runs from Swakopmund to the border. The skeletons are those of ships washed up by the massive gales which come in here from the mid-Atlantic. They have thrown up many a ship, from passenger vessels such as *Dunedin Star*, wrecked during the Second World War, to small fishing boats, abandoned to disdainful crews of cormorants drying their feathers on the spars. Nor are these the only skeletons on the Namib coast. The whalebone shelter of a long-gone Bushman contrasts with the rusting frame of an old oil rig. Above all, there are the ghost towns of the early diamond days, Kolmanskop and Elizabeth

Bay. Dried and preserved by the desert air, their Edwardian-style rooms are filled with drifts of sand, their streets with stunted desert plants.

This inhospitable shore was first glimpsed by Portuguese navigators at the end of the Fifteenth Century. In 1484, Diogo Cão put ashore at what is now Cape Cross, north of Swakopmund. Legend has it that he mistook the local seals for people. He erected a limestone *padrão*, a stone column topped by a cross, which informed the seals of their conquest in Latin and Portuguese: 'Since the creation of the world 6684 years have passed, and since the birth of Christ 1484, and so the illustrious Don Johannes has ordered this pillar to be erected by Johannes Canus, his knight.' It was a memorial in more senses than one, for Cão himself died shortly afterwards.

Three years later Bartolomeu Dias and his small squadron sailed past on the same quest, the search for a route around the southern tip of Africa. There were few landmarks for his chart. The bay he named 'Golfo da Conçeicão', 'Conception Bay', was renamed by the Dutch for the large number of whales seen in the area and is today known as Walvis Bay. Further south Dias found another bay, and this he called 'Angra das Voltas', 'Bay of

12. *Many marine and wetland birds, such as this flock of flamingoes, flourish in the bird sanctuary near Walvis Bay.*

the Tacks', to remind himself of the difficulty he experienced in tacking out of it. Apparently beset by similar difficulties, later navigators rechristened it 'Angra Pequena', 'Narrow Bay'. On the bay's south-western point, which now bears his name, Dias planted a *padrão*. Like that of Cão, it has been replaced by a replica set in concrete. It bears witness not only to where the Portuguese stepped ashore, but to where they abandoned an unwanted hostage, one of four black women who had been kidnapped on the West African coast.

For over a century the south-west coast of Africa remained a place to be sailed past on the way to other destinations. But the cetacean inhabitants of the area had not gone unnoticed. By the late Eighteenth Century British, American and Norwegian sealers and whalers had begun regular raids. It was these forays which stimulated the first official possession of what is now Walvis Bay. In 1793 the Dutch at the Cape, realizing that a potential asset was being plundered behind their backs, despatched a vessel to enforce the twelve-mile coastal limit. Their control of the bay, however, was brief. The British invaded the Cape and, with the same motive as the Dutch, that of securing the sealing and whaling for

themselves, hoisted the Union Jack at Walvis Bay.

The Europeans' foothold on the territory was tenuous. Long before their arrival the inland plateau had been settled by Bantu-speaking peoples. These had come down from the north, with tribes such as the Ovambos and the Kavangos occupying the fertile regions in the north-east, and the Hereros settling the barren Kaokoveld in the north-west. During the Eighteenth Century the Hereros had moved further to the south, leaving the Himbas and Tjimbas to take over the territory they had vacated.

By the early Nineteenth Century this steady southward migration had encountered opposition from the south, mainly from the Hottentots. Dutch occupation of their traditional lands had driven many of them across the Orange River, where they had displaced the indigenous Bushmen. They were divided into clans such as the Nama, and included groups of mixed stock such as the Witboois, led by the fiery Hendrik Witbooi, and the Basters, Dutch settlers with Hottentot wives.

All these jostled for control of the land. Friction regularly erupted into warfare, particularly violent between the Hereros and the Nama. It was not long before the

men at Walvis Bay began profiting from this unrest, with a traffic in arms from the seaboard to the interior.

In the mid-Nineteenth Century German Rhenish missionaries attempted to introduce the concept of Christian brotherhood, with mixed results. They heralded the start of a more general German colonization of the country which, inevitably, aroused conflict with British interests centred at Walvis Bay.

The great nineteenth-century 'scramble for Africa' was enacted in miniature on this desert shore. For many years Walvis Bay had remained unacknowledged by the British government. Then, in 1878, the warship *Industry* sailed into the bay to annex the settlement together with a surrounding area of 1 165 square kilometres. A magistrate sent up from the Cape Colony, William Palgrave, was given the unenviable task of controlling illegal whaling and gun-running.

With the British entrenched at Walvis Bay, German ambitions turned elsewhere. In 1883 an enterprising tobacco merchant from Bremen named Adolf Lüderitz sent an expedition to the Orange River. In his name a strip of land extending from the mouth of the Orange River to just north of Angra Pequena was purchased from the Nama chief at Bethanie. The following

13

13. Abandoned during the 1920s, the once-thriving diamond centre of Kolmanskop in the Diamond Area near Lüderitz is now a 'ghost town', preserved by the dry desert air.
14. Including rose quartz and red jasper, a selection of stones glistening on the beach at Möwe Bay is a reminder that this is one of the richest mineral areas in southern Africa.

14

15

15. In its heyday Kolmanskop boasted shops, saloons, hotels, and even an opera hall graced by imported stars from Europe. Now only sand and silence fill the buildings, deserted by the miners as new discoveries were made in the south. **16.** The Benguela Current exacts a price in return for its profit in fish, as attested by the wreck of Montrose II, washed up on the Skeleton Coast during a storm in 1973 and still well preserved some 10 years on.

year the German government, at Lüderitz's instigation, sent a couple of gunboats to take formal possession of the territory by hoisting a flag and firing off a 21-gun salute. Lüderitz himself, however, had little time in which to enjoy the acquisition, since he disappeared soon afterwards in the course of a prospecting expedition. In his honour, Angra Pequena was renamed 'Lüderitzbucht', the 'Bay of Lüderitz'.

Diplomatic agreement was finally reached over the boundaries. Germany was to have the territory of 'Süd-West Afrika' at large, while Britain would keep the enclave of Walvis Bay, the only fully navigable natural harbour on the coast.

One result of this division was the creation of the harbour and town of Swakopmund, some 30 kilometres north of Walvis Bay.

The lines thus drawn on the map lasted until the First World War. An attempted German invasion of Walvis Bay in 1914 was quickly headed off by a detachment of the South African Police. Forty thousand Union troops were shipped to the bay, Swakopmund was bombarded, and the German forces, heavily outnumbered, were forced into retreat. They sustained a defensive campaign for a further year against odds which included aeroplanes and newly devised armoured vehicles, before capitulating near the

town of Otavi. The Peace of Khorab, signed on 9 July 1915, brought to an end the 31-year rule of Germany in South-West Africa, and in 1919 the territory was mandated to South Africa by the Treaty of Versailles, as part of the spoils of war.

Over half a century later, German culture and influence remain strong, particularly in the towns of Lüderitz and Swakopmund. These are fascinating places, with an atmosphere found nowhere else. Typical nineteenth-century Baltic towns, they seem to have been transposed to an alien shore. The result is a unique juxtaposition of landscape and architecture. Swakopmund, in particular, has many beautiful and well-preserved

17

18

buildings, creating a counterpoint of half-hipped roofs and Bavarian-style onion towers. A feature of the town is its magnificent *fin-de-siècle* railway station, built for the first train to Windhoek in 1902. Even the old town prison is palatial, at least from the outside!

In recent years, underground water has been used to turn Swakopmund into the nearest thing to a garden city in Namibia. Lüderitz, though, remains the definitive image of a gardenless city. Despite being regularly shrouded in clammy sea mists which breathe inland morning and afternoon, it supports not a blade of grass. There is no fresh-water supply here, and every drop consumed by the town's 4 000 inhabitants has to be piped from a borehole at Khoicheb, 100 kilometres distant.

Walvis Bay makes a contrast both in style and scale with the two German towns. With a present population of about 26 000, it is the second largest settlement in the territory as a whole after Windhoek, the Namibian capital. With its thousand metres of wharves, its rows of cranes and derricks and its clattering factories, it is an unlovely place, except perhaps in the eye of a fisherman. For Walvis Bay is the centre of the fishing industry on the Namibian coast. In the Benguela Current are found the heavy plankton blooms which live on the nutrients of the upwelled water drawn to the surface by wind and currents. On the plankton depend the shoals of fish and, indirectly,

17. *The loneliness and bleakness of the Namibian shores are captured in this view of Terrace Bay.* 18. *Guano platforms at Walvis Bay have been specially constructed to remedy the lack of rocky islands in the area. Seabirds nest on these 'artificial islands' in preference to the local sandy beaches, depositing large amounts of guano, rich in fertilizer nutrients, that make a valuable and easily collected harvest.*

the colonies of rock lobster which make a major contribution to the local economy.

Times for the fishing industry have been better. In the early days fishing was simple and catches relatively small. But in the years after the Second World War there was an unexpected 'fish boom', centred on Walvis Bay. This boom was based on exploitation of a new catch, that of the pelagic pilchard, *Sardinops ocellata*. In those days the pilchard shoals of South-West Africa were among the largest in the world. Lurking in deep waters by day, they surfaced at night to feed on the plankton, and to be captured by the million in the purse-seine nets of the fishermen. Factory ships able to work outside the then twelve-mile limit, spotter planes and advanced depth-sounding and fish-detecting systems combined to stimulate bigger catches and increase profits. The good times rolled as the annual catch soared, reaching a staggering 1,4 million tonnes in 1968.

But this was over-fishing on an unprecedented scale. The shoals began to dwindle, and it was not long before there was a precipitate collapse. Only a complete ban on pilchard fishing in 1974 saved the animal from extinction on the South-West African coast. Since then the industry has turned to the smaller anchovy to keep bankruptcy at bay. Though controls are now stricter, there are signs that this species, too, is under considerable stress.

Man is far from the only animal on this coast dependent on the wealth of the upwelling. Untold numbers of birds, including the jackass penguins and cormorants clustering the offshore islands, rely upon it. Perhaps its most visible beneficiaries, though, are the seals.

The Cape fur seal is the only species endemic to southern African waters and is found from Namibia around to Algoa Bay. Relentless sealing once depleted their

20

19

19. Created under conditions of great pressure and temperature, this gem diamond lay for some 90 million years in the bedrock of the ancient seashore before being brought to light by large-scale modern mining technology. Huge mechanical bowl-scrapers clear some 10 tonnes of overburden for every carat recovered. **20.** The mineral resources of the territory include the sea's contribution in the form of salt, which is collected from pans bulldozed in the sand near Swakopmund. Sea water is pumped into the pans, allowed to evaporate and then the crust of salt left behind is carefully scraped up. **21.** Swakopmund is enhanced by fine German colonial architecture from the turn of the century, including this elegant railway station, built in 1902 as the terminus of the line from Windhoek. **22.** Like Swakopmund, Lüderitz has a strong German colonial atmosphere and architecture. This view towards 'Lüderitzbucht' reflects the aridity of the town's setting – with a meagre annual rainfall of 18 millimetres and no rivers or dams nearby, the people of Lüderitz are totally dependent on fresh water pumped from a borehole inland.

21

numbers but since it has been controlled the seal population has increased dramatically and is now estimated to be about one million in southern Africa. Major colonies are found on the Namibian coast in places such as Cape Cross and Atlas Bay, where there is an enormous annual gathering of over 180 000 seals. Further to the south, at Black Rock, the Sea Fisheries Research Institute has a study area with an observation post perched on the edge of the cliff above the colony. From here scientists can look directly down on the seals as they arrive

bared teeth take place as the bulls fix the boundaries between their domains. This 'macho' behaviour often turns into outright battles in which the animals inflict apparently fearsome wounds on each other. Mainly on the neck, these bleed profusely, though they heal with surprising speed. Most adult bulls carry a network of battle scars on their necks.

Once the boundaries have been settled, the female seals begin to come ashore. Smaller and lighter in colour than the males, they are promptly rounded up into 'harems' of up to 30 cows. By the time

while the female is at sea. Nine months later, when the mother returns to shore, the pup is ready to be born.

Birth is a simple and straightforward affair for, unlike the human infant, the baby seal is well shaped for a smooth arrival into the world, and into a society which is nothing if not gregarious. Its mother is fiercely protective, though its adoptive father is generally indifferent, being by now otherwise occupied. For within days or even hours of the birth, the next mating takes place. Copulation of seals is very much a one-sided affair, though the female may initiate it by nipping the male on his much-scarred neck. At this signal the bull will lower a mass of heaving blubber onto his mate, all but hiding her from sight. It is not uncommon for a cow to be smothered during the ensuing performance, though she can sometimes signal for survival by again nipping the bull's neck.

Life has its perils, too, for the pups, particularly for those on shore-based rather than island colonies. Roving bands of black-backed jackals infiltrate the colonies, looking for any stranded or momentarily abandoned pups. Having secured one and dragged it away from its mother's floundering reach, the jackals dismember it, tails wagging in a frenzy of aggression. Since they are basically scavengers, lacking the heavily muscled jaws of larger carnivores, and the seal pups have tough hides, this can be a long and bloody process.

The majority of pups, however, survive to take to the sea, where they are completely at home, fast and agile. The seals' main enemy is the shark, though captains of fishing vessels are not above taking a pot shot at them, particularly when they perform their favourite circus trick of jumping over the edge of the purse-seine net to gorge themselves on its contents.

Although the resources of the sea were recognized early, it was only in the Nineteenth Century that the hidden wealth of the shore was discovered. For on the coast of the southern Namib, particularly in the region around the mouth of the Orange River, is found the richest deposit of gem diamonds in the world. No one is certain how these diamonds came to be here. Unlike those mined in the Transvaal, these are found in the bedrock of an ancient sea-coast, laid down beneath a heavy burden of coastal sand. They may have been washed down by prehistoric rivers from volcanic deposits inland, or they may have been formed by volcanic action under the sea. Whatever their origin, it is certain that at

23. *Jackals roam the enormous seal colony at Cape Cross in search of any unguarded pups.*

for the breeding and mating season in mid-October.

The bull seals come ashore first, to stake out their territories. Even on land they are imposing animals, near-black in colour and weighing up to 230 kilograms. Thick fur and skin are padded with a layer of blubber up to 10 centimetres thick. Since seals are built for cold water and not for the heat of the sun, they must return frequently to the sea to cool off. Prime property for the season is therefore down by the water's edge or on the rim of one of the offshore islands. Latecomers are forced to accept inferior sites higher up the beach. Much jostling, barking, and 'boundary displays' with reared head and

they arrive in the colony, these cows are ready to give birth to pups conceived during the previous season's mating, twelve months before, although the gestation period of seals lasts only nine months. If the two important events of mating and birth were to occur at different times of the year, two separate colonizations of the beaches would be necessary. To save effort, the Cape fur seal has compressed the two events into one. It has evolved an ingenious method of 'delayed implantation', in which the fertilized egg of the female is retained in the oviduct for three months after mating. It then descends to become implanted in the uterus and to begin placental growth some time in the past they had extended contact with the smoothing action of the waves. Many of them were carried northwards along the coast by the current, to the area where they were first discovered.

In 1908 a young German railway supervisor named August Stauch was overseeing the clearing of sand from the line outside Lüderitz and told his workers to keep their eyes open for 'pretty stones'. Among the men was one named Zacharias Lewala, who had previously worked on the diamond mines at Kimberley. It was he who, within two weeks of Stauch's instruction, reached down to pick the first diamond from the hard, hot earth.

The discovery triggered a new diamond rush. German officials, throwing colonial dignity to the winds, crawled on all fours across the desert, picking up the stones. A horde of hungry-eyed prospectors arrived and soon fully fledged towns had sprung up around the diamond holdings at Kolmanskop and Elizabeth Bay.

They were places with a lurid energy and vitality. Besides houses and shops, they boasted a more than adequate supply of saloon bars. There was even a theatre to which orchestras and opera stars were imported from Europe. And many of the wild-eyed men went home as rich as their dreams would have them.

The boom lasted in full flourish until the First World War brought a break in the diggings. Post-war depression took its toll, made worse by a glut of diamonds. But the real end of the boom in the Kolmanskop area was signalled by the discovery in the 1920s of larger deposits at the mouth of the Orange River and in the Port Nolloth region, the focus of the present industry.

Many years went by, however, before these deposits could be fully exploited. Only with the development of large-scale earth-moving machinery in the 1960s did it become possible to reach the diamonds, the bulk of which were hidden beneath millions of tonnes of sand laid down over the prehistoric beach.

Of all the images of this coast, that of the Diamond Area, the 'Sperrgebiet', is one of the strangest. Deep valleys are gouged through the dunes by enormous mechanical bowl-scrapers. The overburden thus cleared is piled up to form coffer-dams to hold back the sea, while large pumps drain away the

24. *Dwarfed by the sweep of sea and shore at Jones' Bay, a group of anglers pursue the rich game fishing which is a major attraction of the area.* **25.** *(Overleaf) An other-worldly vista of De Beers' massive diamond-mining operation in the 'Sperrgebiet' north of Oranjemund.*

26

seepage. Once the sand is removed the gravel substratum is broken up by hydraulic excavators to expose the bedrock on which the diamonds lie. Local contract workers, mainly Ovambos, move systematically over the rock face, wielding fingers and brushes to extract the gems. Between them they gather a good handful of diamonds a day. Small in general, but of high quality and brilliance, they add up to a million carats a year and account for a sizeable percentage of Namibia's revenues.

If stones are important to man, the animals have other priorities. In this arid climate water is at a premium, and nowhere more so than in the Namib itself. Here nature has evolved a wonderful variety of ways to conserve the exiguous supplies of moisture. Many plants and animals, for example, have learned to make use of the rare rainfall which may occur after years of drought, and then last only hours or even minutes. Sometimes the earth is so hot that the rain evaporates as, or even before, it hits the ground. Certain plant species wait for this brief supply of moisture, and then grow rapidly. A sparse grassland of *Stipagrostis* species may develop after no more than 20 millimetres of rain has fallen. Animals such as the large desert antelope, the gemsbok, will quickly take advantage of this supply of grass, arriving in large numbers to graze.

These ephemeral grasses contrast with hardy perennial grasses, lichens and dwarf shrubs such as *Arthraerua lubnitzia* and *Zygophyllum stapffii*, and *Lithops*, the so-called 'stone plants', succulents which resemble stones. All these store the rare moisture for long periods in their leaves and roots. Perhaps the most famous exponent of this talent is the magnificent *Welwitschia mirabilis*, its centuries-old leaves curling in fantastic grey-green shapes and providing a home for a suite of dependent bugs. This plant has evolved a system of 'reverse transpiration': whereas most plants draw moisture from the soil and transpire it through the leaves, the *Welwitschia* absorbs moisture through its leaves and stores it in the bulbous tap root.

One of the most remarkable responses to isolated rainfall is found in the desert's

temporary ponds. These may remain dry and seemingly lifeless for years on end. Beneath the hard surface of the mud, however, they harbour the eggs of a wide variety of small creatures specialized to this environment. They include many tiny crustaceans such as Anostraca (fairy shrimps), Conchostraca (clam shrimps), and Notostraca (tadpole shrimps), and the algae and bacteria on which they live.

For these animals the rain, brief as it is, is the catalyst of a rapid cycle of growth and reproduction. For the few days that the moisture lasts the pond seethes with activity. The eggs hatch and the animals grow to full size, mate and lay more supplies of eggs. The larval stage is compressed, and growth is amazingly fast. The tadpole shrimp *Triops namaquensis*, for example, can reach a carapace length of nine millimetres within six days. The eggs produced by sexual reproduction are highly resistant to desiccation and are generated in large quantities. It has been estimated that the *Triops* female lays several thousand eggs in her brief lifetime. As the pond dries and hardens, the adults die, the eggs are preserved, and the ferment of life sinks again from sight.

Besides the ephemeral rainfall there is another, more reliable source of moisture, though it is more localized. This is the water which is brought down by the rivers from inland. In rivers such as the Kuiseb and the Swakop there is an almost yearly flow but not all this water may reach the sea after the initial 'flash flood'. In the case of the Kuiseb, the mouth of the estuary has long been blocked by sand washed into it by the Benguela Current.

The floodwaters, trapped along the river's course, sink slowly into the sand, leaving a series of pools and taking up to 70 years to reach the sea along an underground route. Riverine vegetation grows around the pools, including the nara melon on which many of the Topnaar people depend, and the acacia, the pods of which are a favourite of the gemsbok.

Many animals make use of this water. Some, like the gemsbok, have learned to dig for it when necessary. Others have even devised ways of carrying it, notably the small desert sandgrouse, which nests in shallow holes far out in the desert, sometimes 50 kilometres from a pool. The male sandgrouse drinks his fill at the water-hole and as he wades in it, his breast feathers soak up between 20 and 40 millilitres of water which the bird transports back to his nest. There the chicks drink from the breast feathers, taking up to 3 millilitres of water each, the equivalent of a 30 per cent increase in individual body weight.

The third source of moisture in the desert is that of fog. Thick, cold and clammy, yet another product of the Benguela Current, it rolls in almost daily from the sea. In the immediate coastal region it may deposit up to 45 millimetres of moisture a year, a contrast to the mean annual rainfall of 5 millimetres in the same area. Borne on the sea wind, it is driven inland across the desert, often reaching 100 kilometres from the coast.

A great variety of animals makes use of this supply of moisture. Jackals lick condensed fog from the surfaces of rocks, and in certain circumstances man has

26. *Nutrient-rich waters of the chill Benguela Current and the marine phenomenon of 'upwelling' combine to produce a wealth of plankton, the food base of the once-rich fish stocks on the west coast of southern Africa.*
27. *The stark, sculptural quality of the Namib landscape is shown in the clay cliffs of the Hoanib River, remnants of bygone floods which deposited layer upon layer of sediment.*

been happy to join them. The survivors of the wrecked *Dunedin Star,* for example, kept themselves alive by licking fog water from the wings of an aircraft which had crashed while attempting to rescue them. But nowhere is the importance of this fog in the hard art of survival more apparent than in the central Namib, among the 300 metre-high dunes of the Gobaba.

This magnificent wilderness, apparently inimical to life, in fact harbours a great many small creatures. They depend on the regular precipitation of the fog for moisture, while nutrition is largely provided by wind-blown detritus such as grass and seeds brought down from the mountains by the east wind. Bound together in a complex food web, each creature has its place in the system of the dunes, from the slipfaces to the valleys, or 'dune streets', between them. They include an endemic group of tenebrionid beetles, lizards, silverfish, gerbils and sidewinder snakes. The trapdoor spider preys on beetles and small reptiles, paralyzing them and dragging them down into its burrow to make a living but motionless larder for its young. Another unique creature found here is the golden mole. Long believed extinct, it was recently rediscovered after over 100 years. A mere six centimetres long and totally blind, it is nevertheless a raveningly voracious predator, aptly described as the 'shark' of the dunes.

Some of these animals, including the golden mole, live beneath the surface of the sand and never emerge into the open. Others are nocturnal, such as the desert gecko, a creature with transparent skin and broad, webbed feet which allow it to dig deep burrows below the compacted sand of the dunes. It remains by day in this cool hideaway, coming out to hunt only by night. Other animals, though, spend part of the day in the open. One of these is the Namib sand-diving lizard, which begins the day by emerging onto the surface of the sand when the temperature reaches about 30 degrees centigrade. To build up thermal energy it adopts a special position, its belly pressed to the warmth of the sand, its limbs and tail raised. When its temperature has risen to the required level it sets about rapidly foraging along the slipfaces for plant food. As the morning advances, however, the temperature soars to about 40 degrees centigrade. Now the lizard adopts a stilt-like gait, its body held as high as possible above the sand. At intervals it stops to perform a 'thermoregulatory dance'. Standing on diagonally opposite legs and balancing itself with its tail, it waves the other two legs in the air to cool them.

When this ruse no longer helps, as the temperature reaches its noon maximum of between 40 and 50 degrees centigrade, it escapes by 'diving' with an adroit flick of its tail into the cool regions below. There it remains until the temperature drops again in the late afternoon.

Though it is normally diurnal, this lizard emerges at night when a fog is in the offing, even when the temperature is below its favoured range of 30 to 40 degrees centigrade. The effort is worthwhile, for it can take on water equivalent to 12 per cent of its body weight. Stored in a special bladder in the lower intestine, this will keep it going for many weeks.

Of all these creatures, the tenebrionid beetles have perhaps aroused the most scientific interest. They, too, have ways of regulating the effects of heat. *Stenocara phalangium* has the longest legs, relative to its body size, of any insect in the world. It lives in the valleys between the dunes and on cool mornings, to warm up before the day's foraging, it faces the sun, its abdomen pressed close to the ground. As the sand heats up it raises itself on its stilt-like legs. When the full heat of noon strikes, it climbs up onto a small stone where it stands motionless at full height, its white posterior facing the sun to maximize reflection. Its only concession

28

29

to action in these periods is to defend its perch vigorously against intruders.

But the real speciality of these beetles is the collecting of fog water. For some, such as the small *Lepidochora discoidalis*, the micro-engineer of the dunes, this is a practical matter. When it senses the coming of a fog-bearing onshore wind it scuttles out to build itself a narrow trench, perpendicular to the direction of the wind, which condenses more water than the surrounding sand. When the ridges are saturated the beetle systematically works its way along them, flattening them and taking up the moisture.

Perhaps the most intriguing of all, though, is *Onymacris unguicularis*, the 'fog-basking beetle', which not only gathers moisture, but has evolved an anatomy to assist with the process. Down its back run grooves which converge behind its head. At the first sign of the fog it clambers up to the crest of the dune and there stations itself, facing the wind with its head down and its posterior raised. Droplets of moisture form on its back and trickle down the grooves into the beetle's mouth, providing it with moisture for many days. One of the unforgettable sights of the Namib is of a row of these beetles, patiently waiting as the wind rolls in, bringing the gift of the sea to the land.

28. *The desert plant Welwitschia mirabilis is capable of storing moisture for decades at a time in its large tap root, and survives for hundreds and sometimes thousands of years. It hosts an endemic community of beetles in its seedheads and broad, curling leaves, providing the insects with food and shelter and receiving in return assistance with pollination.* **29.** *Making the most of almost nothing is the high art of the desert shore. Many lizards of the family Cordylidae subsist on insects brought from inland by the wind, and on moisture precipitated from the sea mists.* **30.** *Whale bones arranged as a framework for a shelter bear testament to the preserve of long-gone Bushmen along the Namib coast. These hunter-gatherers were always able to make the most of what nature offered, and the whales washed up on this desert shore also provided a major source of protein, the flesh being buried in larders on the beach.* **31.** *A beetle, Calosis amabilis, glimpsed at Möwe Bay. The insect life of the Namib shore is unique and there is an extraordinary diversity of beetle species, almost all of which are confined to this area. They depend on wind-blown animal and vegetable matter and on the moisture of fogs which they are adapted to gathering in an intriguing variety of ways.* **32.** *Like many other Namib creatures the palmate gecko, with its transparent skin and large, webbed feet, is a nocturnal animal. It lies buried beneath the sand during the heat of the day, emerging by night to forage in the gullies and on the slipfaces of the dunes.*

THE WEST COAST

'LAND BARREN AND UNBLESSED'

Each year in spring, in the region of Namaqualand in the western part of the Cape Province, there takes place a fleeting miracle of nature, the annual appearance of the indigenous wild flowers. Known to botanists as 'opportunists', these plants have evolved by adapting to conditions of extreme aridity and an unreliable and ephemeral rainfall. After the winter rains, from early August to the end of September, their seeds, long hidden dormant in the earth, germinate rapidly and erupt into flower.

The result is a dazzling transformation. Over 350 different species make their appearance almost overnight, in a large-scale spontaneous flower show. Of every conceivable colour, they range from jakkalsblom to botterblom, from bokbaaivygies, sandvygies, gazanias and bittergousblom to viooltjies, elandsvy, bees-sporries, dassiesgousblom and beetle daisies. They carpet the earth from horizon to horizon along the whole coastal strip between mountains and sea. Within a few weeks they set seed and wilt before the full heat of summer.

While they last they soften a hard coast. Although technically this is not a desert region, the coincidence of cold sea and hot shore makes for harsh conditions, hardly improved by the heavy north-westerly gales which regularly pound the coast. Relatively few people live here, and the long northern reaches from St Helena Bay to the mouth of the Orange River and the border with Namibia are particularly bleak. With the exception of scattered fishing villages such as Lambert's Bay and Papendorp and the diamond towns of Port Nolloth and Alexander Bay in the north, the beach runs almost uninhabited for 550 kilometres.

The greatest concentration of human habitation lies to the south, in the region

of the rocky outcrop of the Vredenburg peninsula and Saldanha Bay. Around the peninsula are dotted small fishing villages such as Velddrif and Paternoster, while Saldanha Bay harbours the west coast's major fishing centre, the town of Saldanha itself. With its wharves and jetties bristling into the bay, its rows of factories and canneries, many of them bearing familiar household names, and its all-pervading reek of fish, it is a pungently atmospheric place. But if fishing is an important industry in the area, it is not the only one. A large, modern iron ore export facility bisects the bay nearby, while on the coast some 80 kilometres to the south is the recently completed nuclear power station at Koeberg.

The human settlements have their counterparts in the animal and bird colonies. Reaching 15 kilometres to the south of Saldanha Bay and enclosed by the Donkergat Peninsula, the beautiful lagoon of Langebaan is one of the richest wildlife and marine areas on the southern African coastline and has recently been proposed as a national park. The abundance of its salt-marshes is complemented by a group of islands, the home of large colonies of seabirds. Skaap and Meeuw islands mark the entrance to the lagoon, while Marcus Island lies in the centre of Saldanha Bay, and Malgas and Jutten islands at its mouth. Another important bird colony is found off the coast a few kilometres to the south, at Dassen Island, the home of one of the few remaining communities of the local jackass penguin.

33. *The small west coast harbour of Lambert's Bay hosts many fishing boats, including those visiting from Cape Town, that work the sardine and pilchard shoals in the offshore waters.*

34. *One of the most exposed and storm-battered of the local fishing villages, Lambert's Bay is bathed in cool, rain-washed light.* **35.** *Cold waters notwithstanding, an ardent following has grown around the new sport of windsurfing, pitting human skill against the power of the waves.*

34

35

Early settlement of this lonely coastline was slow, if not outright reluctant. The naming of Saldanha Bay was even the result of an error. In 1503 a Portuguese captain, Antonio de Saldanha, made a landfall at the foot of Table Mountain where he took on water. Thereafter, for a hundred years, Table Bay was known as 'Aguada de Saldanha', the 'Watering Place of Saldanha'. Then in 1601 a Dutch captain, Joris van Spilbergen, unfamiliar with the coast, sailed past what is now Saldanha Bay and assumed it to be the well-known 'Watering Place of Saldanha'. When he arrived at the true place of Saldanha, he compounded the confusion by naming it, with a somewhat obvious piece of inspiration, 'Tafel Baay'.

Despite opposition from all but the Dutch, the name stuck. And in posthumous compensation, Saldanha's name was transferred to a landmark the good captain himself never saw. As an experienced seaman, though, he would undoubtedly have approved of the place. This complex of bay, islands and lagoon made by far the best natural harbour on the west coast, being protected from both the northerly gales of winter and the south-easterly winds of summer. It had only one major drawback – there was little fresh water here. True, there were a few natural springs on the shores of the bay, but they were meagre and invariably dried

up in summer. Soon after his arrival at the Cape in 1652, Jan van Riebeeck visited the area and summed it up without enthusiasm. 'There is no land in the whole world so barren and unblessed by the Lord God', he recorded glumly.

For most of the 154-year rule of the Dutch East India Company at the Cape, activity on the west coast was restricted to sporadic sealing and egg-collecting, incursions by pirates, and attempts at farming, mostly doomed through lack of water. At the turn of the Eighteenth Century, though, the area was briefly the witness of history, with the Battle of Blaauwberg in January 1806. Four thousand British soldiers under General Baird landed at Table Bay and marched into the dunes of the Blaauwberg hills to confront General Jan Janssen's rag-tag force of 1 500 men, comprising burgher troops, Malays and Hottentots, stiffened with a contingent of German mercenaries, the Waldeck Regiment. Given the odds, the conclusion was foregone, the turning point of the battle coming when the supposedly reliable Waldecks took flight.

British attempts to colonize the west coast had little more success than had those of the Dutch. Then in the 1830s Saldanha Bay suddenly sprang into bizarre life. In 1828 a certain Captain Morrell had visited the west coast and four years later published an account of his explorations. The publication might have created little stir but for mention of heavy guano deposits the captain had observed on the offshore islands. It had recently been discovered that these nitrate- and phosphate-rich deposits made excellent fertilizer. Scenting profit, hordes of guano-collectors descended on Saldanha Bay.

Their main target was Malgas Island, at the entrance to the bay, where the deposits were up to 20 metres deep, representing many centuries of excretion by thousands of cormorants and gannets – it was after the 'malgas' or 'mad goose', as the early Dutch settlers had unflatteringly called the gannet, that the island was named. The collectors pegged out the island, separating the holdings with ropes adorned with flags. A small army of hired workmen sweated under the blazing sun, digging, scraping and loading the guano. They even exhumed the mummified body of a French sealer which was sent to Europe and exhibited as proof of the preservative properties of the guano. Around the shore of the bay, rum booths sprang up, and a hearty trade in grog took place. The deposits were soon cleaned out, however, and the island returned to the birds.

In the coming decades, the sharp eyes of prospectors were turned elsewhere, and to other forms of wealth. The end of the Nineteenth and the early years of the Twentieth Century saw the great diamond boom in the Transvaal and South-West Africa. In the 1920s it extended south to the hot, windswept coast of the northern Cape, in the region of Port Nolloth and Alexander Bay where the last diamond rush in the classic nineteenth-century style took place.

With the first discovery of the gems the usual crowd of hopefuls and no-hopers, derelicts and out-and-out desperadoes converged on the area. At first they were spectacularly successful. The diamonds lay on the surface in mind-boggling quantities. One man turned up no less than 487 gems beneath a single flat stone! But it did not take long for the surface deposits to be exhausted. It was clear that many more lay beneath the surface, but the impoverished diggers could not afford the expensive machinery needed to retrieve them.

At this point Hans Merensky stepped in. Well known as a geologist, prospector and diamond expert, Merensky was also a shrewd businessman. He noticed that the greatest concentration of diamonds coincided with beds of gravel containing fossil shells of an extinct warm-water oyster, *Ostrea prismatica*. Having bought

36. *A crowned plover fusses over its clutch of mottled eggs among the spring flowers and dune vegetation at Doring Bay.*

up all the holdings at Alexander Bay on this 'oyster line', he made an agreement with the Diamond Syndicate, headed by Ernest Oppenheimer. Between them the area of Alexander Bay was pegged out, the deal including the sale of their diamonds through the South African government.

Unfortunately, the agreement excluded the ragged army of individual prospectors who were left out in the cold or, more accurately, the baking heat of a desert shore. They reacted by fomenting themselves into a mood of violent rebellion and planned a mass storming of the Syndicate's holdings. Like many a revolutionary mob, however, what they gained in righteous fury they lost in indecision as to the best course of action. While days of heated debate took place at the diggers' encampment, Alexander Bay was quietly surrounded by police armed with machine guns. The hour of decision came and went. The leaders of the rebellion succumbed to an attack of cold feet, and the last dispirited embers of revolt were blown away in 36 hours of a howling sandstorm. The incident marked the historic end of the individual prospector and the swarming, maverick communities he created. From now on the diamond industry wore a three-piece suit and a tin hat, and became respectable.

While diamonds spelled fortune at least for some, in the south another resource, that of fish, was soon to be exploited on a large scale. The problem of water at Saldanha Bay, however, remained unsolved until the Second World War. Then the bay, hitherto the peaceful haunt of birds and fishing boats, became the bolt hole of the British Navy, particularly after the German invasion of North Africa and the sealing off of the Suez Canal zone, and a long-discussed pipeline bringing fresh water from the Berg River was built.

Maximum security precautions surrounded the bay and its entrance was mined. During the next two years Royal Navy warships, many the victims of submarine attack, picked their way in from the savagery of the war in the south Atlantic to the safety of the sheltered harbour. With the turning of the tide in North Africa and the invasion of Italy, the war moved northwards and Saldanha Bay gradually regained its tranquillity.

The tranquillity was short-lived. In the post-war years the town grew rapidly with the start of the great 'fish boom' which included not only Saldanha Bay, but other fishing villages along the coast, from Paternoster to Papendorp. All shared in the new demand for fish and the profits of the upwelling which, at about 30 metres a day, is especially powerful on this part of the coast. Swarms of fishing boats made their way out nightly to the open sea beyond South Head, bringing back the pilchard catch to the canneries spread around Hoedjies Bay. The fleets expanded rapidly, quadrupling their catch between 1956 and 1962, and reaching a peak of over 400 000 tonnes a year.

But, as with the Namibian fishing industry, enthusiasm for gain had blinded the fishermen of Saldanha Bay to the effect on the pilchard shoals of these large catches. By the mid-1970s, the pilchards were in full decline, taking the fishing industry with them. In compensation, and despite warnings from fisheries experts, quotas were raised. The result of this was a full-scale slump. Since then, greatly reduced quotas on the pelagic catch and new controls on mesh sizes of the nets have allowed both the fish and the industry which depends upon them to survive, though a final safe estimate for a 'maximum sustainable yield' has yet to be found.

The economic health of the area has been boosted by the introduction of new industries. One of the most important of these centres around the iron ore export facility built by ISCOR (the South African Iron and Steel Industrial Corporation). Projecting into the bay from its eastern side and protected by a breakwater which reaches from near Saldanha to Marcus Island, it handles about 20 million tonnes of ore a year, brought down from the mines at Sishen in the north-western Cape. A railway network carries seemingly endless trains of the mineral to the facility, from where it is transported by conveyor belt directly into the ship's hold. Iron ore is bright brick-red, and not surprisingly this has become the dominant shade in the jetty area, where the water has turned the colour of the ore.

38

39

Even the local seagulls, ignoring 'official' notices to avoid *rooi water*, sport bright red feathers!

Iron ore, if highly visible, is harmless to the ecology. But other aspects of local industrial development have aroused much debate among environmentalists, particularly with regard to the long-term effects on Langebaan Lagoon and the bird islands.

The lagoon has a uniquely rich food web which differs not only from that of the seashore, but from that of estuaries, too. Whereas most lagoons are formed as fresh-water enclaves by rivers running into estuaries, Langebaan Lagoon was formed by prehistoric changes in the level of the sea. With the fall in sea-level the area was isolated by the ancient dunes which now form the Donkergat Peninsula. The water in the lagoon is therefore both tidal and salt. It is also of exceptional clarity. The mouth of the lagoon is populated by colonies of white clams, and these filter-feeders screen the incoming tidal water, clarifying it in the process. Low levels of nutrients in the water reduce the phytoplankton population and this further enhances the clarity, accounting for the fact that relatively few fish live in the lagoon, apart from large numbers of sandsharks in the shallows.

The main source of nutrition comes not from the sea, but from the salt-marshes. The plants here are dominated by such species as those of the genus *Sarcocornia* which grow quickly to maturity in spring and early summer, and die back with the heat of midsummer. They form beds of decaying vegetable matter which are attacked by bacteria. These break down the material into a 'detrital soup' which in turn is the food for a great number of marine species. About 550 species of invertebrates, almost double the number in any other lagoon on the southern African coast, have been recorded here.

It is these small creatures which support the knots, turnstones, sandpipers, sanderlings and many other wading birds in the lagoon. In the summer months

37. *Returning from a fishing trip, a gannet prepares to touch down at its nesting site among the closely packed hordes on Malgas Island.* **38.** *A group of cormorants sit astride their nests atop a guano-stained boulder.* **39.** *The most northerly of the world's penguin species, jackass penguins, like these on Dassen Island, are now rigorously protected. Although these birds are not rare, current populations are a fraction of the size of original ones.* **40.** (Overleaf) *Tidal marshes which form the southern extension of Langebaan Lagoon are the key to the food supply of a vast variety of invertebrate species and, in turn, of the wading birds which live on them.*

some 55 000 birds gather here. Of these, over two-thirds are of one species, an immigrant from the Arctic, the curlew sandpiper. This medium-sized wader with its delicately curved bill and slightly hunched silhouette has its breeding grounds in Greenland and Siberia. With the onset of the northern autumn the birds begin the long journey to the south, where they will spend the summer fattening themselves ready for their return to the breeding grounds during the European spring – though many of the younger birds may over-winter at Langebaan and only migrate the following year.

Curiously, one marine species which no longer occurs here naturally is the oyster. Remains of a once abundant species have been found, but it died out approximately 2 000 years ago. In recent years an imported species of oyster has been introduced, and under the aegis of the Fisheries Development Corporation, aquaculture of these oysters takes place at the village of Churchhaven, on the western bank of the lagoon. Here the animals are grown on trays suspended below the surface of the water from which they filter their food. The future of the project is uncertain, however, since the proposed status of the lagoon as a national park will bar it to commercial enterprise, even when, as in this case, it is harmless to the ecology.

A more pressing question is the future of the bird colonies. Skaap Island is the home of a colony of black-backed gulls, one of the largest known of this species, while noisy masses of cormorants have settled on Jutten Island. Marcus Island supports two major bird societies: some 10 000 jackass penguins share the island with the largest-known resident population of the rare black oyster-catcher. These colonies pale, though, in comparison with Malgas Island, at the entrance to the bay, which is inhabited by vast jostling hordes of cormorants and gannets. The latter, numbering about 45 000, have raised territorial defence to a high art. Many duels take place, conducted with stiletto-sharp beaks.

41. *Near the compact coastal settlement of Port Owen, the mouth of the Berg River has been diverted and is maintained by breakwaters to allow fishing boats permanent access to the sea.* **42.** *Hardy dune flowers, Didelta carnosa, cling to the shore at Papendorp, near the mouth of the Olifants River.* **43.** *Elands Bay, with Verlorenvlei in the background, spells the intimacy of village, sea and nearby estuary.* **44.** *A wreck abandoned in the shallows of Saldanha Bay and the Grielum humifusum flowers in the foreground form a typical west coast contrast.*

When not squabbling, they maintain social order with elaborate rituals of appeasement, involving much oriental bowing and scraping. By common consent, the birds leave an open strip of ground, a kind of runway, near the edge of the island, from which they can take off on fishing trips. As they make their way down to the runway through the throng, they perform a repeated gesture of conciliation. The bird 'sky-points', raising its beak to expose the vertical black stripe on its throat as a sign of vulnerability.

If protection has allowed the gannet and cormorant colonies to expand rapidly in recent years, the jackass penguin has not fared so well. Otherwise known as the Cape or black-footed penguin, it is the most northerly of the 17 species of penguin. Its main breeding ground is Dassen Island, off the coast south of Saldanha. On this flat, sandy island it breeds in some 20 burrow areas around the perimeter. Once numbering about two million, the colony has been decimated by many years of egg-robbing and removal of the guano which sheltered the eggs from the sun and marauding gulls. Despite protection, its numbers have not recovered, and have now fallen to some three per cent of the original count.

In recent years Saldanha Bay has seen a number of collisions between industry and ecologists over the birds. One *cause célèbre* was that of the new iron ore jetty. Access for the ore-carrying ships required a deeper channel past Malgas Island to the sea. Blasting to enlarge the channel killed many thousands of fish. The local seabirds flocked to take advantage of this free feed, only to be killed in their thousands by the next blast. Protest from scientists and wildlife groups caused the blasting programme to be spaced out to allow the flocks to disperse between explosions.

Protest was also aroused by the building of the causeway between Marcus Island and Saldanha which acts as a breakwater protecting the export facility. Requests were put forward that a predator-proof fence be erected on the causeway, to prevent rats, meerkats and jackals from reaching the island. These were ignored, with the result that a horde of predators found its way along the causeway to wreak havoc in the colonies, killing many thousands of young birds. For a while the road along the causeway was flanked by cyanide guns, but these menacing objects have now been removed and a predator-proof wall has been erected, allowing the birds to rebuild their colonies.

Perhaps the most spectacular and most publicized industrial innovation on the

44

west coast in recent years is the nuclear power station at Koeberg. Firm bedrock was one reason for the choice of this site, and the other was sea water. A nuclear power station uses about 70 million litres of water a day for cooling. For many, haunted by the idea of a 'China syndrome', the site is altogether too close for comfort to the city of Cape Town, 30 kilometres to the south. Consensus among scientists, however, is that the plant will introduce proportionately less radiation into the atmosphere than can be absorbed in an afternoon's tanning on a granite rock. A more pressing, if as yet long-term, problem is that of the disposal of the radioactive waste. A site has been purchased in arid Namaqualand for the safe storage of low and medium level waste products.

As the station goes on line in 1984, its effect on the local marine life is being watched by scientists with interest. The large outlet pipes will return the water to the sea further up the coast. Though it will not be radioactive, it will marginally raise the sea temperature in a two kilometre-long strip along the shore, reaching about half a kilometre out to sea. Under this stimulus, many of the marine creatures may change their life-styles. Rock lobster, for example, will probably grow larger and more quickly, though their life span may be shorter. Mussels will also grow fatter, and cultivation of oysters and shrimps has been mooted, following the example of aquaculture near coastal reactors in America and Australia.

Marine biologists are far from the only scientists with an interest in this part of the west coast. Field study has brought to light a fascinating picture of prehistory

here in a number of important sites, one of which lies a few kilometres inland from Saldanha, at Langebaanweg.

In the 1950s this bleakly arid landscape was the scene of large-scale phosphate mining. In the course of excavations in 1958, a mine employee found a fossil tooth which had belonged to a long-extinct, four-tusked, elephant-like gomphothere, *Anancus*. Originating in Africa about 40 million years ago, it died out a mere two million years ago. It is believed to have lived in this area during the late Tertiary period, from about 10 to 15 million years ago.

The find caused great scientific excitement. Excavations were carried out by the South African Museum, resulting in the discovery of a vast treasure of fossil animals. These were matched by more finds at Arrisdrift, just south of the Orange River, which yielded remains from an earlier period, about 20 million years ago.

The Langebaanweg fossils allowed palaeontologists to reconstruct an image of the west coast as it was at the time of the great ice ages, when much of the world's water was locked in the polar ice-caps, lowering the sea-level. The Proto-Berg River flowed down from the inland plateau to a sea then many kilometres further out. This broad coastal zone with its moist, temperate climate supported rich forests and swampy grasslands, traces of which were left in the form of fossilized pollen.

The swamps and fern-forests were the home of a wide variety of animals. *Anancus* was one of these but there were many others, including small creatures such as the ancestor of the dassie, *Prohyrax*, as well as the tiny pika,

46

Kenyalagomys, a kind of mouse-hare. Primitive ruminants included the small, hornless chevrotain, *Dorcatherium*, and the deer-like *Climacoceras*. These lived off the vegetation and in turn became the prey for carnivores such as the bear-dog, *Amphicyon*, and a particularly menacing sabre-toothed cat. Larger denizens of the coastal grasslands were the three-toed horse, *Hipparion*, the herbivorous sivathere, the okapi-like giraffid,

45

47

48

Palaeostragus, and the enormous rhino, *Ceratotherium*. Dominating all these was the awe-inspiring giant cave-bear, *Agriotherium africanum*. Weighing up to 1 000 kilograms, this carnivore stood several metres high. It originated in Eurasia during the Miocene, before moving down into the bowl of southern Africa about six million years ago.

The bulk of these creatures, unable to adapt to changing conditions, lost the struggle for survival. Other animals took their place, among them the ancestors of modern man. A few kilometres from Langebaanweg is the site of an early habitation of *Homo sapiens*, a cave at Baboon Point, overlooking Elands Bay. Situated about 80 metres up a cliff, it has a fine view of the Atlantic, a few minutes'

45. *Some thirty kilometres north of Cape Town and operational in 1984, the country's first nuclear power station at Koeberg is built on firm coastal bedrock. Intake pipes which provide cooling water are sheltered by the arms of a specially constructed breakwater.*
46. *Gutting the catch at the end of a hard night's haul on the 'Kelp Coast'.*
47. *Buffeted by strong wave action, fragments of the large alga Ecklonia maxima, one of the dominant species in the large west coast kelp forests, break off and release mucus and particles into the water, providing a food base for bacteria and many marine animals.*
48. *A young rock lobster in a west coast sanctuary emerges warily from concealment.*

walk away. When man first came to this cave, though, the sea may not even have been in sight. The earliest, that is the lowest, deposits at the bottom of the cave midden have been dated to 150 000 years ago. At that time the earth was still in the grip of a major ice age, and the sea was as much as 25 kilometres further out than it is today. *Anancus* and his friends had long gone, but there were many other animals living on the coastal plain, as indicated by the bones of antelope which predominated in the first layers of the deposit. Buck continued to form a staple part of early man's diet for many thousands of years. But, at about 11 000 years ago, a hiatus is found in the cave record which coincided with the end of the last global ice age. A thaw followed, accompanied by the retreat of the ice-caps and a rise in the sea-level. The sea moved inland, swamping the coastal grassland and driving its fauna inland. Antelope bones therefore disappeared from the cave record.

Deprived of one form of sustenance, early man found that another had been brought to his front door – that of the sea. In the upper layers of the midden the bones of marine animals predominate, with remains of seals, penguins, cormorants and gannets. There are also traces of eelgrass, *Zostera*, probably used as bedding.

Man had come to know and use the sea. He found names for its plants and animals, its winds and currents. If the northern part of the west coast is still the 'Diamond Coast', the southern shore is that of the 'Kelp Coast'. It is no misnomer, for the marine life of the west coast is dominated by dense underwater forests of seaweed. There are a number of species, including the abundant *Laminaria schintzei* in the north and *L. pallida* to the south, but the most important is the fast-growing *Ecklonia maxima*. This enormous plant provides the framework within which lives a host of other plants and animals. Its dim-lit forests reach as far as three kilometres out to sea. Anchored to the sea-bed at a depth of up to about 12 metres, the thick, rubbery stem is supported at the surface by a gas-filled bulb from which band-like fronds radiate. These receive the sun's rays, providing energy to induce photosynthesis of the kelp's fibres.

Few animals feed directly on *Ecklonia*. Wave action is fierce here, making it difficult for animals to settle on the plants, although three specialized herbivores have learned to do this. The limpet *Patella compressa* occurs only on *Ecklonia maxima*. Highly territorial, it limits its own colonization of the plant to relatively small numbers, thus preserving its food source. The small alikreukel, *Turbo cidaris*, is more common. It can feed on the kelp, but wave action limits its excursions up the stem. A third herbivore, the perlemoen, *Haliotis midae*, has a more original way of using the kelp. It attaches itself to the rock at the foot of the plant. Raising its shell and part of its foot, it traps fronds washed under it by the waves, then feeds on them at its leisure.

For most of the animals, food is supplied by the kelp indirectly. Wave action constantly trims the larger fronds, releasing fragments into the water along with large quantities of mucus, and it is on these that the food chain is built. The mucus supports bacteria. Filter-feeders such as oysters and mussels live on the bacteria. Rock lobsters eat the filter-feeders, and are themselves the prey of octopuses. As well as being a food source, the kelp has a further use as a shelter for the animals, buffering the force of wave action. Nor is it of importance only underwater. The winter gales tear the *Ecklonia* from its anchor and, buoyed up by its air-filled bulb, it floats to shore. There it becomes food for creatures such as sea-lice and sand-hoppers, as well as offering shelter for many other species.

Besides the kelp, the main source of nutrition is that of the upwelling. Its very abundance, though, can sometimes backfire, as has been demonstrated by the phenomenon known as 'red tide'. This is caused by certain round-celled planktonic organisms, in particular *Noctiluca* which has a red pigment used to detect a light source. When in large enough concentrations it can be seen as a reddish coloration in the water, and is visible at night by its phosphorescence. In itself it is harmless, but when upwelling occurs more strongly than usual, dense blooms of this plankton grow. When concentrated even more by an onshore wind, they can lead to a red tide. *Noctiluca* gradually consumes all the available nutrients and then dies, becoming the prey of bacteria which in their turn deplete the water of oxygen. In this anaerobic environment mass mortalities of fish, rock lobster and many other forms of marine animal may occur. In effect, the food web is destroyed from below.

One of the biggest red tides on record occurred in 1966 at Elands Bay. It spread for some 50 kilometres along the coast, resulting in the death of many thousands of marine animals, particularly in the rock lobster sanctuary at St Helena Bay. Unlike most red tides it was formed not from *Noctiluca*, but from another species, *Gonyaulax grindleyi*. Nor was oxygen depletion the cause of the deaths, for oxygen levels in the water remained high throughout the tide. But the plankton grew in such density that it clogged the gills of the marine animals, literally suffocating them. It took almost a decade for the biomass in the area to recover from this latter-day plague.

If an explanation has been found for the red tides, another marine tragedy remains a mystery, that of the stranding of whales. This strange phenomenon has often been recorded on the southern African coast. Early travellers on the west coast observed the Khoisan peoples camped next to beached whales on which they lived for weeks or even months, in spite of the decomposition of the carcasses. The majority of these strandings were of single animals, but there have been cases where entire schools of cetaceans have been washed up. Two such cases occurred on the west coast in almost exactly the same area and in remarkably similar circumstances.

In 1936 a school of 58 false killer whales became beached at St Helena Bay and were found along a 1 500-metre stretch of the beach. Sixteen of them, though, were concentrated in one

49. *The forces of wind and sea have carved out a fantastic group of rocks south of Papendorp.*

particular spot. Forty-five years later, on 19 August 1981, a second stranding took place, almost duplicating the first. On this occasion 65 false killer whales were found strewn along the shore of St Helena Bay. The overall distribution was wider, covering about 93 kilometres, but the greatest concentration of the animals took place only 200 metres from the similar concentration of 1936.

Since whale strandings are completely unpredictable they have rarely been witnessed. These particular strandings took place on a lonely and uninhabited part of the coast and it was several days before the news reached local scientists. A detailed record was made of the 1981 event, including the sex of the animals, their approximate age, and the structure of their teeth. Of the 65 whales, the majority were females, though only one was found to be pregnant. Only seven were small enough to be classified as calves. Many had encrustations of worms around the ear openings, but these were discounted as having any direct bearing on the reason for stranding.

From a mass of theory and speculation on these and other strandings, few hard facts or tenable explanations have emerged. A deep underwater valley, the Cape Submarine Canyon, which runs perpendicular to the coast for about 100 kilometres, ends near St Helena Bay. It is believed that this may have helped to direct these normally deep-water creatures inshore. This, however, fails to explain their behaviour after stranding. They suffer great distress, and death by exposure in the broiling sun is protracted,

50

taking up to a week. Yet an almost universal feature of these beachings is the whales' persistent refusal to return, or allow themselves to be returned, to the water. The majority of those put back in the sea almost immediately beached themselves again.

Thus no conclusive answer to this mystery has been found. The strongest contender for an explanation is that of disease, particularly one affecting the animals' sonar system, but as little is known of cetacean diseases, such an ailment itself remains hypothetical.

If nature is capable of catastrophe, man can sometimes imitate nature, and even add something of his own. A prime example of this talent occurred on 6 August 1983, when the Spanish oil tanker *Castillo de Bellver* caught fire 40 kilometres off the coast to the west of Saldanha Bay. This enormous ship, 334 metres in length and weighing 271 540 tonnes, carried over a quarter of a million tonnes of crude oil, worth almost R65 million. The fire began at about half past one in the morning, starting on the port side and soon spreading to take control of the ship. Forty minutes after the outbreak of the fire, Captain Alfonso Civera and 31 of his crew took to *Castello*'s four life rafts. By now the vessel was a raging inferno, with flames and clouds of oil-laden smoke rising hundreds of metres into the night sky.

South African Navy and Air Force rescue units quickly picked up the crew. One oil-soaked crewman was plucked from the sea by helicopter and another was rescued by boat. Three members of the crew, however, remained missing.

In the early hours of dawn Safmarine's powerful tug *John Ross*, accompanied by two harbour tugs from Saldanha and two Kuswag anti-pollution vessels carrying chemical oil dispersant, arrived at the scene. As *John Ross* approached *Castillo* with the intention of sending a party aboard, the vessel suddenly split in two with a thunderous explosion, sending the tug into a hasty retreat. Thousands of tonnes of oil belched from the two halves of the stricken ship.

51

52

Fires continued to rage in the stern section as the two halves drifted apart but by mid-afternoon had abated in the bow section. Then, at about half past eight in the evening, with another violent explosion, the stern sank, taking some 100 000 tonnes of oil with it. The bow section, containing 60 000 tonnes of oil, continued to float, its nose pointing to the sky. By early the next morning it had become cool enough to allow a helicopter to lower two salvors onto its upraised anchor. After several hours of precarious work, perched 20 metres above a churning, icy sea, they managed to secure three heavy tow-lines from *Castillo's* anchor chain to *John Ross*. During the next week the tug slowly pulled the bow north-west away from the coast. About 80 kilometres west of Cape Columbine two explosive charges were detonated in

the ship's side and the last of *Castillo de Bellver* sank from sight.

However, the disaster was far from over. Left in the ocean was an enormous oil slick, representing the bulk of the ship's cargo. Gradually spreading to cover an area of over 1 000 square kilometres, it spelt potential ecological disaster for the west coast nearby. In response, an urgent rescue operation was mounted. In the following weeks several hundred oil-soaked penguins, cormorants and gannets were treated at the SANCCOB (South African Foundation for the Conservation of Coastal Birds) station in the Cape Peninsula. But if bad, this was infinitely better than had been expected. Strong north-westerly winds normally prevail on the west coast in August and would undoubtedly have driven the slick ashore, had they occurred. By a quirk of nature,

50. *This group of false killer whales was among the school of 65 animals stranded at St Helena Bay on 19 August 1981.* **51.** *The setting sun adds a romantic glow to the large iron ore export facility jutting from the eastern bank of Saldanha Bay.* **52.** *A representative selection of the ephemeral spring glory of the Namaqualand flowers, soon to fade under the summer sun.*

however, unseasonal south-easterly winds blew during the critical period. Slowly the oil slick drifted out into the open ocean, to be broken down and dispersed by the sea water.

On this occasion the usually dreaded south-easter prevented ecological disaster on an apparently barren coast that, despite its harshness and relative paucity of habitation, is still vulnerable to the hand of man.

THE CAPE PENINSULA

'CABO DA BOA ESPERANÇA'

On 16 January 1971 an historic gathering took place on the blue waters of Table Bay. Fifty-eight ocean-going yachts, sailed or towed from all around the country and including many overseas competitors, congregated here, in the midst of great public rejoicing.

It was the start of the first Cape-to-Rio yacht race. The shores of the bay and the slopes of Signal Hill were jam-packed with people and cars. The harbour itself was thronged with spectators from all walks of life, all passionately and vicariously absorbed in the excitement of this epoch-making race, in the sleek beauty and elegance of the boats, and in the challenge of competition. To all of this was added a strong spice of danger, for the sailors had 3 000 kilometres of the south Atlantic ahead of them, as lonely and elemental a place as any on earth.

At 4.30 sharp that afternoon the Mayor of Cape Town fired the starting gun, and the race began. Precisely 23 days and 42 minutes later the first competitor crossed the finishing line in Rio de Janeiro harbour. Back home, the news of *Ocean Spirit's* triumph was greeted with all the joy of a royal birth. And subsequent races have been greeted with no less stir, enthusiasm and discussion.

Cape Town and its people played host on this occasion, a rôle not new to them. For this is a city with a long tradition of hospitality, as well as a deep bond with the sea. Its history has seen many seafaring men, from early explorers such as Dias and Da Gama to Van Riebeeck and his companions planting a new society on the sandy shore where the modern city now stands.

Its beauty enhanced by the magnificence of its setting, the city lies enclosed between the bay and a group of mountains, in a broad valley flanked by Signal Hill and Lion's Head to the west and Devil's Peak to the east. Behind looms the brooding presence of Table Mountain itself. One of the world's great creations of nature, the mountain can be seen from up to a hundred kilometres away, a smoke-blue shadow against the azure sky of Africa, beckoning a welcome already.

53. *A nineteenth-century island in the contemporary perspectives of the Cape Town docks, the old clock tower in the Victoria basin was once the headquarters of the Royal Cape Yacht Club.*

It rises 1 000 metres, not to a peak but to a straight-line plateau, a hypnotic configuration which constantly draws the eye upwards. Its moods are many, its sandstone face a pattern of light and shadow, shifting from one moment to the next. It generates its own special weather effects, especially in the summer months when the prevailing south-easterly winds bring moisture which condenses along the plateau to lay the famous 'table cloth' of cloud.

But the city, the bay and the mountain are only a few of the elements which make up the complex of the Cape Peninsula and its surroundings. These comprise a kind of 'appendix' to the southern African coast, isolated by the expanse of the Cape Flats from the rampart of the Cape folded mountain range 40 kilometres away. From the Table Mountain massif the land continues southward, narrowing down to Cape Point and forming a rocky claw that projects from the subcontinent 50 kilometres into the Atlantic. The mountains of the Cape Peninsula fall steeply into the sea, but a variety of small villages and settlements, each with its own character, clings to the narrow coastal shelf. On the west side, facing the Atlantic, are Sea Point and Camps Bay with their Mediterranean flavour, still within easy reach of metropolitan Cape Town. Further south are Llandudno and, beneath the dramatic Karbonkelberg, the fishing village and harbour of Hout Bay. From here Chapman's Peak drive, with its splendid if vertiginous views, leads down to Noordhoek, Kommetjie and the small holiday village of Scarborough, once known as Schuster's Bay.

On its eastern side, the Peninsula forms one side of the expanse of False Bay. Here another row of villages hugs the steep shore from Muizenberg, at the juncture of the Peninsula and the Cape Flats, southward through St James, the fishing harbour of Kalk Bay, Fish Hoek, and

the naval harbour of Simon's Town, operational headquarters since 1957 of the South African Navy.

At the southern tip of the Peninsula some 40 kilometres of the coastline and the wild and wind-scoured land it encloses have been set aside as the Cape Point Nature Reserve. Once a group of five farms, it was declared in 1939 and handed over to a resident population of duikers, ostriches and baboons. These cast a wary eye on the many thousands of the human animal who make their way every year through the reserve to the historical and geological climax of the Peninsula, Cape Point.

Rising high over a restless ocean, buffeted by incessant winds from all quarters of the compass, this lonely spot draws people from all over the world. It is a place of history, of adventure, of the long-nurtured dreams of the sailors of old, of the Portuguese, Dutch, English and French. For them this was the feared 'Cape of Storms', the 'Cabo Tormentoso', which was also the 'Cabo da Boa Esperança', the 'Cape of Good Hope', representing the turning point of the southern seas as they voyaged east.

Now the descendants of Dias and Da Gama are solemnly warned by notice not to feed 'Los Baboons', while the heirs

of Van Riebeeck take the bus *Flying Dutchman* up the hill to the base of the old lighthouse, built in 1860 but long since disused, except as a platform for

54. *The unmistakable profile of Devil's Peak and Table Mountain, seen from Blouberg at dawn.* **55.** *The rhythm of horses exercising on Bloubergstrand counterpoints with a ponderous oil tanker, a familiar sight around the Cape coast.* **56.** *Equipped with a foghorn as well as an 850 000 candle-power light, the cheerfully candy-striped lighthouse at Mouille Point is one of the oldest still in operation.* **57.** *A spectacular panorama from Signal Hill across the docks and Table Bay, with a fog rolling in from the sea.*

54 55 56 57

visitors. Far down below, the waves break over the granite reefs of the Dias Rocks and Bellows Rock. It was here that the Portuguese vessel *Lusitania* foundered one foggy night in 1911, with the consequence that a new and automatic lighthouse was built on the rocks, almost at sea-level. Its lamp, until 1978 the world's most powerful, is capable of delivering a 20 million candle-power warning to passing ships.

Complementing the outcrop of the Cape Peninsula is the 'miniature sea' of False Bay. A thousand square kilometres in extent, it is flanked by mountains, but its bayhead abuts on the dunes of the Cape Flats. From Muizenberg a·long scimitar of white-gold sand stretches away eastwards. Nearby is Sandvlei with its water-side development, the Marina da Gama, and the large lake of Zeekoevlei, once the haunt of hippos but now the scene of dinghy sailors and windsurfers. Long gone from Zeekoevlei, hippos have recently been introduced in the neighbouring bird sanctuary of Rondevlei. A few kilometres further along the bay, Strandfontein is the site of another bird sanctuary which, unlike that at Rondevlei, developed without official assistance. The Strandfontein Sewage Works generates an abundance of small creatures living off the bacteria, and these supply the food for many marine and wetland birds.

Beyond Strandfontein, the sweep of the bayhead is almost uninterrupted. About half-way along are the Swartklip cliffs, but sandy beaches such as that at Macassar predominate thereafter to the seaside resort of The Strand and, tucked into the north-eastern corner of the bay beneath the mountains, the harbour of Gordon's Bay. On the eastern shores of False Bay are a number of holiday and retirement settlements such as Rooi Els, with its tranquil estuary, and Pringle Bay, with its fine beach and thick fynbos vegetation. Finally, at the south-eastern corner rises the sentinel of Hangklip.

Out in the bay is Seal Island, a small rock platform which supports a densely packed community of about 50 000 Cape fur seals. Hunted for generations, they were almost wiped out on the island by the turn of the century. With official protection from 1949 onwards, the population pendulum swung back. By the

58. *Along with five other local Moslem tombs, the kramat at Macassar on the northern fringe of False Bay is revered as a holy place. Erected in 1925, it marks the original burial place of Sheik Yussuf of Macassar, a prince of the East Indies exiled to the Cape by the Dutch in 1694.*

59. *A view of the elegant halsgewel of Groot Constantia, a restoration of the late eighteenth-century house built on the site of Governor Simon van der Stel's original historic home.*

influence on waves entering the bay from the open sea. As they encounter this barrier, the waves pile up against it, then converge again behind it with increased force. This effect is carried 30 kilometres across the bay from Rocky Bank to the far shore, between the mouth of the Steenbras River and Cape Hangklip, where it can strike in the form of isolated freak waves many metres high. Well stocked with fish brought in on the same currents, these waters attract many anglers. Some, forgetting danger in the excitement of the catch, are swept from the rocks by 'killer waves', and are remembered in a bleak row of crosses on the shore.

It was into these unreliable conditions that the first explorers sailed at the end of the Fifteenth Century. Dias came past early in 1488, and experienced the wrath of the 'Cabo Tormentoso' when his ships were blown out to sea for five weeks. Others soon followed his pioneer route around the tip of Africa, including the first to step ashore at Table Bay. In 1503 Antonio de Saldanha explored the sandy valley and climbed the mountain. From its summit he was able to look down to Cape Point, which he recognized from its description. After him, the bay was named the 'Aguada de Saldanha', the 'Watering Place of Saldanha'. The name survived until 1601 when the Dutchman Joris van Spilbergen made a landfall here. Like Saldanha, he had lost his bearings and marked the bay as 'Tafel Baay' on his charts.

On the heels of the Portuguese and the Dutch came the English, the first of whom to see the bay was Sir Francis Drake, in 1580. The narrator of *Golden Hind's* voyage recorded that it was '. . .the most stately thing, and the fairest Cape we saw in the whole circumference of the earth'.

Water was available here, and meat could be had by bartering with the local Hottentots. The bay became a regular stopping-place, with messages left under special 'post-office stones'. Soon the idea of a permanent settlement was conceived. In 1620, two English captains took possession of the bay in the name of their king, James I. They presented the resident Khoisan with an English flag, and piled a cairn of stones on the Lion's Rump, later to become Signal Hill. Pleased with their acquisition, they reported:

'We, Andrew Shillinge and Humphrey Fitzherbert. . . upon a good concert and by a consultation holden on shore, the first of July, 1620. . . in the Bay of Soldania, have taken quiet and peacable possession of the Bay of Soldania aforesaid for, and in the name of King James.' Their myopic monarch, however, repudiated their

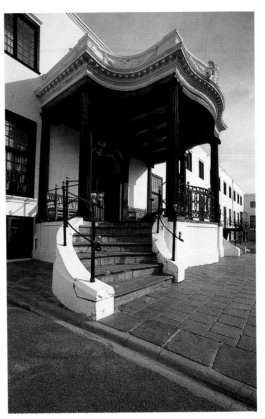

60. *The Kat Balcony in Cape Town Castle, built in the late Eighteenth Century, is a product of the combined skills of the French architect, Louis Thibault, and the German master-carver, Anton Anreith.*

action, in spite of their recommendations that the area was fertile, well-watered and offered good opportunities for whaling.

With the English out of the running, the Dutch took the opportunities instead. Like the English, they had long had experience of 'Soldania', not all of which was welcome. In March 1647 the Dutch East Indiaman *Haerlem*, on its way home with a valuable cargo of spices from the Orient, ran aground in Table Bay. The spice cargo and some of the crew were transported back to Holland but 60 men stayed behind to continue the salvage of the vessel and were rescued the following year. Among the rescuers was a young ship's surgeon named Jan Anthonisz van Riebeeck who, while the ship was picking up the stranded crew, took the opportunity to explore the area and make a considered assessment of its potential for settlement. On his arrival in Amsterdam and partly on the basis of his report, Van Riebeeck was given the job of setting up the first permanent community on the shores of 'Tafel Baay'. He was given a clear brief by the Council of Seventeen, the powerful executive committee of the Dutch East India Company in Amsterdam. They wanted a limited settlement only at the Cape. It was to act as a service depôt for the fleet, as a refreshment, quarantine,

mid-1950s their numbers had reached the 50 000 mark, and 15 000 pups were arriving each year. With barely an inch of rock visible and the colony offering heavy competition to fishermen in the bay, the authorities began a careful culling programme to keep the population stable, treating the seals as a renewable resource.

The whole area from Table Bay around to False Bay is an important transitional zone between the west and south coasts. This is particularly evident in the change of temperature from the western side of the Peninsula to the False Bay side. While winter temperatures are about equal, in summer the False Bay waters are 8 to 10 degrees centigrade higher than those of the western seaboard, one of the steepest temperature gradients recorded in an area of this size. The differential is at its most acute in the region of Cape Point, and it is here, too, that the most turbulent currents and winds occur. The mingling of the cold Benguela Current and the warm waters of the Agulhas stream, descending the east coast from the tropics, results in violent storms compounded by thick mists.

The interaction of coast and currents produces another effect, that of so-called 'killer waves'. At the entrance to False Bay a shoal called Rocky Bank, although invisible from the surface, has a profound

61

62

63

64

61. *The vagaries of the Peninsula's coastal weather demand great skill and dedication from local volunteer lifeguards. Here they practise riding the breakers at Llandudno.* **62.** *Waves crash in an age-old rhythm, relentlessly buffeting the unyielding granite of the Peninsula's shoreline.* **63.** *Many of the Peninsula beaches are well suited to the excitement and challenge of surfing, particularly in the winter months.* **64.** *On the windy shore where Van Riebeeck once vainly attempted to plant wheat, blocks of flats now rise in the suburb of Sea Point.*

revictualling and repair station at the half-way mark on the long voyage between Holland and the East Indies.

Accompanied by his wife and about a hundred Company servants of various ranks, Van Riebeeck put into Table Bay with his fleet of three ships in April 1652. His first concern, while the settlers were still living on the ships, was the building of a timber fort on the shore, by the mouth of the river that ran down the valley. A cluster of simple houses and workshops soon grew up around the fort. By the beginning of 1658 a sturdy wooden jetty had been erected, and by 1671 fresh water for the ships was being piped to the end of it. Company gardens and vineyards were planted in the valley, and crops were sowed. Within a few years men were released from the Company's service as Free Burgher farmers, to begin the long process of opening up the interior to the plough. After the Commander's departure on promotion to the East Indies in 1662 his successors rebuilt the fort, this time as a five-bastioned stone castle, finishing it in 1679. Its cannons were trained across the bay, in the direction of possible intruders.

By the early Eighteenth Century small settlements had spread around the Peninsula and False Bay shores. Hout Bay was a source both of wood and of fish. At Kalk Bay lime was burned to make whitewash for the local Dutch-style houses with their gables and reed thatch. Whaling also took place from the village, and hardly a house in the area did not have some evidence of this activity, with fences, walls and even steps being built from whalebone. At Muizenberg, in the north-western corner of the bay, the Dutch East India Company established a military outpost. One of its commanders, Wynand Muys, is believed to have given his name both to the nearby mountain and the village below.

Expansion into False Bay was partly stimulated by the weather in Table Bay, which was exposed to the north-westerly gales of winter. In 1720 a storm swamped almost the whole fleet, causing great loss of life. Attempts were made to build a breakwater, but these were all washed away. From 1741 Company regulations bound the shipping to anchor in False Bay during the winter months and a small battery and a repair depôt were set up in Simon's Bay.

It was a storm in Table Bay which led to a still-remembered act of heroism, that of

65. *The resilience of the granite base of the Cape Peninsula is reflected in this collision of sea and rock at Chapman's Peak.*

Wolraad Woltemade. Little is known of his early life. It is believed that he may once have been a soldier in one of the local command posts but by the 1770s he was an old man, retired to the life of a humble dairyman on the shores of Table Bay, where he had a cottage. He kept a few cows and goats, a smattering of chickens, and a horse.

The horse shared Woltemade's fate, and that of the remaining men on the wreck of the Company's ship *De Jonge Thomas*. On 3 June 1773 a gale blew the ship onto a reef near the mouth of the Salt River. Trapped in the foundering vessel, the survivors signalled wildly to the shore for help. Ignoring the advice of the other onlookers, Woltemade mounted his horse and rode it out into the sea. Against the surge of the storm, they worked their way out to the wreck. There the old man instructed the sailors clinging to spars and rigging that they must come no more than two at a time, and that they must hang on to the horse. Thus he carried 14 men back to the shore, two at a time for seven trips. But by now *De Jonge Thomas* was beginning to break up, and those left on board panicked. When Woltemade came back for the eighth time on a now exhausted horse, a confusion of hands pulled both man and animal beneath the waves.

Within a few years of the wreck of *De Jonge Thomas*, the Dutch East India Company itself began to sink. The great days of the merchant empire were long over, and troubles at home were starting to sap its energy. In 1794 the French Army overran Holland and the House of Orange fell, to be replaced by the puppet régime of the Batavian Republic. It was this development which, indirectly, led to the first British take-over of the Cape the following year.

The British assumed that having conquered Holland, the French would automatically annex her colonies. In the case of the Cape this would mean a major threat to the eastern trade route and growing British interests in India. Accordingly, they despatched a fleet of nine warships under Vice-Admiral Sir George Elphinstone, carrying about 1 600 soldiers under the command of General Craig, to rescue the colony from this dire possibility.

In June 1795 they sailed into False Bay and anchored off Simon's Town. Messages were forthwith conveyed to the Dutch Governor, Abraham Sluysken, that they were come to save the colony from their common enemy France, whose fleet, it was intimated, might appear on the horizon at any minute.

Sluysken was under no illusion as to what this amounted to; in modern parlance, he was being made an offer he could not refuse. His only defence was to temporize for as long as possible. Tension mounted as the parleying came to a stalemate. Then on 3 August a squad of the local Hottentot soldiers, known as Pandours, fired on a party of British sailors who had come ashore. It was little enough, but it gave the British commander all the excuse he needed to begin his invasion.

The Dutch, in spite of ample warning, were ill-prepared. Their main strategic strongpoint was the narrow bottleneck of land between the sea and the steep mountain slopes at Muizenberg. Here De Lille, second-in-command of the Dutch garrison, made his stand. Numerically, he had a clear advantage over the invaders, his 3 600 troops comprising a mixture of regular militia, burgher volunteers,

soldiery had thrown a heavy party which had lasted deep into the night before. At the time the British made their appearance they were still in a condition of hangover. To the pounding in their heads was soon added the pounding of guns. The combination was too much for the dazed defenders and De Lille was soon forced to fall back to the banks of the Zand Vlei, beyond reach of the Navy's guns. By four o'clock in the afternoon a triumphant General Craig had occupied Muizenberg.

His position, though, was still far from secure. After the initial retreat – a humiliation for which De Lille was later court-martialled and which is perpetuated in today's suburb of Retreat – the Dutch rallied, and the Governor made ready for a counter-attack. But as he did so the odds swung decisively against him. On 9 August *Arniston* put into False Bay with reinforcements of 400 men, guns and

66. *The spectacular 10-kilometre Chapman's Peak drive follows the division of strata between the Peninsula's granite base and its sandstone superstructure.*

Pandours and Malays. The British, on the other hand, had only half that number.

On the morning of 7 August they landed their men between Simon's Bay and Kalk Bay and, without opposition, marched along the shore towards the defences at Muizenberg, their progress covered by the fleet which sailed parallel to the shore. When they arrived at Muizenberg in the early afternoon they found a skimpy defence manned by a curiously hesitant crowd of soldiers. In spite of the tensions of recent weeks and the obvious imminence of an invasion, the Dutch

supplies. Two weeks later 14 more ships arrived, carrying an occupation force of 3 000 troops. A century and a half of Dutch rule had come to an end.

Having acquired a colony cheaply at the cost of 15 lives and a little hypocrisy, the British then abandoned it seven years later when the Peace of Amiens brought a break in the war with France. Resumption of the Napoleonic conflict, however, brought them back again at the Battle of Blaauwberg in 1806, this time for good. The Navy was moved from Table Bay and domiciled at Simon's Town, which was

67

68

now fortified with a Martello tower on the model the British had observed in Corsica. The town developed a Regency flavour, most evident in the elegant Admiralty House.

The newcomers quickly added a new style to an already colourful and heterogeneous community. Africa, Europe and the Orient met in the leisurely streets of the town by Table Bay, its castle now the seat of the new Governor and the quarters for the British garrison. The work of an immigrant English artist, Thomas Bowler, perfectly captured the flavour of the period, both in the town and in the bay, now the scene of British merchantmen and warships. Other immigrants transplanted memories of the 'old country', among them an Oxfordshire man named Henry Peck, who set up a famous inn overlooking the beach at Muizenberg. He gave his hostelry the beguiling name of 'The Gentle Shepherd of Salisbury Plain'. For the next thirty years he dispensed largesse and introduced the pleasures of the False Bay coast to travellers, presiding in a no-nonsense fashion over a rough-and-ready establishment which nevertheless served good fare and, surprisingly, champagne. Over the entrance to the thatched 'Gentle Shepherd' was Peck's motto, 'Life is but a journey, let us live well on the road'.

From the mid-century onwards the False Bay coast began to gain a definite vogue. The country's first branch-line railway was built from Cape Town to Wynberg in 1864 and in the years following was extended piecemeal along the False Bay coast. The passion for sea-bathing which developed in the 1880s added to the popularity of such warm-water places as Muizenberg, St James, Kalk Bay and the decorous Fish Hoek — the British had banned the sale of liquor in the village since their sailors tended to drown getting back to their ships, and Fish Hoek remains 'dry' to this day.

Daguerrotypes of the period record the gaiety and ease of those days, though the whirl of the south-easter as it curves around the 'instep' of the bay in the summer months remains a familiar link with those Victorian ladies holding down hats and skirts.

Another charming picture is drawn by a 'Lady living at the Castle' in the *Cape Monthly Magazine* for August 1870, when she describes Malay fishermen in Table Bay '. . .pulling up the fish as fast as they can, tucking them up like helpless babies under their left arms, with one jerk of the wrist, and followed by an immediate tap on the head or nose with the club. The boatmen thus seem to be always performing the antics of Punch and Judy. . . and any breezy day you may see dozens of these boats fishing among the shipping in Table Bay and all of them doing a capital business, I am sure'.

If the bay was generous, the weather continued to be a threat to shipping. The first British occupation had seen a violent storm, that of 1799, in which the warship HMS *Sceptre* had been wrecked on 'Sceptre reef'. With the steady increase of traffic the building of a permanent breakwater became an imperative, and in 1860 the Colonial Government set aside a large sum for the project. On 17 September that year Prince Alfred, the fifteen-year-old son of Queen Victoria, tipped the first load of stone.

Nature's answer to this human presumption came when no more than 100 metres of stone had been laid, in May 1865. Grim warning of the impending storm had built up for days beforehand, with lowering clouds, mounting northerly winds and a plummeting barometer. Then, early in the morning of Tuesday, 17 May, the fury of the ocean was unleashed on the bay and its crowded shipping.

At the start captains and crews battled to hold anchor, and the 'anchor-boats' which darted around the bay supplying

replacements for lost tackle did heroic service. But by mid-afternoon all human control over the situation had been lost. Even the largest ships were torn contemptuously from their moorings, smashed against each other or hurled onto the beach where hundreds of appalled spectators watched helplessly. No voices could be heard above the roar of wind and waves, and when night fell the searchlights on the shore made little impression on the gale-swept darkness. One vessel attempted to escape into the open sea, only to be dashed onto the rocks at Green Point, discharging its crew into the maelstrom. Courage or despair, insane acts of heroism, all were equally to no avail.

It took four days for the storm finally to blow itself out. As a cold grey dawn broke on the shore it was possible to count the cost. Sixty people had died, and over a hundred sailors were left destitute on a beach littered with the debris of the week's destruction. The fine new breakwater lay in ruins, a jumble of broken stone. Eighteen large sea-going vessels were lost, including the mail-steamer *Athens*. As a kind of pathetic foot-note, a squealing pig, a chance survivor from one of the wrecks, ran to and fro among the dead and the barely living.

Since the 'Storm of the Century' there have been a number of changes in the contours of Table Bay, many of them concerned with increased protection of shipping. The rebuilt and completed Alfred Dock was inaugurated in July 1870, and the first decades of the present century saw the large-scale reclamation of the Foreshore area. The old profile of the bay disappeared, though Van Riebeeck's statue in the Heerengracht, the Castle and the recently uncovered Wassenaar Dam in the Golden Acre development remain to suggest the contours of the old order. The Alfred Dock has been supplemented by the massive Duncan Dock, with its large

precooling chambers for perishable goods and, more recently, by the Ben Schoeman Dock which has containerization facilities. Understanding of the way in which heavy wave action takes place has led to new styles of breakwater design.

67. *A rusting hulk, half buried in sand, is all that remains of* Kakapo, *washed up in Chapman's Bay near Noordhoek on 15 May 1900.* **68.** *A study of sand-covered kelp fronds, thrown up on the beach by a storm. Half-buried, they are a food source for sand-hoppers, which in turn are eaten by sanderlings and white-fronted plovers.* **69.** *A lonely vista of the beach at Noordhoek, looking towards Kommetjie.*

69

The existing Table Bay breakwater has been extended with many thousands of 'dolosse', large 20- and 50-tonne concrete tetrahedrons which, by virtue of their angled planes and open formation, effectively disintegrate and disperse wave energy.

Today Cape Town is the country's second largest port after Durban. The biggest export is that of the Cape's fruit, amounting to almost a million tonnes of fresh fruit and over 300 000 tonnes of canned fruit annually. The bulk of the country's high-quality table fish is also brought here, to be canned and exported. Many of the major fishing companies have their headquarters in the large office blocks on the Foreshore, as do other bodies related to the industry, including the Sea Fisheries Research Institute and the Fisheries Development Corporation.

Besides fisheries research, many other forms of science connected with the sea are represented in and around Cape Town. South Africa's first marine biological station was set up at St James in the 1890s. Since then, the wealth of marine life around the Peninsula has been the subject of intensive study, much of it centred at the University of Cape Town, where there are flourishing departments of Oceanography, Zoology and Environmental Studies. The departments of History and Anthropology seek clues to man's prehistory on the coast, while the Department of Geology has made studies of the origins of the Cape Peninsula itself.

As mountain formations go, the Cape Peninsula is relatively young. About 800 million years ago a dark slate, referred to by geologists as 'Malmesbury Shale', was laid down in sedimentary deposits in the area of what is now the western Cape. Some 250 million years later igneous granite, molten material crystallized at great depth, was forced from below this shale level to the surface. Composed of coarse, light-coloured crystals of silicates,

72   73

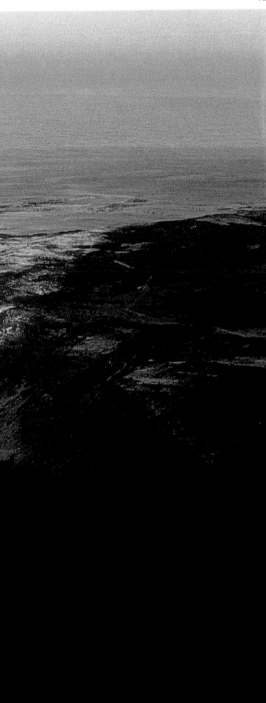

feldspar and quartz, it formed an uneasy partner with the shale through which it was injected.

On rare occasions temperature and pressure were sufficient to fuse the mutually incompatible shale and granite. An interesting example of this fusion is Darwin's Rocks at Sea Point. In June 1836 the young Charles Darwin, already pondering upon the concepts which were to bear fruit as the *Origin of Species by means of Natural Selection,* arrived in Table Bay on the brig *Beagle.* The ship's naturalist, his interests included the study of geology, and his inspection of the contact zone of the two rock types at Sea Point reinforced many of his speculations on geological evolution.

The mountain range formed by this first upheaval was gradually eroded level. Then, between 400 and 500 million years ago, the land became submerged beneath the sea. Over many millions of years sand was deposited at the bottom of this new ocean, to an almost incredible depth. In places the Cape folded mountain range, derived from this deposition, reaches more than 3 000 metres, and once rose even higher. Gradually, however, the sea retreated, baring the rock formation of compacted sea-sand known as Table Mountain Sandstone.

Thus, on the granite and shale base a massive superstructure of sandstone was erected. The demarcation between the two levels is clearly visible across the face of Table Mountain, continued through

70. (Previous page) *A navigator's view of the imposing crags of Cape Point, with Dias Rock in the foreground.* 71. *The succession of bays and headlands leading to Cape Point on the Atlantic side of the Peninsula.* 72. *The ubiquitous dassie, a familiar sight in the Peninsula mountains, is an incongruous relative of the elephant.* 73. *A lone chacma baboon forages on the stony Cape Point shore, one of the few places in the world where baboons are known to feed on intertidal organisms.*

Lion's Head and Devil's Peak, and is particularly well revealed along the Chapman's Peak drive, where the road follows the geological division for many kilometres.

Seismic upheaval and the work of the oceans thus created the original structure of the Peninsula. Since then, however, it has been considerably altered. The erosion of wind and waves has sculptured the rock, more quickly where it is soft, more slowly where it is hard granite. Vast areas were carved away to leave the low-lying Cape Flats and to isolate the Peninsula, an isolation increased by periodic rises in the sea-level which turned it into an island. Erosion gradually modelled the familiar outlines of Table Mountain and its companions, a process which is still going on and, notwithstanding the hardness of the rocks, is surprisingly rapid. Indeed, it has been estimated that at the present rate most of Table Mountain will have worn away in the next ten million years!

Against the upheavals of the earth's crust, the affairs of man and the animals appear properly dwarfed. An image of the fauna and flora of about 20 000 years ago has been reconstructed from remains found in the Swartklip cliffs, on the northern edge of False Bay. Here an accumulation of fossil bones was discovered, believed to have been left originally by hyenas which lived during one of the last great ice ages. Then the shoreline extended beyond Cape Point and Cape Hangklip, and today's False Bay was low-lying temperate grassland. Among the remains found were those of the extinct giant Cape horse and the giant buffalo, along with the relics of more familiar animals, known either historically or still surviving elsewhere. These included the quagga and the white rhino, as well as wildebeest and springbok. Together with those of grazing animals were found bones of hippopotamus, clawless otter, water mongoose and reedbuck, showing that streams or fresh-water pans must have punctuated this broad, open plain.

With the coming of the thaw the bay came into existence again. By this time man was well established in the area, and one site in particular appears to have been congenial. This is a cave overlooking the sandy valley which links Fish Hoek and Kommetjie at the southern end of the Cape Peninsula. Once known as the Schildersgat, or 'Painter's Cave', it is now called Peers Cave, after the two men who were responsible for its excavation.

Bertram Peers and his father Victor lived a few minutes' walk from the cave.

74. *The Atlantic Ocean provides the backdrop for this group of recently introduced zebra on the windy heights of the Cape Point Reserve.*

Enthusiastic amateurs, they began in the mid-1920s to dig in the cave. Expecting little at first, they soon uncovered stone tools, weapons and ostrich-shell beads, as well as great quantities of mussel shells. Then, in 1927, they hit the archaeological jackpot, with the discovery of a complete skeleton. Small in stature, it was estimated to be some 15 000 years old.

'Fish Hoek Man' had arrived. The first major find of its kind in this part of Africa, it caused a great sensation. Further excavation revealed two more well-preserved adult skeletons and one of a small baby. Unhappily, the methods used by the Peers, while enthusiastic, were crude by present-day standards, and their records were primitive. Thus, much of the potential value of this exciting discovery in terms of the analysis of the levels of the cave deposits and their more precise dating was lost for ever.

One of the important food sources of early littoral dwellers such as Fish Hoek Man was that of stranded whales. Most strandings are of single animals but entire schools have sometimes beached, as happened in 1936 and 1981 at St Helena Bay on the west coast. One of the largest recorded examples of this baffling phenomenon took place on 24 December 1928, on Long Beach at Kommetjie. This stranding was unusual in that at least part of it was witnessed. The foreman of a local farm was out at about five o'clock in the morning with his greyhound, hunting for hares, when suddenly he became aware of a great commotion at the edge of the bay. After a moment he noticed the whales, which appeared to be standing up in the water, filling the air with their cries.

Within a few hours the beach was littered with more than a hundred bodies. As is almost universal with these strandings, the whales could not be induced back into the water, and instead died of exposure in the summer sun over a period of about a week.

The event aroused great public interest, compassion and, unfortunately, rapacity. Almost immediately a large crowd of souvenir hunters began sawing and hacking out the teeth of the whales, though on occasion the practice was known to backfire. One small boy seated himself astride the tail of an apparently dead whale and dug his penknife into its flesh, only to find himself an instant later six feet up in the air! Finally, however, the decomposition of the corpses drove away even the most determined, and the Kommetjie municipal workers were left with the malodorous task of disposing of the remains.

The False Bay shore was the scene in 1966 of another kind of marine mishap, that of a 'red tide'. Unlike the similar case at Elands Bay, the plankton on this occasion was the normally non-toxic *Noctiluca*. Strong onshore winds concentrated both the plankton and the nutrients of the upwelling, and a heavy 'bloom' occurred. At night this was clearly visible in explosions of green phosphorescent light as the waves fell on the shore. During the next few days the wind fell and, in the sluggish currents at the northern end of the bay, the plankton was unable to disperse. Having used up all the available nutrients, the plankton then died. With the subsequent breeding of bacteria on the decayed organisms the dissolved oxygen in the water was used up, causing widespread mortalities of fish and other marine life.

A 'red tide' may be beyond man's control, but other aspects of the False Bay waters and shore are subject to human influence. In particular, the question of the management of fish stocks has aroused much debate in recent years. Because of the shallow nature of the bay,

commercially important demersal species such as kingklip and hake are rare here, and bottom trawlers are not permitted to work the bay. Until recently the catch consisted largely of pelagic species caught in purse-seine nets, but a steady decline in these shoals resulted in increasing restrictions being placed on the local fishermen. Finally, in November 1982, a total ban was imposed on purse-seine fishing for pelagic species in False Bay.

If the fish are declining, the human population in the area is expanding rapidly, particularly on the nearby Cape Flats where a 64 per cent increase is predicted by the year 2 000. A heavy increase of effluents into the bay will inevitably follow, including that of sewage. As demonstrated at Strandfontein, this is not necessarily harmful to the wildlife, but it is hardly attractive to swimmers or sailors. At present the bay copes easily enough with the load. In the windy months of summer the 'residence time' of the water in the bay is usually about four to six days, though it is longer in winter, and the turbulence created by waves, tides and currents cleans out the bay. The general drift of the currents is clockwise, but this is not always predictable – counter-clockwise eddies in the Gordon's Bay area tend to have the effect of sending the effluent back where it came from.

If sewage, within limits, can be fitted into the marine food web, industrial effluent is another matter. Here again, expansion of the community on the Cape Flats is likely to have a long-term effect. The industrial discharge into the bayhead at present derives mostly from canning works and chemical and fertilizer companies, and there is no doubt that more large-scale industrial concerns will be developed here in the future. The extent to which False Bay will be able to dispose of the additional waste matter is a question to which only time can supply an answer.

The threat to the balance of the sea has its counterpart on land, and nowhere more so than in the survival of the local fynbos vegetation, the richest concentrations of which are found along the mountain fringes. Where the mountains stand back from the sea, as in the stretch between Rooi Els and Cape Hangklip, water draining from the slopes supports many varieties on a shelf of Table Mountain Sandstone. This 'tall moist heathland' is dominated by ericas such as the Prince of Wales heath and mealie heath. Besides ericas there are members of the protea family such as *Mimetes hirtus*, flowering shrubs such as *Leucospermum bolusii*, and the white swamp daisy *Osmitopsis asteriscoides*.

Unfortunately, many of these beautiful plants are under threat from so-called 'plant invaders'. During the Nineteenth Century, in order to bind the constantly shifting dunes which made crossing the Cape Flats a five-hour nightmare, a number of plants were imported from Australia. They included the Australian wattle, here rechristened rooikrans, sweet hakea, and the ubiquitous Port Jackson bush. They did their work all too well. The Port Jackson and the rooikrans now almost entirely dominate the once denuded Cape Flats. Not satisfied with this conquest, these tough, fast-growing plants have also begun to invade the fynbos territory on the mountain slopes.

Sweet hakea, for example, has become an increasing pest on the west side of the bay, particularly between Miller's Point and Simon's Town. The fynbos has little chance against such competition, though the authorities, with the aid of volunteer 'hack groups', have managed to limit the more aggressive of these take-overs.

A more insidious threat to the fynbos comes from an unexpected quarter. In 1980 it was discovered that about 20 per cent of the indigenous species have their seeds dispersed by ants, in a process known as myrmecochory. The ants concerned are three of the five local species, the brown house ant, the pugnacious ant and, to a lesser extent, the black garden ant. Plants from about 30 of the fynbos families produce seeds which have a sweet, oily appendage called an elaiosome. Attracted by its smell, the foraging ants carry the seeds underground to their nest, and there they eat the elaiosomes. The seeds, still viable, remain in the upper galleries of the nest, a few centimetres below the soil surface, where they are protected from fire, rodents and insect predators. When veld fire burns the living plants overhead, removing the competition for sunlight, the seeds germinate and new growth begins.

This age-old co-operation between plant and insect, however, has long been under siege from an intruder. In about 1900, during the Second Anglo-Boer War, the Argentine ant was brought from South America in fodder imported for the British horses. Since then this highly aggressive insect has systematically displaced the local ant species, and in doing so has posed an indirect but powerful threat to the fynbos. Instead of carrying the seeds underground, it eats the elaiosomes where it finds them. Left exposed on the surface, the seeds fall prey to passing rodents and other insects.

The cycle of growth and regeneration is thus broken at a crucial point. Progressive retreat of the fynbos has already been witnessed in areas dominated by the Argentine ant. If urban expansion and pollution have all too visible effects on the ecology, this two millimetre-long creature promises to wreak an equal havoc on one of the country's most precious natural assets.

75

76

75. *Sunrise over the Hottentots Holland mountains silhouettes the naval port installations across Simon's Bay. Long the South Atlantic base of the Royal Navy, since 1957 Simon's Town has been the logistic and operational headquarters of the South African Navy.* **76.** *Gaily coloured bathing huts add a sedate Victorian note to the beach at St James.*

77

77. *One of the several crosses erected in memory of anglers drowned by freak 'killer waves' on the treacherous eastern shore of False Bay. In the distance is the dramatic landmark of Cape Hangklip.* **78.** *False Bay in a serene mood. Sunrise at Muizenberg beach captures the anticipative pleasures of a day's fishing.*

78

79. *Some 550 million years old, these rocks near Simon's Town show the characteristic formation of the Peninsula's granite foundation where it meets the sea.*
80. *A whaling centre in the Eighteenth Century, the charming old fishing village of Kalk Bay continues to depend on the fish stocks, particularly snoek, in and around False Bay.*

79

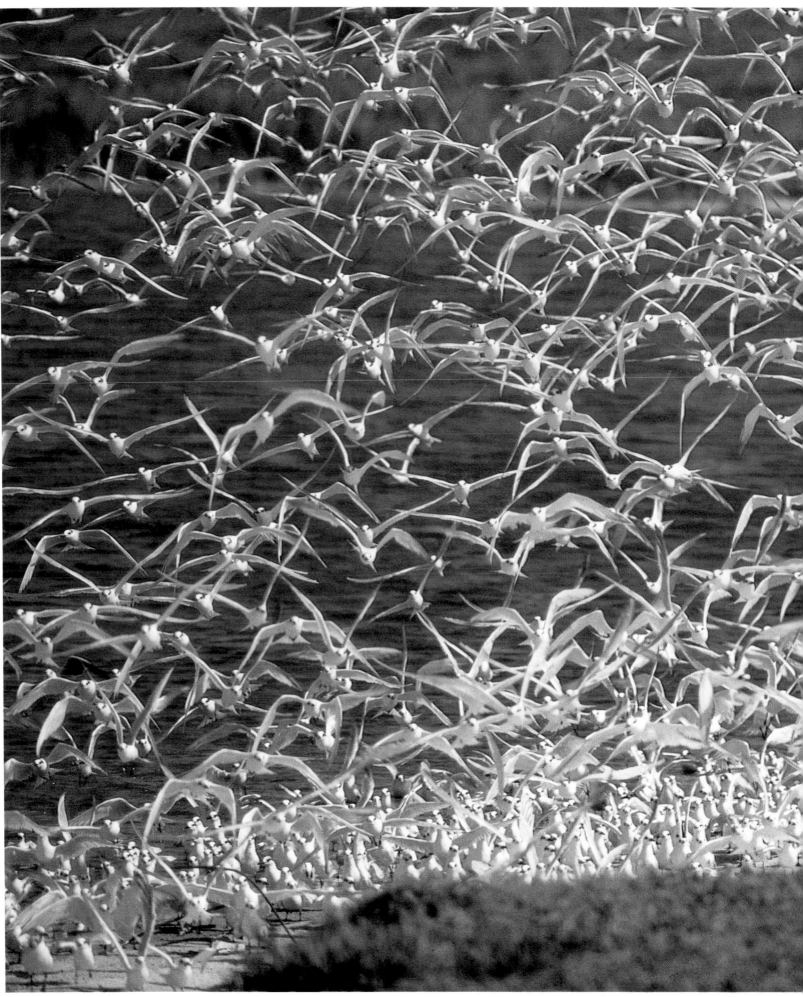

81. *An abstract pattern of threshing wings as a flock of terns takes to the air.* **82.** *Showing off the striking design on its back, a white-breasted cormorant preens its wings.* **83.** *Well known for their habit of gleaning insects disturbed by browsing livestock, the cattle egret also feeds on shrimps, molluscs and fish.*

82

83

THE SOUTH COAST

SHIPWRECK SHORE

As the climax of a mighty continent, Cape Agulhas leaves much to be desired. Low cliffs back away from the shore, leaving a rough stretch of wind-stripped heath around a ragged group of holiday houses and shacks. There is no clear headland, only a series of wet black reefs running parallel into the sea, the water churning between them among pebbles and broken shells and the pink carapaces of moulted crayfish.

This bleak and lonely place is the most southerly point of Africa, and was long the goal of western man's dreams in the high Renaissance. The first recorded sighting was in 1488, when Bartolomeu Dias named it Cape Saint Brendan, since the discovery took place on the saint's name day, 16 May. The title of 'Golfo das Agulhas', or 'Gulf of Needles', was originally attached to what is now the nearby Struisbaai, but was later transferred to the headland. The name

84. *A southern right whale breaches, hurling itself out of the water to crash back with an explosion of spray. This once-in-a-lifetime photograph was taken by marine biologist Dr Peter Best while conducting his annual census of southern right whales.*

seems at first ambiguous, since the rocks in the area, while intimidating enough, hardly resemble needles. However, the explanation lies in the magnetic forces in the area — early pilots noticed that at this point their ships' compasses recorded the true and magnetic poles as one.

The land leading down to Cape Agulhas is a broad, low-lying plain. The main road linking Cape Town and Mossel Bay deserts the coast here for several hundred kilometres, cutting off this segment of land and its wild coastline, one which is still remarkably unspoiled. Scattered villages lie mostly within a day's drive of Cape Town, particularly in the stretch up to Walker Bay where the mountains still hug the shore. Here are popular holiday settlements such as Betty's Bay, Kleinmond, Onrus with its 'restless' river and shore, and Hermanus with its lagoon, Kleinriviersvlei. The northern edge of this 800-hectare expanse of water is the scene of a major attraction for sailing enthusiasts, the Hermanus Yacht Club. With a large membership, mainly from Cape Town, the club runs an eight-month season from October to May which reaches a climax in the famous Hermanus

Easter Regatta. Besides sailing, 'getting away from it all' in this area means fishing, swimming and surfing, walking in the mountains or along estuaries such as those of the Bot River and the Klein River, or exploring the older parts of the charming small fishing communities dotted around the coast.

This is the region of the southern extension of the continental shelf, the Agulhas Bank, 60 fathoms deep and reaching 250 kilometres to the south, with its concentrations of pelagic fish. The largest harbour on the south-west coast is that of Gansbaai, at the southern end of Walker Bay. Once enjoying the expressive name of Gansgat, this little community of hardy fishermen received a boost during the Second World War, when a factory was built to process shark liver oil, with its high vitamin A content. Today this vitamin is synthesized and demand for the liver oil has fallen away, though sharks, particularly the vaalhaai, continue to be caught here and dried for export.

Although less spectacular than in many other parts of the southern coastline, the landscape here is of great interest to geologists. The twin agencies of wind and

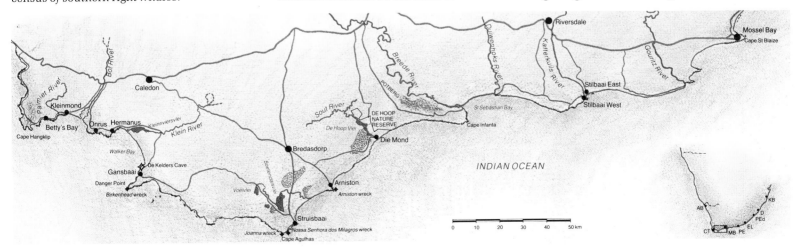

English vessel *Joanna*, headed for Surat in the East Indies, ran aground north-west of Cape Agulhas. She was still fast on the rocks when the sun rose, and Captain William Browne and his men set about building makeshift rafts to paddle their way to land. After 10 days' walk along the shore the first three Englishmen arrived at the Dutch East India Company's settlement at the Cape. Commander Simon van der Stel immediately became alert to the possibility of salvage and forthwith sent Ensign Olaf Bergh and a party of men to the wreck. The ship had been badly mauled by the waves but Bergh managed to retrieve a substantial

water have eroded many caves in the compacted 'beach rock' which comprises the coastal terrace, the best-known being probably 'Waënhuiskrans', 'Wagon-house cave', at sea-level in the cliffs below the fishing hamlet of Arniston. Opinion is divided as to the number of wagons, double-decker buses or other forms of transport which could be contained in this enormous, booming cavern. What is certain is that it is not to be entered lightly, for the sea is still at work here, and even at low tide access is far from easy.

A smaller but no less interesting example of nature's handiwork is to be found near the community of Die Kelders. One of the 'cellars' in question is a large sea-level cave once known as the 'Drup Kelder'. Lady Anne Barnard, who made a day trip to it on 8 May 1798, gave a vivid impression of the cave, with sidelights on the complications of sight-seeing at the turn of the Eighteenth Century. The humour and observation of her account are spiced with the dangers of possible leopards, which she calls 'tigers', precipitous cliffs, and the bone-strewn gloom of the cave itself:

' . . . in the distance appeared stupendous hills of white sand, over which we had to cross,' she wrote. 'Many tremendous mounds of sand did we ascend and descend, our wheels above the axle-trees, and at last we reached a curious cave of petrifactions, called the Drup Kelder – or rather we arrived in the neighbourhood of it, for it took us some time to discover the path, which was steep and dangerous, and had to be done on foot. Sometimes this path was only two feet broad, with a precipice at the side, in which I must assuredly have been dashed to pieces had I fallen; no ascent of the Table Mountain was equal to the dangers and horrors of this. At the cave's mouth there lay sundry bones, but we could not judge what animal they belonged to. Tigers often infest it, and feast on what

they drag inside; it was, therefore, necessary to fire a gun before we entered the cavern, and to have plenty of light to intimidate the creatures. Unless in greatest want no savage animal will attack a man; the guides remarked by the trembling of the horses that they had smelt tigers near about, but we saw none. We had fortunately brought a tinder-box, and the gloom of the cave was soon illuminated by some wax candles which I packed up after my last party in Berkeley Square – you will remember! They little thought, those candles, when their tops had the honour of shining upon some of their Royal Highnesses, and in your right honorable face, that their bottoms would next illuminate the Drup Kelder in South Africa.'

If the shore had its leopards and precipices, the sea held greater terrors. Beset by wayward currents and powerful gales generated deep in the Antarctic waters, this is one of the most dangerous reaches of the southern African coast. Probably more wrecks are concentrated here than in any other region, spanning a full five centuries of navigation. In a small museum in Bredasdorp, a few kilometres inland, many memorials to the victims of the Cape Agulhas shore are collected.

The Shipwreck Museum is a fascinating and a haunting place. In these quiet rooms are preserved the relics of many of the almost 200 wrecks claimed by the south coast. Here, too, is a record of the many human responses to the crisis of the sea. Two early incidents illustrate not only the plight of the stranded but also the often ambiguous attitude of those on the shore.

In the early hours of 8 June 1682 the

85. *A lowering sky over white, windswept dunes on the exposed shore near Arniston warns of an impending storm.* **86.** *Seen here from one of the caves in the eroded beach rock, the fishing hamlet of Arniston takes its name from the tragic wreck of an English transport vessel lost in the bay in May 1815.*

85

86

quantity of booty, to the value of some 28 000 gulden, from which the men were paid a handsome reward. By this time the crew of *Joanna* had gratefully departed on a passing English vessel, indifferent to the fate of their gold, a lesser treasure than their lives.

Something of the same pattern was repeated a few years later with another wreck, that of the Portuguese ship, *Nossa Senhora dos Milagros*. This time, though, there were interesting complications. To begin with the ship was carrying unusual passengers, a contingent of Siamese emissaries laden with greetings and expensive gifts for Louis XIV of France and the Portuguese court. Among them was one Occum Chamnan, who left an account of the wreck and its harsh aftermath.

The ship ran aground near Cape Agulhas, not far from the spot which had seen the wreck of *Joanna* four years earlier. With no food, the survivors set out to walk to Table Bay, living as best they could off raw shellfish. Succour in the form of a tribe of Hottentots appeared but turned out to be a grave disappointment, particularly for the Siamese. It was the custom among early voyagers around the southern coast to barter with the Khoisan in coins of low value, to avoid spoiling the market. The Portuguese bought a cow with their copper small change, but the bewildered Siamese found their gold and diamonds contemptuously spurned.

When the small group of bedraggled men finally reached the Cape, Simon van der Stel, spurred on by rumours of gold and jewels on the wreck, busied himself secretly organizing Bergh and his men for another profitable salvage. The results, however, when the party finally arrived back at the Castle, were less than expected. Van der Stel cast a rueful eye over the few small cannon and the bales of muslin and sailcloth that had been retrieved; of the rumoured treasure of gold and diamonds there was no sign.

The Commander, however, must have carefully scrutinized Olaf Bergh's bland countenance and detected something therein of which he became suspicious. As rumours of theft began to circulate, he caused several of the salvage experts, including Bergh, to be rounded up and thoroughly questioned after the seventeenth-century fashion. Under this probably far from gentle encouragement, Bergh revealed the spot in his garden where a drinking cup, two saucers of gold and a flask of musk were buried.

His passion for the treasure of the Orient cost Bergh several years of exile in the Indies. A congenitally buoyant character, however, he soon surfaced again, to be found back in the Cape in 1695, in command of the garrison. As if this were not irony enough, he lived to buy up Van der Stel's model estate of Constantia after the Governor's death. There he spent the remainder of his days, a living proof of the vagaries of fortune.

Advances in ship design by the beginning of the Nineteenth Century were no guarantee of immunity from the devastation of the southern gales. A grim reminder was provided by the fate of the British transport vessel *Arniston* which had left Ceylon for England in early April 1815. Crew and passengers numbered 350 and included 19 women, 33 children and a group of invalid soldiers.

Off the south coast, towards the end of May, *Arniston* ran into a violent gale which tore away most of her sails, leaving her with little power of manoeuvre. On 29 May, driven by a powerful south-easterly wind, the ship came within sight of land. By the next day it became clear to Captain Simpson that he was trapped in a wide bay and, with little chance of escaping back out to sea, had no option but to make for the shore at the safest-looking place. Unfortunately, he was unaware of the shallow depth of the bay. About two kilometres from the beach the ship suddenly ran aground, tilting over to windward. Simpson ordered the guns to be cut free and jettisoned, but the ship remained unmoved. It was now about eight o'clock in the evening, and the gale began systematically to dismantle *Arniston*. Water poured in below decks, drowning most of the invalid soldiers outright. In a few moments the mainmast was torn free and keeled overboard. Screams of terror, cries for help – all were lost in the rending of timbers and the roar of wind and waves.

When dawn broke on the shore there

87. *The colours of rust and sand blend in the beached wreck of an old floating dock.*

was little to be seen. Of the 350 people on *Arniston*, only six sailors had succeeded in swimming to the beach. These bewildered and disorientated survivors, hoping to find their way to the Cape, set off in the wrong direction. After four days of walking an endless beach and living off shellfish they turned back, arriving at the scene of the disaster again three days later. Here they found a cask of oatmeal washed up, and the ship's pinnace. While eating the one and attempting to repair the other, they were found by a farmer's son, Jan Swartz. Almost immediately, rescuers converged on the bay. They were met by a grim sight. For kilometres along the beach lay over 300 bodies of the drowned, of men, women and children. As one observer reported, there were 'mothers with their children, husbands with their arms still locked around their wives', lying where the sea had cast them up.

If there were acts of heroism on *Arniston*, they were lost in darkness and oblivion. Forty years later another British ship was to go down on this coast, to leave behind an heroic legend and to become perhaps the most celebrated of all the wrecks off southern Africa. This ship was the ill-fated *Birkenhead*, at the time of her launching in 1845 the largest ironclad ship in the Royal Navy. Originally intended as a frigate, she was used instead as a troopship, and it was in this capacity that she came to her famous end on the night of 25 February 1852.

Birkenhead had left Simon's Town a few days before, having stopped to take on coal. On board, besides a crew of 131 officers and men under Captain Salmond, were 487 soldiers, including 14 officers. Most of the soldiers were young recruits, signed on a few weeks before embarkation and destined for the Eighth Frontier War, then being waged inland from the settlement at Algoa Bay. Besides the men, there were seven women and 13 children.

Unlike that of *Arniston*, *Birkenhead*'s doom was unconnected with bad weather. The sea and sky were calm, with only a slight breeze. Once Cape Hangklip had been passed, the captain set the course and speed at a little over seven knots before retiring below.

The course set by Salmond skirted the shore, but it took no account of the vagaries of the underwater reefs in the area, then little charted. It was one of these reefs, about a sea mile to the south-west of the all too aptly named Danger Point, that *Birkenhead* struck just before two o'clock in the morning of that mild summer night.

From the first impact to the final disappearance of the ship took little more

than half an hour. The rock ripped open *Birkenhead*'s bow plates, letting the sea into the forward troop deck where most of the sleeping soldiers were drowned. In the rest of the ship several hundred men were thrown from their hammocks and, in plunging darkness, they struggled half-clothed through the hatchways to the deck.

In the same first violent moment of panic and confusion, Captain Salmond managed to make his way from his quarters onto the bridge. There it took little to tell him what had happened. His

88. *Commercial fishing in the old style, from a small open boat, still persists at Stilbaai.*
89. *A group of fishermen on the weathered old wooden jetty at Stilbaai clean their catch by dunking it in the water.*

answer was a desperate gamble, but one which failed tragically to come off. He ordered the engine-room to reverse the engines, in an attempt to pull *Birkenhead* off the rock. With luck, this might have worked. In the event it simply increased the already gaping lesion in the ship's belly. The bilge was flooded instantly, followed by the engine-room. While *Birkenhead*'s great engines were doused behind them, the engine-room crew fled upwards for their lives.

By now the huge ship was little more than a helpless carcass, rocking to and fro with the blows of the waves. On the quarterdeck several hundred wild-eyed and frightened young soldiers were marshalled and told to keep quiet. In an attempt to stem the tide the captain asked one of the officers, Major Seton, to send men down to the chain pumps. Sixty doomed men went down. The gunner, a Mr Archbold, set off flares which added an eerie light to the scene, but after a few minutes they gave out and the deck was plunged once more into darkness.

By now it was clear that nothing could save the ship. The captain ordered the boats to be lowered and the women and children brought out. The events of the next few minutes were half lost in confusion. As with almost all sea-going ships till modern times, there were not enough boats to take everyone on board. *Birkenhead* carried two cutters, two gigs, one dinghy, a pinnace and two paddle-box boats. Of these, only the cutters and one of the gigs had survived the crash. The first cutter, under the command of coxswain John Lewis, was lowered into the sea. But as it went down a number of soldiers jumped into it from the ship's gunwales. To keep priority for the women and children the cutter pulled away while the second cutter, carrying the seven women and 13 children, was lowered into the water, followed by the gig. All three boats moved away to wait within range of the sinking ship.

Captain Salmond climbed up into the mizzen rigging to call out that all officers and men who could swim should try and make for the boats. The instruction, however, was almost immediately countermanded by the army officers in charge, Captain Wright and Lieutenant Girardot, who ordered the men to stand fast where they were. Their explanation, that they were afraid the men would swamp the boats with the women and children, was given no test of proof. In a few moments, while the troops stood to forlorn attention in the welter of the quarterdeck, the ship abruptly broke in two and sank.

In the chaos of sea, men and wreckage that ensued, many were sucked down into the vortex of the sinking ship. Some managed to save themselves by clinging to pieces of the wreck, others reached the boats, while still others swam for the shore. Of these latter, few made it to the beach. The thick kelp near the shore entangled many of them, others were killed on the rocks, and many sank from exhaustion and drowned.

The men, women and children in the cutters were rescued the next day by a passing schooner, *Lioness*, on her way from Algoa Bay to Cape Town. The gig managed to reach the shore at Walker Bay. Later *Lioness* returned to the wreck to find that *Birkenhead*'s mainmast still showed above the water, with 44 exhausted men clinging to it. Together with some 50 souls who had managed to reach the shore, the total of survivors came to 184. They were the lucky ones. Altogether, 445 people had died on *Birkenhead*.

The survivors were taken to England, and in May 1852 those from the Navy were courtmartialled at Portsmouth. They were not only exonerated from all blame, but were commended by the Court for the 'steadfastness shown by all in the most trying circumstances'. The judgement of public and press which followed was even more fulsome. The tragedy of errors became ennobled with a glow of heroic sacrifice, at the heart of which the idea of 'women and children first' took pride of place. On the windy shore where the fragments of *Birkenhead* were washed up, however, little remains besides rock and fynbos and a plaque which records the stark essence of the tragedy:

'In memory of those who perished in H.M.S. Birkenhead, 26th February, 1852.

The ship, carrying reinforcements for the Eighth Kaffir War, struck a sunken reef approximately 1⅓ sea miles south-west by south from this point.

Nine officers, three hundred and forty-nine of other ranks and eighty-seven of the ship's company lost their lives.

Every woman and child was saved.'

90. *As evening approaches, a couple of fishing boats pass the light at Stilbaai's harbour entrance, bound for the heavy fish shoals of the Agulhas Bank.* **91.** *Viewed from its old harbour, the fishing and holiday town of Hermanus is overlooked by brooding mountains.*

90   91

A disaster area for man, however, may be a haven for other animals. Under the influence of the southern gyre of the Agulhas Current, the water here is relatively warm, and the rocky shores harbour a great variety of marine creatures. If the kelp stands are not as thick as those found on the west coast, there are nevertheless abundant growths of a variety of algae in the low infratidal zone, including such species as the prickly-bladed kelp *Ecklonia biruncinata*, and *Bifurcaria brassicaeformis* which thrives on heavy wave action. As always where algae are present, colonies of their consumers occur, including urchins such as *Parechinus angulosus*. Sharing the rocks with the algae are dense concentrations of the characteristic red-bait, a creature much used by anglers as bait, and favoured by those fish which can

form a kind of miniature 'garden' around each limpet. The limpets feed on the algae but do not completely destroy their food source. Under the stimulus of this constant 'grazing' the algae grow even faster, supporting a very high population of *Patella cochlear*. The problem of the resulting over-crowding has been solved in a unique fashion, for in the intervals between feeding the juveniles climb on the backs of the adults, one on top of the other, forming a sort of living tenement and leaving space for the recovery of the gardens. This partnership has led to an astonishingly high limpet population – up to 2 600 have been counted on a single square metre of rock surface!

The upper reaches of the shore are the realm of the barnacles, which give their name to the upper and lower Balanoid zones. The lower of these zones has a

annual visitors to the south coast is the southern right whale, which can grow to a length of 15 metres and weigh up to 55 tonnes. Despite its size, this is a docile and slow-moving creature, with a top speed of little more than six knots. The combination of these factors, together with the fact that once killed it remains floating, made the southern right whale a favoured target for whale hunters in the past – indeed, it is believed to have been given its name because it was 'right' for hunting. It has been strictly protected since 1935, and legislation introduced in 1980 prevents harassment as well. It is now an offence to approach to within 300 metres of a southern right whale, and in the event of one surfacing close by it is necessary to depart forthwith to more than 300 metres' distance.

Of an estimated world population of

92

93

break it open, for it has the rare ability to synthesize a protective coating of tunicin, a cellulose-like substance. The rock pools at this level of the shore are inhabited by many starfish, including the spiny *Marthasterias* which has a novel way of dealing with its preferred prey of black mussels. It uses its tube feet to prise open the shell of the bivalve, then extrudes its stomach into the animal to digest it.

Further up the shore is the Cochlear zone, named after the animal which dominates it, the pear limpet *Patella cochlear*. These creatures have evolved a symbiotic relationship with a number of species of tiny red algae which grow to

further range of algae, including species of the *Gigartina* and *Gelidium* genera, but supports a relatively limited number of animals, among them the limpet *Patella longicosta*, and winkles such as *Oxystele sinensis*. In the rock pools are found many anemones, as well as the scavenging whelk *Burnupena*. The upper Balanoid features barnacles, limpets such as *Patella granularis* and *P. oculus*, and winkles such as *Oxystele variegata*. At this height on the shore the algae begin to give way, though the sea lettuce *Ulva* and the knobbly *Iyengaria* can be found.

The warmth of the water attracts large animals as well as small. Among the

about 5 000 animals, some 500 now live in South African waters. They move inshore in the spring and early summer to mate or to calve. Walker Bay is a favourite mating ground where single adults are often seen from mid-August to October, but where cow/calf groups can also sometimes be observed. About 70 per cent of the local calvings, however, take place further to the east, in the area between Arniston and Cape Infanta, off the coast of De Hoop Nature Reserve. As she moves ponderously through the warm shallow waters inshore, rolling and wheeling with the calf by her side and coming up at regular intervals to 'blow', the right whale

94

95

92. *Evidence of a rich shore life, two limpet shells lie on the stony beach at Cape Agulhas, together with sea-urchin tests and a cuttlefish bone cast up by the waves.* **93.** *Fish traps have long been a feature of the southern coastline, many of them surviving from the time of the Khoisan. This contemporary example is at Skipskop.* **94.** *The view from the end of Africa. First navigated by Bartolomeu Dias in 1488, the lonely headland of Cape Agulhas is now marked by a lighthouse and a radio beacon.* **95.** *Life in a south coast fishing village is as stark and exposed as the coast itself. Flapping washing adds colour to the lime-washed cottages at Arniston.*

mother is a living landmark to be long remembered.

The abundance and variety of life on the shore is matched by that of the coastal strip itself, particularly its vegetation. This part of southern Africa has a Mediterranean-type climate, with winter rains and hot, dry summers, conditions which exact special adaptations from the local flora to retain water through the dry season. The result has been the evolution of the indigenous group of plants known as the 'fynbos'.

The unique qualities of these plants have long been recognized by botanists, who group them together in one of the six 'floral kingdoms' of the world, the Cape Floral Kingdom. Though it is the smallest of these kingdoms, taking up only about four per cent of the country's land surface along the Cape mountain ranges and coastal belt, fynbos is distinguished by a remarkable concentration of species. There are at least 8 550 species of flowering plant here, of which some 6 250 are found nowhere else. The best-known are probably the magnificent Proteaceae, with more than 320 different species, and the Ericaceae which has 605 species, including the heaths. Of the 860 South African Iridaceae species, the majority are found in fynbos areas, adding substantially to their floral wealth.

Many of these plants are now endangered, by plant invaders such as wattle and pine, by agriculture, and perhaps above all, by the ever-present hazard of fire. Official protection and the dedicated labours of gardeners and botanists, however, have created a number of fine wild-flower reserves on this part of the coast. The area around Betty's Bay contains the highest known concentration of fynbos species and many are protected in the Harold Porter Botanic Reserve, which includes the beautiful Disa Kloof with its waterfall and dense indigenous trees. At Hermanus the Fernkloof Nature Reserve is a 171-hectare sanctuary for plants, birds and animals.

The best-known as well as the most discussed wildlife area on the south coast, however, is that of De Hoop Nature Reserve, centred around De Hoop Vlei, some 50 kilometres to the east of Cape Agulhas. Long and narrow, De Hoop Vlei extends from north to south for about 15 kilometres, averaging about half a kilometre in width, and is fed from the north by two small rivers, the Sout and Potteberg. Landlocked at the southern end, it is separated from the sea by about two and a half kilometres of rolling white sand dunes.

The water level of the vlei has varied

dramatically at different times in the recent past. The average annual rainfall, mostly in the winter months from March to October, is about 450 millimetres. Drought or flood can alter this pattern, and De Hoop Vlei has seen examples of both. The worst drought in recent memory occurred in 1975, when the vlei dried up completely, with a resultant heavy toll on the breeding populations of the bird colonies. At the opposite extreme was the flooding which followed heavy rains in 1957. Hemmed in by the coastal dunes, the overflow spread in a huge sheet of water over almost 3 500 hectares of the coastal plain, reaching a maximum depth of about six metres. The flood waters lasted for up to two years in some places, causing much rejoicing among the aquatic birds, followed by a massive population explosion. Local ornithologists also rejoiced, at the first large-scale breeding in South Africa of the greater flamingo.

Even in normal times the brackish water of the vlei supports a veritable 'who's who' of birds, more than could easily be listed. Some 220 of the south-western Cape's 370 bird species are found here, of which 104 have been recorded as breeding at the vlei. Flocks of coots are common, as are two of the local duck species, the Cape shoveller and the yellow-billed duck. Wading birds include the elegant grey and black-headed herons, the yellow-billed egret and the familiar cattle egret, the smallest of the white egrets. Egyptian geese in particular do well here, taking advantage of an incidental food source provided by grainlands stretching away from the northern edge of the vlei. After the harvesting of the wheat, oats and barley at the end of the year the grain left in the stubble attracts thousands of these geese to the area. They also congregate at the vlei for their post-nuptial moult in summer, when they are left flightless for several weeks.

The shores and hinterland of the vlei are no less interesting than the vlei itself. A rich fynbos vegetation is complemented by enormous white milkwood trees, some of them centuries old, which provide nesting sites for the local fish eagles. These majestic birds divide the territory of the vlei between them, feeding off the Mozambique tilapia and varying their diet with an occasional coot.

Besides birds, the fynbos provides shelter for many animals. Duiker, steenbok and grey rhebuck have been supplemented by eland, springbok, bontebok and mountain zebra imported from the surrounding areas. Small-spotted genet, large-spotted genet, Cape mongoose

96. *One of the many fynbos species that adorn the coastal areas of the southern Cape, Erica plukenetii is but one member of the amazingly diverse and numerous Ericaceae family.*
97. *The protea family is one of the glories of the Cape Floral Kingdom. Of the 320 recognized species, Protea neriifolia is one of the best known and occurs in abundance on the southern Cape mountains.*
98. *Believed extinct for many years, the beautiful and striking marsh rose, Orothamnus zeyheri, now grows in the Kogelberg Forest Reserve and in the Hermanus mountains.*
99. *Between July and December the flowers of Leucospermum prostratum can be seen along the coastal flats around Hermanus.*
100. Mimetes hirtus *grows in profusion on the well-watered slopes of Aasvoëlkop.*

98   99

100

and striped polecat are common and Cape fox can still be found here, while populations of water mongoose and clawless otter tend to vary with the level of water and the abundance of food.

A series of cliffs and ridges lying parallel to the coast borders the northern part of the vlei. Known locally as 'hardeduine', they are composed of compacted 'beach rock' which has been eroded over the ages, and many deep caves have been formed in them. One of particular interest to zoologists is the 'bat cave'. Situated on the eastern side of the vlei, its entrance looks out over the bush that flanks the shore and is 15 metres above the water level. During the Second World War, when fertilizer was scarce, the farmer who then owned the land around the vlei exploited the deep bat-guano deposits, and in doing so opened the entrance from a bare metre in height to the present gap of four metres.

The cave penetrates 470 metres into the cliff. About 40 metres from the entrance a sharp bend in the tunnel effectively reduces the air flow to the deeper parts of the cave, including a large domed chamber 200 metres further in. Enhanced by the body heat of the bats themselves, the midsummer temperature in this chamber can reach over 30 degrees centigrade. The combined effect of the temperature and the uniquely pungent aroma of the animals is enough to daunt all but the most devoted bat-lover. For the bats themselves, however, conditions in this 'fine and private place' are ideal for the maternity colony which collects here.

There are 28 known species of bat in the Cape Province, the most common of which is Schreiber's long-fingered bat. Of the six known breeding places of this animal in the Cape, the most important is that at De Hoop Vlei, where a population of well over 100 000 congregates in summer to breed in massive maternity

roosts. Besides this dominant species, four other insectivorous bats occur here. Two are horseshoe bats, Geoffroy's horseshoe bat and the Cape horseshoe bat, while breeding populations of the mouse-eared bat and the common slit-faced bat bring the probable summer population of this single cave to about 150 000.

Together with the general deterrents of heat and atmosphere goes the hazard of contracting the disease histoplasmosis. This is caused by the fungus *Histoplasma capsulum* which is found in many of the world's warmer climates. It particularly favours the nitrogen-rich environment provided by any kind of guano, including bat-guano. A number of forms of infection result from inhaling the spores of the fungus, of which the commonest is acute benign pulmonary histoplasmosis, or 'cave disease'. Its symptoms are similar to those of influenza and last for a few weeks. This curious disease was caught *en masse* by a group of nine visitors to the De Hoop cave in October 1977. Though usually mild and never fatal, it is enough to persuade most people to leave the bats in peace.

In 1956 the vlei and its surrounding riverine bush were bought by the Cape Provincial Administration, which then substantially enlarged the area of land under its control with the purchase in 1980 of the farm 'Dronkvlei' and the Potberg mountain. A complex of vlei, coast, dune and mountain habitats were thus brought together as the present De Hoop Reserve. Among the creatures now included in the reserve are a colony of Cape vultures which breed in a rocky kloof on the Potberg mountain. Once common and widespread across southern Africa, this species of griffon vulture feeds exclusively off carrion, and its numbers have declined drastically before the advance of agriculture. Its traditional habitat has been ploughed and planted

with wheat and other crops, wild animals have been supplanted by domestic animals, and food shortages and general unpopularity with farmers have been compounded by other hazards of civilization, such as electrocution on power lines. Today the vultures depend almost entirely on fortuitous stock deaths among the local sheep.

Records by ecologists at Potberg over recent years have reflected the erratic and declining nature of the breeding colony there. The highest number recorded was 111 in 1972 and a decade later the population had dwindled to about 55. In 1982 only 17 eggs were laid, of which 10 hatched but only four birds survived past the fledgling stage. With a premium on available food, the juveniles, lacking in experience and socially inferior at what carcasses are available, struggle to survive. It has been proposed to help the younger birds by providing carcasses at special 'vulture restaurants', but the practical and financial implications of this move have yet to be fully worked out.

The vultures are not the only threatened species at De Hoop. A recent survey of the flora and fauna resulted in a list which included, among the plants alone, six endangered, 14 vulnerable, and 56 rare species. Many of the pressures which have led to this situation are irreversible.

To the hazards of civilization which threaten the reserve a new one has recently been added. On 16 March 1983 it was announced through an unscheduled leak to the press that the government intended to expropriate about 55 000 hectares of land between Arniston and Cape Infanta, to be handed over to the government-linked company Armscor as a missile site. Of the total, 38 000 hectares

101. *An octopus ambushes a crab on the rocks near Arniston.* **102.** *Fish hanging out to dry in the sea wind at Kassiesbaai, near Arniston.*

was private land, while the balance of 18 000 hectares was to be taken from De Hoop Reserve. The area also included the fishing village of Skipskop. The site was to extend along the coastal strip and was to be divided into three main areas: at the western end, near Arniston, would be the missile-launching area; to the east of this would be an intermediate zone; and at the eastern end of the site would be the 'impact zone', on what is now the farm Elandspad. The eastern slopes of the Potberg were to be granted the dubious privilege of stopping any missiles which failed to land on the designated target.

The rationale for the choice of this site was apparently the work of the Armscor computer which, having been informed that the missile site at Lake St Lucia on the northern coast of Zululand was being phased out, was instructed to look for a new area. Criteria for the decision were that the land must be cheap, 'bad' for agriculture and situated far from the country's borders; that it must have an amenable climate and be on the coast to allow for the testing of long-range and sea-skimming missiles; and it must be within reach of a major city, as an incentive to draw highly qualified personnel.

On the bases of these criteria the computer picked out the heartland of the Cape's ancestral ecology. Reaction was immediate. A storm of public anger and protest was aroused at the prospect of such an installation in such an area, and a flood of letters and memoranda, as well as a petition containing 18 000 signatures, landed on various administrative and ministerial desks. It was pointed out that no consultation with ecologists had taken place, no 'need and desirability' survey had been carried out, and the Cape Department of Nature and Environmental Conservation had not been approached.

The result was that the government belatedly agreed to a study of the effects the proposed missile site would have on the environment. A commission set up under the chairmanship of Dr Douglas Hey included the chairman of Armscor and a number of well-known scientists.

From the outset the commission admitted that it was in an invidious position. It was being asked to put the horse back in front of the cart without, of course, disturbing the cart. Moreover, it was allowed little time in which to assess the information it was given, to collate it fully, or to find new information. None of the scientists on the panel was qualified

103. *Attended by the inevitable crowd of gulls, these fish-drying racks are found in the old harbour at Hermanus, now a national monument.*

to review the specifically military determinants in the choice of site. On certain security matters, the members were sworn to secrecy.

The report of the Hey Commission was released on 6 December 1983. Immediately accepted by the Cabinet, it contained many hopeful points. The farmland to the west of De Hoop Vlei will be incorporated into the reserve, bringing the complete wetland ecosystem within its boundaries. Five kilometres of beach to the east of Waënhuiskrans will remain open to the public. A five kilometre-wide strip of sea east of Waënhuiskrans will be closed only when necessary and then in close co-operation with the local fishermen. Armscor personnel will not be granted access for angling or other recreational purposes to areas restricted to the public. Research scientists and students will continue to have access to the area, subject only to safety and security precautions. All low flying over the reserve will be prohibited. No form of military exercise besides the testing of missiles will take place. There will be no vehicle testing, troop manoeuvres, tracking, parachuting or sea-landings. No underwater weapons such as mines, depth charges, torpedoes, explosives or sonar and associated acoustic research devices will be set off. No missile-testing will take place into or over the sea during the calving season of the southern right whales between 1 June and 31 December each year. All activities will take place

outside the breeding season of the Cape vultures, and no vehicles will be allowed up the Potberg. Strict fire regulations will be enforced. Moreover, it will take three to four years for the range to be set up, so the villagers of Skipskop will have time 'to adjust to the changed circumstances and for an orderly process of resettlement'.

A major accomplishment of the Hey Commission is that the management of the entire area will fall under the Cape Department of Nature and Environmental Conservation, which intends to both increase the number of nature trails and implement a greater control of the invasive alien vegetation. The details on public access to the reserve, however, remain somewhat cloudy. Free access will no longer be allowed, and entry will be by permit only, a proscription which needs clarification. A further cause for debate is the provision of ecological services in the area. The report recommends the appointment of a 'site ecologist', to be responsible for a botanical and zoological survey of the region and for monitoring the ecology every five or 10 years. Many ecologists consider this inadequate and would prefer to see an independent team of scientists forming a permanent 'Standing Review Committee' and working in close conjunction with the Armscor personnel to provide regular reports on any changes in the wildlife. Only in this way can it be guaranteed that what has been accepted on paper becomes a living reality at De Hoop Vlei.

104. *The broad sweep of De Hoop Vlei.* One of the most important wetland areas on the south coast, the 15 kilometre-long vlei is central to the De Hoop Nature Reserve and is home to some 220 bird species, despite regular and sometimes severe fluctuations in the water level.
105. *Set in beach rock on the eastern side of the vlei, the bat cave at De Hoop harbours up to 150 000 bats during the summer breeding season. The dominant species in the cave is Shreiber's long-fingered bat, but there are also colonies of Geoffroy's horseshoe bat, the Cape horseshoe bat, and the mouse-eared and common slit-faced bats. High temperatures and humidity in the cave, as well as the plentiful supply of insects in the surrounding area, are among the reasons for this being the most important bat roost in the Cape Province.*

106

107

106-108. *As man with his guns and fences encroached upon their territory, the larger species of antelope gradually disappeared from this southern area of the Cape Province, either moving eastward or, like the blue antelope, becoming extinct. Some former inhabitants have been successfully reintroduced to the De Hoop Nature Reserve and such species as bontebok (**106**), springbok (**107**) and the rare mountain zebra (**108**) can again be seen grazing the fynbos vegetation.*

108

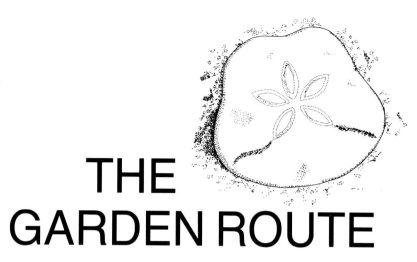

THE
GARDEN ROUTE

OYSTERS AND ELEPHANTS

On the shores of the lagoon near the town of Knysna is a sight that would have gladdened the hearts of the Walrus and the Carpenter. This is the Knysna Oyster Company, founded in 1948. Started with the help of a Dutch oyster farmer, the company is now a flourishing commercial concern, growing many thousands of oysters each year. Much of its development has taken place in conjunction with research by the Fisheries Development Corporation which runs an oyster hatchery nearby. Since 1963 the Corporation has studied methods of rearing fine, fat oysters in the – as yet – unpolluted waters of the lagoon.

The oysters are induced to spawn artificially by raising the temperature of the water. Great quantities of minute swimming larvae are produced and then fed on cultures of phytoplankton until they grow large enough to settle and to metamorphose into miniature oysters, called 'spat'. Once well established, the spat are handed over to the Knysna Oyster Company to be raised to commercial size. They are suspended from wire racks in the lagoon, well clear of the mudbanks to

prevent the young oysters from being smothered by sediment disturbed by mud-prawns. Safely ensconced, the oysters filter tiny particles from the water and grow for about two years before being collected for canning and distribution. Originally the local species *Crassostrea margaritacea* was farmed, but it proved unreliable and has been replaced by a more successful import from Japan, *Crassostrea gigas*.

Profitable aquaculture of this kind would not be possible without the generosity of the clear, dark waters of the Knysna lagoon. But the oysters are only one of a myriad of marine and estuarine species which are found here. They in turn are part of the larger bounty of what has long been popularly known as the 'Garden Route'.

In its wealth of both wildlife and visual beauty of every kind, this part of the coast is unique. From Mossel Bay to Cape St Francis stretches a mosaic of sea and lakes, of rivers and estuaries, and of mighty indigenous forests unsurpassed on southern African shores.

Many thousands of people visit this

area every year, staying at towns such as George, Knysna or Plettenberg Bay, or at small holiday villages such as Wilderness or Sedgefield. Here the pleasures of sailing, swimming or surfing are enhanced by the warmth of the Agulhas Current. There are many secluded beaches, as well as quiet places in the villages where the visitor can absorb the leisurely pace of seaside life, wander around the old jetties, look in on the local craftsmen and woodcarvers, or buy souvenirs such as the well-known 'pansy shells', common on this part of the coast. On the shores of the lakes and estuaries are old and often romantic hotels, such as the inimitable 'Fairy Knowe', on the banks of the Touw River.

For the angler or nature-lover the Garden Route is a feast. The major lakes in the stretch between George and Knysna – Langvlei, Rondevlei, Swartvlei and Groenvlei – are saline to varying degrees,

109. *Thickly forested slopes lead down to the rocky shores at the mouth of the Bloukrans River, a hazard to be negotiated on the Otter Trail.*

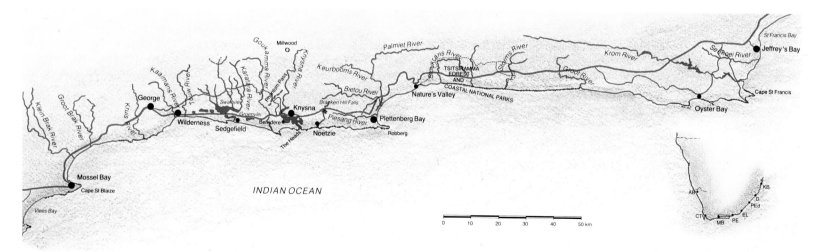

110

111

Tsitsikamma sound a deeper and darker note. They are awe-inspiring and unforgettable. In this dry and generally barren subcontinent little more than one per cent of the land is afforested, and this is one of the few areas where the rainfall is heavy enough – it can reach an annual 2 500 millimetres – to support dense forest growth. And the two forest communities of Knysna and Tsitsikamma combine to create a vast shadowy realm extending almost 180 kilometres along the coast and up to 20 kilometres inland to the foot of the Outeniqua mountains. Over the rolling hills and valleys of the coastal terrace sprawl some 40 500 hectares of indigenous forest, which includes dense stands of yellowwood and stinkwood, of blackwood, saffronwood, white alders and Cape chestnuts. They grow in a profusion enhanced by thick creepers and by beds of ferns such as are found in the 'Val van Varings', a valley of giant ferns in the heart of the woods. Many of the trees, particularly the yellowwoods, reach a great age and grow to astounding heights, and a number of these 'patriarchs' have become popular tourist attractions. Near Woodville, for example, is an enormous yellowwood 600 years old, 31 metres high, with a girth of nine metres. Another, known as King Edward's Tree, is over 700 years old, and reaches 46 metres from the ground before branching.

For the visitor, after the sunlit world outside, to enter the woods is to penetrate a mysterious and twilit place. In many areas the forest is all but impenetrable. Few people live here, few know the forest from the inside. Many parts of its shadowy depths remain to all intents unexplored. As in most great forests, relatively few large animals live here, though there are a number of forest-dwelling antelopes. In the dense canopy birdlife, too, is limited, though the Knysna loerie may be heard, and occasionally seen, among the branches. With its vivid plumage and crest, this distant relative of the European cuckoo inhabits a restricted area of the forest where are found the fruit and berries upon which it depends.

To the speculative eye of the early settlers these forests seemed an unlimited resource, to be had for the chopping. The first white men to set foot here, however, were more intent on staying alive than on exploiting this new-found land. On 3 February 1488 Bartolomeu Dias, after having lost sight of land during weeks of storm, made a landing near what is today known as Mossel Bay. On his charts he named the bay the 'Angra dos Vaqueiros', or the 'Bay of Cowherds', on account of

110. *Mossel Bay, the main harbour on the south coast, has a history dating back to the days when Portuguese explorers put in here for water and supplies.* 111. *A few kilometres from Wilderness, these holiday houses under their wooded bluff overlook the dark, peat-coloured waters of the Kaaimans River.*

with the exception of Groenvlei, also known as Lake Pleasant. Girt with thick stands of reeds, the fresh water in this lake has no visible source, but it is speculated that it comes from springs at the eastern end. At Rondevlei there is a Nature Conservation Research Station, and on the Goukamma River – from the Hottentot for 'little' or 'fat' water – is another protected area, the Goukamma Nature Reserve, which is primarily a bird sanctuary. Given the wealth of food in the lakes it is not surprising that some 174 different bird

species have been recorded here. They range from sunbirds, red-winged starlings and Cape canaries, which live in the reeds and bush around the lakes, to aquatic birds such as kingfishers, water dikkops, black-backed gulls, yellow-billed ducks and Egyptian geese.

Over the coastal lakes area presides a further element in the dazzling natural variety of the Garden Route. After the stark, windswept spaces of the west coast and the fynbos-clad cliffs of the south coast, the forests of Knysna and the

the Hottentot herdsmen he and his men had spied on the shore. On landing, with hopes of bartering for meat and filling their casks with fresh water, they found the 'vaqueiros' to be decidedly unfriendly. Pursued by a hail of stones, the Portuguese tumbled back into their boats and set sail for further up the coast in search of a less stony reception. Later navigators were luckier. Vasco da Gama, for example, landed on the same spot on 20 November 1497 and managed to trade amicably enough.

For several years the bay, with its cattle and fresh-water springs, was used by the Portuguese merchant fleet as a stopping-place on the route to the Orient. In 1500 one Pedro de Ataíde set a precedent by leaving a letter in one of the large milkwood trees down by the shore. The message was collected the following year by João de Nova when he put ashore to collect water. He also set up a small shrine nearby, making this the first place of Christian worship in southern Africa. According to one chronicler, a later refinement to the Portuguese postal system was the innovation of a boot, dangling from the milkwood's branches, in which messages could be 'posted'. Today a plaque marks the spot and, to perpetuate the tradition, a boot-shaped post-box has been placed nearby. Messages were also scratched on stones, and a cast of one of these is preserved in the local museum.

The main base of Portuguese operations was further to the north, at Delagoa Bay, and it was left to the men of the Dutch East India Company to develop and exploit this part of the coast during the Eighteenth Century. In 1767 the first tiny settlement was begun at Mossel Bay, with a granary to store wheat received from neighbouring farms. Further to the east a small outpost of the Company was also set up at what the Portuguese had called 'Bahia Formosa', the 'Beautiful Bay', a romantic name which was soon to be supplanted by that of a Governor of the Colony. In 1778 Baron Joachim van Plettenberg, in a carriage drawn by eight magnificent horses and with another coach and five ox-wagons bringing up the rear, made a tour of the eastern frontier of the Dutch colony. At Bahia Formosa he put up the obligatory pillar bearing the Company's arms and renamed the bay after himself, making sure that his name was included in the inscription on the cross. The change was not universally appreciated; the French traveller François le Vaillant wrote contemptuously of 'This wretched monument . . . a paltry post, erected to the vanity of an individual.'

In 1776 a certain Commandant Mulder and 16 assistants set up a woodcutters' post where the town of George now stands. They were the precursors of a strange community of men, the *houtkappers,* who were to belong to the forest for the next two centuries and to become part of its shadowy lore. Living deep among the yellowwoods, rarely rising above abject poverty, they worked their sawpits, their *kraansae,* in the forest clearings, supplying a steady flow of timber to the coastal towns.

Among these was Knysna, whose name, appropriately enough, is believed to come from the Khoisan for 'place of wood'. Its foundation and early development were very much the work of one man, to whom legend still clings. Despite popular belief, George Rex was not the illegitimate offspring of King George III of England, and he never made any such claim. Little is known of him before his arrival at the Cape in 1797, during the first British occupation, when he was appointed Marshal of the Vice-Admiralty Court, Notary Public to the Governor and Advocate to the Crown. He set up house with a young woman named Joanna, the widow of a well-to-do merchant, taking on her children at the same time.

When the first British occupation came to an end Rex elected to stay on at the Cape. His official functions now over, he purchased the farm Melkhoutkraal on the shores of Knysna lagoon and arrived to take it over in style. Accompanied by Joanna and her four children, he travelled in a coach drawn by six horses and impressively done up with a coat of arms on its sides. Riding alongside was a supporting cast of retainers and friends. The arrival of this cortège at Knysna seems to have made a deep impression on the local inhabitants, and it was not long before rumours were abroad about Rex's royal origins (a mixed blessing, one imagines, since by this time George III had gone stark mad).

Whatever his origins, Rex had left them well behind. A man of energy, he soon transformed his new property. He rebuilt the old farmhouse, which had been burnt down in a Xhosa raid some years before, in sumptuous style and called it 'Old Place'. Around it were laid out gardens and orchards, vineyards and groves of oak trees; nearby was a blacksmith's shop and a watermill. He bred silkworms in plantations of mulberry trees and farmed ostriches, organized sealing expeditions to Plettenberg Bay and sent his men into the forests to cut timber. Within a few years he had expanded his original purchase to 10 000 hectares, almost the whole of today's Knysna area.

His activities as a timber merchant drew him into partnership with another

112. *One of the gems of the Garden Route, the picturesque village of Wilderness is built around the lagoon at the mouth of the Touw River.*

immigrant, a retired shipwright named James Callander who lived in a small cottage near The Heads. Together they tried to interest successive governors, both Dutch and British, in the development of a port on the banks of the lagoon to export their timber. The major drawback to this scheme was the narrowness of the channel between The Heads which connects the lagoon and the sea. Finally in 1817 the Cape Government sent the naval brig *Emu* to test the passage. Unhappily, the ship struck a submerged rock and had to be abandoned. A second attempt, with *Podargus*, was luckier, and soon the new port was a thriving concern. The cluster of buildings began to expand, and in 1825 Lord Charles Somerset proposed officially to found a town, to which Rex contributed 121 hectares of his land.

By now he was well established. On the death of Joanna he married her daughter by her first marriage and added to an already large family, the final count being six sons and seven daughters. The girls, sent to Cape Town to acquire education

and social polish, made sensible marriages to ambitious young men such as Lieutenant Thomas Duthie, who married Caroline Rex and settled on the farm Belvidere on the western banks of the lagoon.

George Rex died on 3 April 1839. Though Old Place no longer stands, his grave is a popular place for visitors in search of the spirit of Knysna. Enclosed by a stone wall and shaded by two pine trees, it is close to the site of his house.

Parallel with the growth of Knysna was that of George. The settlement's formal establishment took place in 1811, when the British Governor, the Earl of Caledon, declared a new magistracy. Adrianus van Kervel was appointed *landdros* to the town, named George Town after King George III, and the first erven were given free to six woodcutters whose job it was to supply building materials. The site was laid out on a generous scale, beginning with the main street, York Street, and Meade and Courtenay streets, all of which were over 80 metres wide. Van Kervel also decreed that the new streets should be

lined with trees, 'not only for ornament but for defending passengers from the scorching rays of an almost vertical sun'.

The result was a pleasant, leafy village, a staging post and an administrative centre which in 1837 was elevated to the dignity of a municipality. Like Knysna, it became a major centre for the timber industry in the nearby forests and, besides elegant town-houses, soon boasted some fine official and religious architecture. The Dutch Reformed Church, consecrated in 1842, was the first to be built, and was followed by the first Roman Catholic church in South Africa, the Church of St Peter and St Paul. In 1850 George achieved the distinction of being probably the smallest city in the world, when Bishop Robert Gray, founder of the Diocesan College in Cape Town, consecrated the Cathedral of St Mark.

Despite all this progress, at mid-century mark these were still remote and scattered communities, difficult of access by land and not always easy to reach by sea. Then in 1867 work was begun on a new route through the forests, under the supervision

113. *The dramatic sandstone outcrops of The Heads guard the entrance to the 22 kilometre-long Knysna lagoon and estuary.*

of the celebrated engineer, Thomas Bain. The result, built by convict labour, was the 82-kilometre mountain road linking George and Knysna. Largely superseded by the modern coastal road, it remains a remarkable feat of engineering and one which affords many scenic splendours, from the crossing of the Kaaimans River to the Phantom Pass which leads down to Knysna – the 'phantom' in question being a common local moth.

The opening up of the forests brought new and sometimes unexpected developments. In Queen Street in Knysna is preserved a house with a red tin roof, a nineteenth-century relic transported intact from its original site deep in the forest. This yellowwood cottage, now a museum, was once part of the gold-prospecting town of Millwood, a few kilometres from Bain's road.

In 1886 an inspector of roads reported alluvial gold in a number of streams in the forest. Then, in August of the same year, a man named John Courtney found gold reef in the hills and triggered the start of the rush. Within a few weeks more than a

115. *The vivid flame red of a Knysna lily on the banks of the Bloukrans River.*
116. (Overleaf) *The rugged shore between Brenton-on-Sea and the Knysna Heads testifies to the eroding power of the waves.*

thousand men had appeared and had hacked out a clearing. Soon they were busily ripping up the earth to get at their dreamed-of fortunes. By the end of 1887 a strange, raffish town had erupted in the heart of the forest. Machinery had been laboriously brought in, trenches and shafts had been dug or blown out using dynamite. Some forty mining companies were hastily thrown together, dominated by the Oudtshoorn, Bendigo and Temperance syndicates. To help relieve the burden of real or imagined wealth were three banks, 25 shops, and seven hotels, including the notorious Morgan's Canteen. There was also a police station, a post office, and three newspapers. Such entertainment as could not be obtained in the saloons was supplied by the Royal Music Hall.

Alas, all this was founded on nugatory

nuggets! After the initial excitement it was reluctantly established that the supplies of gold were meagre at best. It became dangerous to mention a find, however small. One young man named Jim Carruthers seems to have committed this error one night in Morgan's Canteen, over one drink too many. His fellow dreamers followed him home, robbed him and beat him to death.

It was not long before Millwood itself began to die. The mining syndicates collapsed one by one, their demise speeded by finds on the Witwatersrand which siphoned off the prospectors. Unwilling to face final extinction, the town lingered on until as late as 1924, when the goldfield was officially deproclaimed. Now little remains. All the buildings have gone, rotted in the humidity of the well-watered forest. Of the once-proud Millwood Hotel only a decayed and overgrown verandah lives on. Survivors of gardens and orchards linger in clumps of flowers and fruit trees. The abandoned workings can still be seen, though they are slowly disappearing as the forest closes in. Pieces of rusted machinery peer out from an undergrowth choked with leaf humus. An old steam engine is being throttled by advancing trees. Perhaps the most forlorn memento in this place left behind by time is the Millwood cemetery, and even that is being reclaimed by nature. Only two of the inscriptions are still legible, one recording the last resting place of a young man from London, the other that of a woman described as a 'perfect wife and mother'.

The world of the prospectors may have been fragile and ephemeral, but other

114. *Designed in imitation of the Norman style, the Belvidere Church was built in 1855 on the farm of Captain Thomas Duthie, son-in-law of Knysna's well-known benefactor, George Rex.*

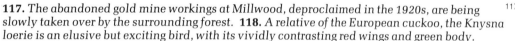

117. *The abandoned gold mine workings at Millwood, deproclaimed in the 1920s, are being slowly taken over by the surrounding forest.* **118.** *A relative of the European cuckoo, the Knysna loerie is an elusive but exciting bird, with its vividly contrasting red wings and green body.* ⁱ¹⁷ ¹¹⁸

communities on this part of the coast have shown tenacious longevity. The so-called 'Albany culture' of the early Khoisan littoral dwellers is at its richest in the stretch running eastwards from Knysna through Cape St Francis to the mouth of the Klasies River. There are many sites, both in caves and in the open, from which researchers have assembled a tantalizing glimpse into a life-style of great antiquity. One of the densest concentrations of the remains of these people has been excavated on the Robberg Peninsula at Plettenberg Bay.

On this rocky promontory five deep caves and numerous shallow shelters protected what was once a substantial Middle Stone Age society. The first modern excavation of these caves was by Thomas Bain who, when not engaged in road-building, collected a number of stone implements from Robberg. These he catalogued and in 1886 sent to the Colonial and Indian Exhibition in London. More recently one of the larger caves was excavated by the Reverend W.G. Sharples, whose fine haul of relics included more than a hundred bone points, a notched bone shaft, pieces of pottery, a drilled fragment of tortoiseshell, and a piece of wood with traces of red paint. The discovery of five skeletons, one of which had been buried with two pieces of pottery of either European or oriental provenance, aroused much excited speculation. Another skeleton was found with a necklace of ostrich eggshell beads, and yet another, buried at the rear of the

cave, had been covered with a burial stone and four large limpet shells.

The first fully recorded and scientifically controlled 'dig' at Robberg, however, was carried out between 1964 and 1971 in the Nelson Bay cave on the south side of the peninsula. It was a joint operation by teams from the Department of Archaeology of the University of Cape Town, the University of Louvain in Belgium, and the University of Chicago. Professor R.R. Inskeep of the University of Cape Town supervised the project during the first few years, and Dr Richard Klein took over during the 1970 to 1971 season.

The Nelson Bay cave is a commodious Khoisan residence measuring 20 metres across the mouth and 30 metres deep. Many of the other caves have been disturbed by guano-collectors and the Nelson Bay cave was chosen at least partly because it was relatively undisturbed. The excavations during the first three seasons were limited to the upper midden layers at the cave mouth, and to a narrow, deep cutting made to plumb the full depth of the deposits. The rewards of the dig in terms of material were gratifying in the extreme. In the first six weeks' work alone, well over a million fish remains were found, from tiny vertebrae to fins, teeth and jaws. There were skeletal remains of a wide range of animals, both marine and terrestrial, from seals and seabirds to antelope, wild pig and buffalo, while at a deeper level relics of now extinct species such as the quagga, giant buffalo and giant hartebeest were

discovered. Throughout the deposits stone tools and weapons were turned up, as well as quantities of large quartzite flakes used to break bones, cut up the quarry and for scraping skins.

One particularly important find from the first season was that of the skeleton of an 11-year-old child, laid on the right side with the arms bent and the hands under the chin, and the knees bent so that the feet were under the buttocks. A finely made, double-ended bone point was found between the right pelvis and a large grinding stone, assumed to be a burial stone, which had been placed over the pelvis. Some bones from the skeleton were radiocarbon-dated at the University of Louvain to about 700 BC, making this the first accurately dated human skeleton found in South Africa. In all, three burials, of an adult and two children, were discovered, together with stone artefacts, shells, and quantities of ostrich eggshell beads.

From this mass of evidence a rough picture of the changing fortunes of the inhabitants of this cave, within the context of their surrounding culture, has been built up. On a number of sites, mostly open sites such as have been found in the dunes at Robberg, Early Stone Age hand axes have been recovered. The bulk of the remains in the complex of caves, however, comes either from the Middle or Late Stone Ages. Thus the Nelson Bay cave may have been occupied as early as 70 000 years ago, but the majority of finds come from two periods, the first from about 8 000 to 6 000 years ago, and then from about 3 000 years ago onwards. There is a conspicuous and as yet not fully explained gap in the record between about 6 000 and 3 000 years ago.

During this long progression many climatic changes took place, and these, as in many other caves around the southern coast, had their effect on the life-style of the cave people. The major event was the ending of the last great ice age, between about 18 000 and 12 000 years ago. Before this period the sea was probably about 80 kilometres to the south of Robberg, and a grassy coastal plain supported the large animals such as wildebeest and buffalo whose bones are found in the deeper midden levels. As the temperature rose so did the sea-level, and the bones of grassland animals diminish, with a concomitant increase in marine remains, of fish, seals, dolphins and seabirds, as well as in the shells of countless thousands of mussels and limpets.

These shells tell a fascinating story, the result of scientific detective work aided by radiocarbon dating. Changes in the mussel population, for example, record changes in the climate. Until 8 000 years ago the remains of black mussels prevail. Thereafter they gradually disappear and are replaced by brown mussels which, in general, are warm-water creatures, while black mussels prefer lower temperatures. As the seas warmed with the end of the ice age, the brown mussels extended their territory southwards, replacing the black

mussels which now dominate the colder west coast waters.

Study of the limpet shells has given scientists clues to the migration patterns of the cave people. Depending on the temperature of the sea water, varying concentrations of oxygen isotopes are built up in the shell of the limpet as it is laid down by the living animal. Sophisticated techniques, developed to measure the ratio of these concentrations many thousands of years later, reveal that the great majority of the limpets in the cave died in winter. A cross-check on this seasonal gathering has been provided by measuring seal jaw-bones from the midden. The bulk of these came from seal pups killed at about six months of age. Since seal pups are born in summer, it is argued that the cave-dwellers spent the summer inland when game was plentiful, and migrated to the coast when pickings were slimmer in the winter season. Limpets cast a sidelight on early ecology too. It appears that the larger limpets were gradually removed from the shore, leaving much smaller animals in the upper layers of the midden – an intriguing example of early over-exploitation of marine resources.

The inroads made by the Khoisan, however, were modest compared with the impact of modern man on the Garden Route. Nowhere is this more evident than in the encroachments on the lagoon and estuary at Knysna, the richest environment of its kind on the South

African coast. Geologically, it was formed during the Pleistocene, when the whole of this coastal belt was submerged. With subsequent elevation, rivers cut deep valleys and gorges in the plain. A period of subsidence followed, during which valleys such as that which now encloses the Knysna basin were drowned and gradually filled with silt and sediments. Over these deep deposits the Knysna River of today continues to run, bringing down its burden from the mountains above. The well-wooded banks of the valley offer little opportunity for erosion, and an annual rainfall of approximately 900 millimetres is spread fairly evenly across the seasons, making for a steady flow of water.

At Charlesford, about 20 kilometres inland from The Heads, the river reaches the upper end of the estuary and from this point its water becomes tidal and saline. Then, after flowing through a deep, rocky gorge, the river opens into the estuary proper, where the tidal exchange is remarkably high, about 90 per cent of the water being exchanged with each tide. The final 12 kilometres encompass the lagoon, which broadens to about three kilometres across, with its salt-marshes and complex of islands dominated by Leisure Island and Thesen Island. At the mouth of the lagoon, between the sandstone outcrops of The Heads, there is considerable turbulence from the incoming sea which, on this part of the coast, has a temperature generally between 15 and 20 degrees centigrade. Waves up to a metre high are common, and provide an important effect in the dynamics of the estuary as a whole.

There are many different kinds of habitat here, compressed into a relatively narrow area. In the upper reaches of the estuary a mixture of mud and sand occurs, with the proportion increasing in favour of sand lower down. The combination of a high tidal exchange and the complex sedimentation laid down here over the ages has created a wide variety of opportunities for marine animals. Some 350 different species of invertebrates and fish have been recorded in the Knysna basin, more than in any other comparable area. They include 40 species of fish, 12 of crabs and 69 of marine worms. Many filter-feeders congregate at the mouth of the lagoon, where plankton is brought in from the sea. Besides oysters, these include the barnacle *Tetraclita serrata*, the mussel *Perna perna*, and the giant

119. *The shy and rarely seen Cape clawless otter feeds mainly on fish and crabs, but sometimes also on octopus.*

horse mussel *Atrina squamifera*. The latter, as much as 30 centimetres long, has long golden byssus threads which, it has been suggested, were the inspiration for Jason's legendary golden fleece.

Further up the lagoon a major source of food comes from the salt-marshes, with their reeds and plants such as the eel-grass *Zostera*. These die and break down to provide the food on which many marine creatures live, in their turn supporting many fish and birds. In the upper mud channels the dominant filter-feeder is the mud-mussel *Arcuatula capensis*, which depends not only upon the plankton suspended in the water, but also makes use of plant detritus. Aquatic plants also occur here, including angiosperms and seaweeds such as *Enteromorpha* and *Ulva* between the tide-marks. These support a relatively small number of animals, among them winkles, and crabs such as *Sesarma catenata*. A curious and common creature also found in the lagoon is the sea hare *Notarchus*. Reaching about 10 centimetres in length, this slug-like animal festooned with tassels is bisexual and is known to mate in twos, threes, fours or even more.

The lagoon is an important place of sojourn for the juveniles of many open-sea fish. Shoals of pilchards, accompanied by their predators, are often found here, along with species such as kob, spotted grunter, leervis, white steenbras, mullet, and many others. Bottom-dwellers include flatfishes and rays, as well as those which conceal themselves in the weeds, such as klipfish and pipefishes. Among the latter is the Knysna sea-horse, a creature found almost solely in this lagoon. Another notable local species is the Knysna mud crab which, measuring up to 30 centimetres across, is the largest shallow-water crab in southern Africa. It is armed with massive nippers capable of crushing a finger.

All these animals and plants create a web of life of great complexity. Of major ecological importance, the Knysna basin is not officially protected, and is becoming more and more vulnerable to man's influence. Its high tidal exchange and the salinity of the water prevent it from being exploited for dams and for agricultural use, but it is increasingly subject to the pressure of waterside homes and holiday shacks and the annual influx of tourists. Reclamation of the wetlands for building purposes easily disturbs their delicate balance. Recently ecologists managed to quash a proposal for a marina on the shores of the lagoon, but while specific restraints can sometimes be imposed, the general pressures remain.

Other areas of this part of the coast, however, are well protected, one being the magnificent and unique Tsitsikamma Coastal National Park which runs along 67 kilometres of wild and beautiful coastline. On land it is 1,6 kilometres wide, and it reaches a further 800 metres out to sea, thus encompassing both

marine and terrestrial ecosystems as they meet at the shoreline. Of particular interest to the marine biologist, a fascinating complex of climatic and geological influences is at work here. In general, this is a dramatically steep shore, swept by powerful waves which make life perpetually insecure for the intertidal

creatures. Thus a wealth of those animals which specialize in hanging onto rocks for their livelihood occurs. Nine species of limpet alone are found here, from the rosy-flecked *Patella miniata* to the giant *P. tabularis*. Many animals flourish both in size and in number, among them the alikreukel, a gourmet delicacy elsewhere but here protected, and filter-feeding creatures, notably mussels, barnacles, reef-forming tubeworms and red-bait, all of which rely on the surging waves to deliver their food supply. The local birdlife, too, is abundant, with more than 200 recorded species, including 35 of seabirds.

A good way to see many of these animals is to take the famous Otter Trail which runs the full length of the Park from Nature's Valley to the Storms River mouth. The first trail of its kind in the country, it follows the shoreline closely. The route is marked out with otter emblems, includes four overnight huts, and provides a three- to five-day walk through some of the country's finest coastal scenery. Its attractions include a number of cave middens, a guano cave, some spectacular waterfalls, and perhaps even a glimpse of the shy animal after which the trail is named, the Cape clawless otter, a protected species which lives retiringly on crab, octopus and fish. A further feature of the route is the recently opened Underwater Trail. Laid out in a bay near Goudgate, this features interpretive underwater plaques and can be 'swum' under the supervision of a trained diver and ecologist.

An extension and complement to the Coastal National Park is the Tsitsikamma Forest National Park, which runs parallel to it between the sea and the Tsitsikamma mountains. Proclaimed in 1964, it is small in comparison with the forests which stretch eastwards from Mossel Bay, some 476 hectares of indigenous forest out of a total of about 40 500. It abuts on the coastal scrub forest of the Coastal National Park, and in places reaches down to the sea.

The apparent richness of this ancient forest is to an extent illusory. True, there are a great many species of plants and trees here, the latter including the Outeniqua yellowwood, stinkwood and ironwood, Cape beech, white pear and candlewood among the larger species. Between these grow smaller trees such as mountain saffron, num-num, rock elder, tree fuchsia and red currant. Besides the 122 woody trees and shrubs, there are many other bulbous plants, lianas, lichens and mosses, as well as 14 different species of fern. All these are in competition for a limited amount of nutrients. For while the rainfall is heavy here and engenders these forests, the soil is poor and deficient in many essential chemicals. The result is what is called a 'closed nutrient cycle', in which every particle of nutrition is used to the full and constantly recycled. The yellowwoods, for example, have developed a network of small roots

120. *Oyster beds at low spring tide in Knysna lagoon. With some 350 known fish and invertebrate species, this lagoon is the richest on the southern coastline.* 121. *The beautiful Bracken Hill Falls are enclosed by forest vegetation.*

around the bole of the tree to absorb nutrients from decaying vegetation.

Over the past two and a half millennia this region has become increasingly dry and, notwithstanding the rainfall, moisture is at a premium in the forest. The dense canopy of leaves helps to 'seal in' much of this moisture, and the edges of the forest are protected by a 'buffer zone' of shrubby plants which both helps to keep in the moisture and wards off invasion from the surrounding fynbos. But the balance is a delicate one, and sensitive to any change. The cutting of a new road through the forest, for example, can cause a wound which may take decades to heal. Thus, the trees and plants tend to keep to themselves what little nutrition is available. They can ill afford to lose leaves and shoots, and many have developed high concentrations of chemicals which make them unpalatable to animals. Not surprisingly, there are few creatures here. Nocturnal bushpigs, small-

123

spotted genet, mongoose and small rodents live on what is left to them by the forest.

Of all the animals which have made their home in the shelter of the forests, perhaps the most famous and certainly the most fiercely debated are the elephants of Knysna. Now hovering on the brink of extinction, their history has been a brutal one. When European settlement of the Cape began in the mid-Seventeenth Century there were many thousands of African elephants across the subcontinent. Essentially grazing animals, they did well in the broad savanna conditions to which they were ideally adapted. But the advance of man was swift in its effect on the elephants. In 1702 the last in the south-western Cape was shot at Tiervlei, 10 kilometres from Table Bay. By 1750 they had been wiped out or driven away from the cultivated areas up to Mossel Bay and through to the Karoo.

Those that survived retreated into the

forests of Knysna or into the thorn-brake of Addo, further to the east. There they found a natural refuge in which, since they were no longer competing directly with man, they were for many years left in peace. Then in the Nineteenth Century came the era of the big-game hunter, and the invention of the modern rifle which made courage a safe bet. And the courage of men such as Alfred, the second son of Queen Victoria, received ample proof in Africa.

His second visit to the Colony featured a hunt which took place in the Knysna forest on 11 September 1867. Accounts of the heroism displayed, including that of the Prince, are mixed. He was supported by 40 other guns in his assault on the elephants. Notwithstanding this fire-power, the hunters succeeded only in wounding most of their quarry, driving the animals into the forest to die. The Prince, to the relief of all, did manage to 'bag' an animal. The dead elephant was

125

indulgently measured at about four metres to the shoulder, which would have made it the size of a mastodon – the record confirmed height for an African elephant is 3,5 metres.

Though evidently inaccurate and probably sycophantic, the measurement soon gave rise to a legend. The reputed size of the Knysna elephants whetted the appetite of other hunters, who came to the forest to try to beat Alfred's record. In fact, they spent the next six decades trying, and with devastating effect. In 1876 growing public concern about the future of the elephants led to an estimate of their population, and it was found to be between 400 and 500. The hunting continued unabated, however, and as late as 1907 a guide-book advised sportsmen not to come to Knysna without their guns, adding that the elephants were 'not likely to become extinct'.

In fact, they were already well on their way to extinction. A severe decline had

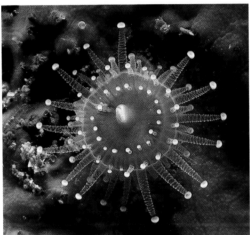

124

taken place since the 1870s and in 1902 it was estimated that about 50 animals were left. By 1904 there were only 20. For several years this number remained stationary and was given as the probable population in 1908, when the elephants were declared Royal Game and given belated official protection. Perhaps the last assault on them was that of Major P.J. Pretorius in 1920. Pretorius had been given official sanction to reduce the number of elephants in the Addo thorn-brake, in the course of which exercise he had succeeded in almost wiping them out altogether. Public outcry had halted the carnage at Addo, but Pretorius had been licensed to shoot one last bull in the Knysna forest, for 'scientific purposes' for the South African Museum. In the event, the hunt claimed two bulls, a cow and a calf.

In 1925 the number of elephants was down to 12, and subsequent surveys in 1951 and 1969 saw a continuing decline.

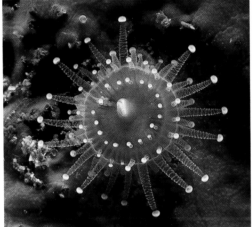

126

By now it was evident that forces other than natural were at work, including poachers and the local smallholders whose properties border the forest. The latter, irritated by the elephants' occasional raids on their produce, were not above shooting them. One of these tragedies was the killing of one of the forest's largest bulls, named 'Aftand' on account of a broken tusk. This huge animal had grown too old to forage effectively in the forest and had taken to helping himself from nearby fields. His carcass was found, ineptly butchered at close range with a high-powered rifle. His tusks had been hacked out and an ear and a foot chopped off.

A survey carried out in 1980 by the Department of Forestry caused sharp public reaction when it was announced that there were only two elephants left. Further search brought one more animal to light. It had been seven decades since the elephants had been officially

127

protected, and angry questions were asked about the quality of this protection. It was also asked what could be done to save the dying herd.

At this stage, it seems, very little can be done. The suggestion was put to the

122. An unexpected patch of colour is highlighted where the rocky banks at the Storms River mouth fall sheer into the water. **123.** The sandy anemone Bunodactis reynaudi has enlarged 'fighting' tentacles around its mouth to help it defend its rock space against other anemones. **124.** The tests of the short-spined sea urchin, Echinodiscus bisperforatus, are popularly known as pansy shells and have become an unofficial symbol for the Knysna region. **125.** The sight and sound of the restless sea are constant companions along the thickly wooded paths of the Otter Trail. **126.** Corynactis, the strawberry anemone, displays its characteristic successive rings of knobbed tentacles. **127.** The vivid colours of a soft coral, Parerythropodium purpureum, typify the beauty of the Underwater Trail in the Tsitsikamma Coastal National Park.

128

Minister of Environmental Affairs that three Addo elephant calves should be introduced to the forest. It was turned down, causing fresh debate, much of it revolving around the question of the uniqueness of the Knysna forest elephants.

They are, in fact, not unique at all, and are certainly not a separately evolved forest-dwelling species of elephant. As a number of scientists have pointed out, the animals were initially driven to live in the forests by outside pressures. This was not their chosen habitat, even though it did afford them temporary protection.

Elephants are not well equipped for browsing the leaves of trees. Moreover, the quality of the food provided by the forest is questionable. Though they appear rich enough to support verdant vegetation, the soils here, as in the Tsitsikamma forest, are poor in total nutrients and are particularly deficient in certain important micro-nutrients. Unlike the thorn trees of the Addo, the foliage provided at Knysna is low in nutritional value, giving little return for a large output of energy. Over a long period this deficiency can lead to a lowered reproductive power coupled with an

increased mortality. Consequently, to increase the herd with imported animals is likely only to postpone the extinction which is inevitable.

The fate of particular species such as the elephants attracts much public attention. Contemporary ecological practice, however, is concerned not only with the part but even more so with the whole, with the country's representative ecosystems. Although much has already been lost on the Garden Route, the two national parks here will preserve some of its ancestral grandeur inviolate into the future.

129

128. The caves of the Robberg Peninsula, seen across Nelson Bay, were long an important occupation site of Khoisan coastal dwellers. Recent excavations have revealed much about the life-style of these early people, in particular that they spent the summer inland and in winter moved to the coast to find their food along the shore. **129.** Once the site of a Norwegian whaling station, Beacon Island was connected to the mainland in the 1940s and is now adorned by a large holiday complex. **130.** The Noetzie, or 'black' River gives its name to the small settlement nearby, where an eccentric property developer has introduced a medieval note in counterpoint to rock and sand. **131.** (Overleaf) A dizzying suspension footbridge spans the turbulent mouth of the Storms River in the Tsitsikamma Coastal National Park.

130

BORDER COUNTRY

WHERE THE SETTLERS LANDED

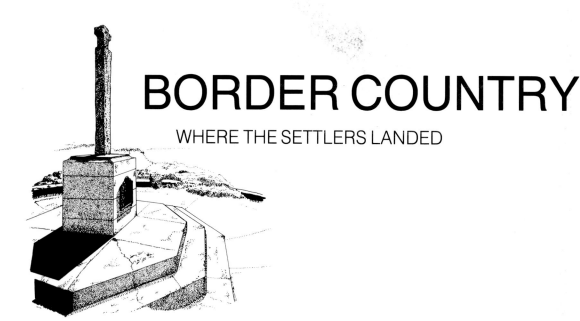

Near the mouth of the Buffalo River an enormous solitary rock, visible for many kilometres, rises like a beacon between sand and sea. Created by the upheavals of the earth when young, time and erosion have left their marks upon it and part of the rock has split and fallen away to form a kind of marine amphitheatre. In this opening the sea is compressed and over the ages has carved out great echoing caverns on the seaward side.

On the map it is marked prosaically as Cove Rock. But for the local Xhosa people it is 'Gompo', a sacred and awe-inspiring place. Here in the caves, they believe, live the chiefs of the legendary 'People of the River and Sea'.

These ancestral beings rule over a spirit world of the water. They live on fish, sand and water, and are believed to be immune to sharks. Their influence reaches far into the land. When the sea reverberates through the caves in stormy weather the local people say the chiefs are talking on their drums. Tradition relates, too, that they are served by a large amphibious monitor lizard which brings fresh cow dung from the nearby hills. This it makes into a ball which it rolls down to the water's edge where the People come up to collect it, taking it to their cave to smear on the floor and walls. Here too are kept the treasures of the sea, gathered from the many wrecks which have been washed up in the area. At night when the tide is high the People come up on the beach to play and to graze their cattle on top of the rock.

'Gompo' is but one landmark on this historic corner of the Cape Province, with its landscape of rolling hills patterned with herds of sheep, Xhosa kraals and tall aloes with their flame-red flowers.

For this is also 'Settler country', long associated with the advent of the British '1820 Settlers' and their struggle to put down roots in a seemingly barren and inhospitable land. Like the Dutch farmers already settled in the area, they came into conflict with the Bantu-speaking people, the Xhosas, Tembus and Pondos, who had descended the east coast of Africa in successive waves in earlier generations. The present division of the region, which includes the satellite state of Ciskei at its heart, reflects the legacy of this historic and violent clash.

Settler society was centred around Grahamstown, inland in the Albany District, but the dominant coastal settlement and outlet for the farmers' produce was Port Elizabeth. Today, with a population of over half a million, 'P.E.' is the country's fifth largest city and its third biggest port, after Durban and Cape Town. Traditional commerce in wool, mohair, hides and skins still takes place through the port, but its principal asset today is heavy industry. Over 700 factories are dominated by two giants of the motor industry, Ford and General Motors, which have production and assembly plants outside the town.

Dry and dusty in summer, the coastal fringe can be the scene of violent storms in the winter months, and of heavy floods brought down from inland by the river courses. In its narrow confine between beach and cliffs, Port Elizabeth is particularly vulnerable. Devastating floods came down here in 1867, 1897 and 1908. Perhaps the worst deluge in recent memory was that which occurred on

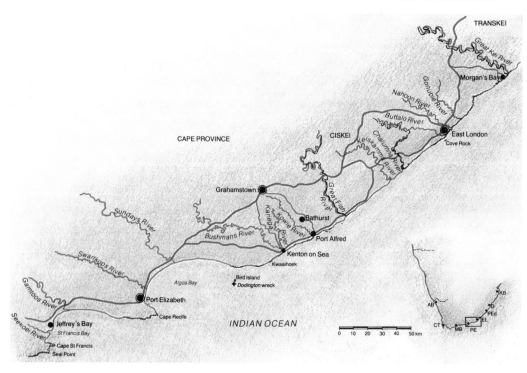

132. *A surfer at Seal Point, popularly known as 'Seals', near Cape St Francis catches an exhilarating kilometre-long ride on the rollers.*

Sunday morning, 1 September 1968, when nearly 430 millimetres of rain fell on the city in a few hours. An overloaded Baakens River burst its banks, washing away roads and houses. Eight people were drowned, and millions of rands' worth of damage was caused. Havoc wrought by the sea is equally devastating. An historic example was the 'Great Storm' of 1902, when a ferocious south-easterly gale wrecked 19 ships on North End beach, a disaster second only to the storm of 1865 in Table Bay.

For most of the year, though, the sea is gentle enough. Its temperate waters host a wealth of fish, examples of which can be seen at the comprehensive museum complex in Port Elizabeth. Besides the well-stocked museum itself, there is a snake park with several hundred live reptiles in residence, a tropical house, and the popular Oceanarium. This features a dolphin lake (two bottle-nosed dolphins named Dimple and Haig were long its stars), a seabird enclosure, a seal pool, and two large tanks housing many local fish and marine invertebrates. A further pleasure of this coast is the bounty of sea shells washed up, particularly at Jeffrey's Bay, where they are the subject of a thriving commerce among the local children. A fine collection of these shells can be seen nearby at the Charlotte Kritzinger Shell Museum.

A few kilometres south of Jeffrey's Bay is St Francis Bay, the scene of less contemplative pleasures. In the eye of the non-surfing beholder there is perhaps little beauty in this lonely and windswept beach, with its long vistas over the Indian Ocean. The land leading down to it is low and scrubby, with yellow dune-grass and *Agathosma* plants, and the headland of Cape St Francis which encloses it is unspectacular. Yet this obscure bay acquired celebrity in the early 1960s, when it was visited by Bruce Brown, an Australian surfer and film-maker.

Brown discovered a hitherto unsung local landmark along the eastern edge of Cape St Francis. This was the massive and powerful waves sometimes generated in this area from the collision of a heavy ground swell at low tide and the north-westerly winds which prevail mostly from May to September. Recorded in his film *Endless Summer*, these entered the surfer's vernacular as 'Bruce's Beauties', and as strong contenders for the title of 'the perfect wave'. Almost overnight, what had been a forgotten corner of the coast became a Mecca for a cheerful subculture of surfing fanatics, coming to 'Super Tubes Point' not only from around the subcontinent but from many other parts of the world, to pit human skill against the abstract power of the sea.

The spirit of adventure, of the duel of man and nature, is of long ancestry on this part of the southern coast. Impelled by the same spirit, Bartolomeu Dias and his men first looked on 'Bruce's Beauties' almost five hundred years ago. At this stage, however, they were probably none too enthusiastic. After ten thousand kilometres of navigation, and having achieved their main object in rounding the tip of Africa, the impetus of the expedition was running out. A few days after passing Cape Agulhas the two caravels arrived at what is now Algoa Bay, where the weary crew decided they had sailed far enough. Dias, obsessed by the desire to find a route to India, extracted one final concession from his men, and they continued on to the mouth of a river, probably today's Keiskamma River. As João de Barros recorded:

'. . . he asked us all to consent to follow the coast for two or three days more . . . But at the end of these days which he had asked for we had done nothing, except that we had arrived at a river which lies 25 leagues beyond the Island of the Cross . . . here we turned back, since the crew began to renew their complaints.'

On 12 March 1488 Dias erected the last commemorative cross of the voyage on a headland to the east of Algoa Bay. In remarkable pioneering research in 1938, Eric Axelson discovered fragments of this original 'Padrão de São Gregorio'. The precious relics are now housed in the Library of the Witwatersrand, but a facsimile of the original stands among the dunes of Kwaaihoek, a mute testimony to one of the most courageous journeys of discovery ever made.

With an increase in traffic, other Portuguese names were soon attached to local landmarks. Today's Algoa Bay is a corruption of 'Bahia de Lagoa', the 'Bay of the Lagoon', and the promontory at the western end was the 'Cape of the Reef', 'Cape Recife'. But beyond naming everything they could see from the offing, the Portuguese showed little further interest in this part of the coast. There was scant shelter, even in the bays, and the local Hottentots appeared to have little to barter.

Tentative settlement began with the Dutch. In January 1690 the Dutch galiot *Noord* gamely approached the Bahia de Lagoa, its captain intent on taking possession of the bay. A violent gale changed his mind, and he hastily retreated. Then, half a century later, one Ensign Beutler chose the hazards of land travel over those of the sea, reaching the bay overland from the Cape. He put up the beacon which gave its name to the Baakens River, till then called 'Kragga Kama', or 'Stony Water', by the Khoisan. But possession of the land was little help in taming the sea, and for many years the shore continued uninhabited except for occasional groups of castaways. Among these was a forlorn band of survivors from the wreck of the British ship *Dodington*, who were marooned on Bird Island in Algoa Bay.

Dodington was an East Indiaman which left Gravesend on 22 April 1755, bound for India. Under the command of Captain Samson, the ship carried 200 soldiers and a supply of cannon, despatched by order of George II for the defence of India. The cargo also contained a large amount of treasure, 36 000 ounces of silver in pieces-of-eight, to pay the garrison and British East India Company servants on the Carnatic coast. Another fortune carried was that of Robert Clive, returning to complete the long series of skirmishes which were to drive the French from India. This treasure amounted to some £3 000 in gold coin.

Originally, Clive himself had booked passage with his gold on *Dodington* but a last-minute change of plan saved his life,

133. *A starfish,* Marthasterias glacialis, *closes in on a winkle.* **134.** *Plough snails of the genus* Bullia *converge to feed on a stranded bluebottle,* Physalia physalis.

135. *Cove Rock, rising dramatically from the shoreline west of the Buffalo River, is a place of magic and myth for the local Xhosa people, to whom it is known as 'Gompo'.*
136. *Superseded by power fishing boats, the sailing fleet at Jeffrey's Bay has now dwindled to this lone survivor, Annette.* 137. *A replica of Bartolomeu Dias' original cross marking the limit of his epoch-making voyage now stands on the lonely promontory of Kwaaihoek, east of Algoa Bay.*

their luck ended, for they had been cast up on an island at the eastern end of Algoa Bay, a forsaken slab of guano-encrusted rock which was often marked on British charts as 'Confused Island'. To the survivors' confusion was soon added dismay. Away in the distance could be seen the low coast of Africa, but on the island itself there appeared to be almost nothing, apart from vast screeching flocks of seabirds. Gradually, however, the sea began to give back a little of what it had taken. Several butts of fresh water were washed up, as well as a welcome cask of brandy. As more objects were cast up on the island, the hope of survival increased. Several live hogs had swum ashore and these were rounded up and covetously looked after until ready to be slaughtered. A set of flints gave the means to a fire, and the splintered timbers of the ship provided the fuel, as well as a possible way out of their dilemma. Among the castaways was the ship's carpenter, Richard Topping, and as more and more timbers appeared he offered to build a boat from them. One of the men had experience as a blacksmith and began making improvised saws and hammers. Stoically, the little community settled down to weather the months in which the sloop would be built.

Life was far from easy. The sea was in a constant state of mutiny. A trip to the mainland in one of the small ship's boats turned into a disastrous confrontation with the local Xhosa, in which one man lost his life and two others barely escaped. Dehydration posed a constant threat, though fortuitous rainstorms provided intermittent relief – the rain was caught in a sailcloth supported on posts, then transferred to water butts. A supply of salt pork which had been washed up ran out, and the local birdlife began to get wise to the newcomers. As the chief mate, Evan Jones, the senior in rank of the castaways, noted in his journal:

'The Pork which Was Washed Upon the Rocks is all Expended. The Birds Which Were so Numerous at our first Coming on Shore, have Entirely left the Island, and the Seals Much Scarcer & Shyer, So that at

if not his fortune. The ship arrived safely at the Cape and rounded Cape Agulhas on 8 July. Here Samson made a fatal mistake, one common in this period. Many of the early charts, in a legacy of inaccurate readings from the Portuguese onwards, assigned the south-east coast of Africa a position further to the west than it had in reality. So when Samson set a course for east-north-east instead of east, he assumed that his ship was set safe on its way to India.

Decisive confirmation of his error in navigation was received at about a quarter to one on the morning of Thursday, 17 July. The night was dark, lashed by a fierce gale. Suddenly the forward lookout

screamed above the roar of the wind, 'Breakers ahead and to leeward!' The helmsman snatched the wheel around, hoping to pull the ship clear, but a moment later *Dodington* struck. The first impact was a light one, but it was followed an instant later by a rending crash as the massive breakers lifted her up and smashed her down on a series of unseen reefs. Thrown onto her starboard side, she broke up in a matter of minutes, and men, gold, silver, cannon, hopes and dreams, all were hurled willy-nilly into a foaming sea.

Only 23 souls out of the complement of 270 on *Dodington* saw the light of dawn. They found themselves alive, but there present have Nothing to live on but an Animal Between Fish & Fowl. There is plenty of them Here and No ways Shy, they Walk As Upright as a Man, These Were Our Food this Day.'

Jones, of course, was referring to the dubious delights of boiled penguin. With starvation almost upon them, the unexpected arrival of the gannet nesting season was a joyful moment. Suddenly the whole island was full of free eggs, and they dined splendidly for several weeks, continuing work on the boat with a will.

On 16 February 1756, after seven months on the island, the boat, a 10-metre sloop, was finally declared finished by the carpenter (who was given an extra ration of grog in appreciation). Launched from a narrow channel at the edge of the island, it was named *Happy Deliverance*. The next morning the castaways stopped to take a farewell look at the dismal rock which had been their salvation, their last action being to rechristen it 'Bird Island'.

There followed 61 days of fraught sailing east and north along the coast against the thrust of the Agulhas Current, until they reached the Portuguese harbour of Delagoa Bay. There, to their delight, they found two British ships, *Rose* and *Snow*, under the command of Captain Chandler, who agreed to take the survivors on to Bombay.

Over the years many attempts have been made to find the treasure left behind off Bird Island, all hinging on survivors' accounts which held that the ship had been wrecked on a reef some distance from the island. But a contemporary local salvage expert and marine archaeologist named David Allen detected a fallacious note in these claims. Familiar with the area around Bird Island and the kind of weather which had assailed *Dodington*, it seemed to him highly unlikely that the survivors could have swum even the short distance from the so-called 'Dodington Rock' under such conditions. A likely reason for the inaccuracy might have been the desire to keep the position of the wreck a secret. Allen believed that the ship could have gone down only on the island itself, a contention supported by the considerable quantities of material washed up.

In partnership with another diver, Gerry van Niekerk, he hired an old trawler, *Etosha*, and they set themselves up on the island in May 1977. Research, cool logic and detective work paid off with startling speed, for almost immediately Allen found the wreck of *Dodington*. Diving down from the dinghy one morning, he found himself gazing through a few metres of green water at a

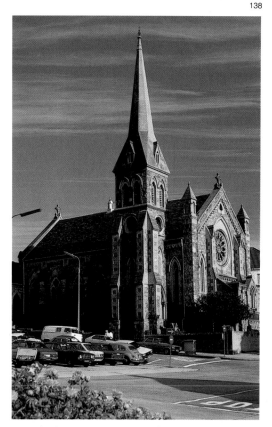

138. *An imposing nineteenth-century Presbyterian church in Settler country, one of the sights of the recently inaugurated Heritage Trail in Port Elizabeth.* **139.** *An example of carefully preserved Victorian architecture in the older part of Port Elizabeth.*

huge mound of copper ingots which he estimated to be about 20 tonnes. On top lay the ship's bow anchor, surrounded by green copper cannons, among them a coral-encrusted, two-metre bronze cannon and, to one side, a patinated brass carronade, a one-metre cannon used to spray shot at close quarters. In all directions around the mound, which was presided over by numerous octopi and shoals of fish, lay the ammunition for the cannon, including large quantities of lead shot, washed to and fro by the waves, and many larger cannon balls.

In a fever of excitement, Allen and his companions set about bringing this dazzling haul to the surface, beginning with the big bronze guns. This had its perils, not least among them the continual interest of *Dodington*'s self-elected custodian, Alfred, a five-metre great white shark. When the first bronze howitzer was finally hauled safely aboard *Etosha* it was revealed to be in almost mint condition, with the initials of George II clearly visible beneath a royal crown.

Soon civil as well as military and naval remains came to the surface. Many of the objects, glued together by sand and oxidation to form conglomerates, had to be prised loose from the sea floor. As well as a brass candlestick and a pair of compasses, numerous smaller objects were retrieved, including some evidently

destined for trading in the Carnatic. Each item was carefully listed, both as to its identity and its position, so that as complete a record of the wreck as possible could be built up.

Then, one Sunday morning, the mounting tension of excitement came to a fitting climax when one of the divers heaved himself out of the water into the inflatable rubber dinghy and emptied out his collecting bag. A glistening stream of silver coins landed in the bottom of the boat. They were Spanish pieces-of-eight, bearing the names of either Philip or Ferdinand and, in Spanish, the legend 'King of Spain and India by the Grace of God'. A hurried examination of the dates on the coins placed them all in the early part of the Eighteenth Century and, to the relief of the divers, none was later than the wreck of *Dodington*.

With 14 tonnes of salvage to their credit, Allen and his team wound off their operation on 18 September 1977, formally bringing their treasures in through the customs at Port Elizabeth. The project as a whole, though, was far from over. Further research both in South Africa and in the naval records in England was needed before it could be confirmed that they had indeed found *Dodington*. Allen shrewdly has not disclosed the exact location of the wreck, for undoubtedly much yet remains to be found in the dark waters below Bird

Island, including the elusive gold treasure of the conqueror of India.

Throughout the Eighteenth and into the early Nineteenth Century settlement along this part of the coast was slow, and increased only when the British occupied the Cape for the second time. Within a few years they had introduced a group of newcomers who abruptly changed the character of the landscape – the '1820 Settlers'.

They demonstrated a classic example of exchanging the fat for the fire. In the wake of the Napoleonic Wars there was much social unrest in Britain, aggravated by poverty and unemployment. And while the French had been defeated, many of their ideas of liberty and equality remained unvanquished. A strong, if distant, reek of revolution filled the British air. In this atmosphere the Governor of the Cape of Good Hope, Lord Charles Somerset, suggested to the British Parliament that an emigration scheme to Africa be set up, specifically to the border area of the eastern Cape Colony. Not only was the scheme intended to provide a distraction if not a relief from the tensions of unemployment and social discontent, but it concealed another motive. The frontier of the Colony was coming under increasing pressure from Bantu-speaking tribes, particularly the Xhosa. The few Dutch farmers in the area had little defence against them, while from the British point of view, military defence of such a remote frontier promised to be expensive. It was the quiet hope of the authorities that a band of English farmer immigrants would provide a barrier to tribal movement.

Lord Charles' proposal was accepted and invitations to join the emigration were posted around the country. The response was overwhelming. Although there were funds available for only 4 000, some 90 000 people, inspired by dreams of land and freedom, applied for 'life in the colonies'. Those finally chosen came from almost every stratum of Regency society. Though many were farm labourers, few had any idea of how to run a farm, nor of the land to which they were going. Nor, of course, were they aware of their quasi-military rôle.

In bitter winter weather they embarked on 21 Naval transports, which set sail in January 1820 on a gruelling three month-long voyage. The relief of finally arriving in Africa was tempered by mounting dismay at the strangeness and bleakness of the landscape and, to English eyes, the oddity of its inhabitants. Fifteen-year-old Eliza Pigot, for example, was examining the shore one day through her telescope when she spied a group of Hottentots. Their nakedness shocked her so much she could only record the vision in her diary in code!

The first ship to arrive at Algoa Bay was *Chapman*, which dropped anchor in the roadstead on the evening of 9 April 1820. She carried a large party of 256 people under Lieutenant John Bailie, as well as 15 from Staffordshire under John Carlisle. Feelings at this moment were mixed. The Reverend William Shaw recorded the immediate impression of many:

'Separated by six thousand miles of ocean from all you were wont to love and enjoy in your native country, and landed on the shore of Algoa Bay – the aspect of which at that time was most barren and unpromising – the hearts of many sank within them, and the enquiry was often reiterated – "Can this be the fine country, 'the land of promise', to which we have been allured by highly coloured descriptions, and by pictures drawn in our imaginations?" We are deceived and ruined, was the hasty conclusion of many.'

They found themselves facing a steep bluff overlooking a near-empty beach. The Baakens River flowed through a nearby ravine down to the sea. On the crest of the hill was Fort Frederick, a fortified barracks occupied by a garrison of some 60 soldiers. Below it were three small stone buildings and a few huts housing the military Commissariat under the command of Captain Evett.

Evett and his Naval opposite number, Captain Moresby of HMS *Menai*, were responsible for the landing of the new settlers, and were joined on 6 June by Sir Rufane Shawe Donkin, the *locum tenens* of Lord Somerset, who was still in England. Since there was no jetty at the bay, the disembarking of the 4 000 new arrivals was a tedious operation. First lowered from the transports into lighters which were rowed to the surf, they were then carried ashore on the backs of soldiers of the 72nd Regiment. Soon a small army of bewildered immigrants had gathered with its belongings on the beach and was organized into a 'tent town'. One of them, Thomas Philipp, made an entry in his diary on 1 May which sums up the prevailing mixture of trepidation and excitement. After announcing the main news in capitals – 'FIRST TROD THE SOIL OF MY ADOPTED COUNTRY' – he went on:

'. . . by moonlight we spread our bedclothes on our trunks and prepared for rest. . . O what a novel night for a civilian – our camp was not many 100 yards from the beach from which it was separated by a sand hill, the Moon shone bright as day – the camp beneath me – a few tents with an unextinguished fire by them – the sea rolling – and the ships in the bay reminded me of an invading army – very different feelings however actuated the population around me – All I hope thankful for the protection shewn them in passing the dangers of the deep, enjoying the escape from a crowded ship even with only the thin covering of the canvass of a tent over them.'

The settlers were given assisted passage

140. *A statue of Queen Victoria presides before the magnificent library, which now also serves as a Tourist Information Centre in Port Elizabeth.*

from the 'tent town' to their allocated 100-acre farms by ox-wagon. A train several kilometres long, laden with their worldly possessions, lumbered away on the long, hot trail inland to the area soon to become the district of Albany, around the settlement of Grahamstown. Here tension and uncertainty turned to open dismay, bitterness and fear, as the settlers surveyed what, compared to the green fields of England, seemed to them a trackless wilderness. The enormity of the task before them and its dangers slowly dawned upon them. Many lost heart and retreated before the prospect, but the majority stayed on, to 'take root or die', as Thomas Pringle, one of the settlers who was to make his mark in newspaper publishing, summed it up. The problems of unaccustomed farming and the struggle for survival were soon doubled by the realization of the hidden military agenda. To the east lay the Xhosa and, inevitably, border skirmishes flared up, reaching a climax on Christmas Day 1834 when thousands of tribesmen swept down on the settlers, killing more than fifty and leaving a trail of smoking destruction. However, against brutal odds and through a series of frontier wars, the Settler society survived.

At Algoa Bay a town and port developed as an outlet for the farmers'

produce and was named by Sir Rufane Donkin in memory of his wife Elizabeth, who had died of a fever in India at the age of 28. At first 'Elizabeth's Town' was little more than a clump of scruffy cottages linked by sandy paths. Enterprising members of the 'nation of shopkeepers', however, soon sniffed commercial possibilities. A merchant named Henry Nourse was given permission by Lord Bathurst, Secretary for the Colonies, to 'form a commercial establishment in the vicinity and in connection with the Settlers'. Captain Evett remained in charge of both the town and the garrison and in 1825, when Port Elizabeth became a magistracy, was instated as Governor Resident. With the greater power invested in him he undertook to improve the housing and in a few years the cluster of four buildings found by the settlers had grown to over a hundred dwellings. With increasing security on the border came prosperity and with it civic pride. In 1862 a Renaissance-style Town Hall went up, and in 1864 a Chamber of Commerce was formed by the local merchants. Today English influence is still strong and the settler heritage is much prized. On the spot where they once sat glumly on their boxes trying to figure out their future now stands an imposing brick campanile, erected in 1923.

Parallel to the growth of Port Elizabeth was that of East London, today a river port with a graving dock and wharves capable of accommodating ocean-going vessels on both sides of the Buffalo River. The town first developed in the wake of the Sixth Frontier War, when British control of the area was extended to the Kei River. In 1835 Colonel Harry Smith, then Chief of Staff to the British Governor, made a trip to inspect the mouth of the Buffalo River as a possible landing place for supplies for the troops. The following year the enterprising George Rex sent his son in the brig *Knysna* to trade at the river. A Union Jack nailed to a tree on Signal Hill was to mark the site of the future settlement.

At first called Port Rex, it was renamed East London in 1847 and incorporated into the Cape Colony. Thereafter, with infusions of settlers, the town grew rapidly, and became the entry point for some 5 000 German immigrants during the 1850s. The newcomers, comprising groups of farmers and veterans of the Crimean War, were given land along the

141. *A few of the many thousands of concrete 'dolosse' which keep the sea at bay on the East London breakwater. It was here in the 1950s that this tetrahedron design was first put into practice.*

142. *The hero of marine science on the Settler coast. The remains of the first historic coelacanth, caught near East London in 1938, are preserved in the city's museum.*

Buffalo River and to the north and east, in the 'Border country' inland. It was hoped that their settlements, some named after towns in Germany such as Berlin, Potsdam and Hamburg, would serve the same quasi-military purpose as those of the 1820 Settlers.

In 1856 work was begun on the first training walls at the mouth of the Buffalo River, the germ of the modern harbour works. The entrance to the harbour was protected by a breakwater whose development in the present century led to an important technical innovation in harbour design, the 'dolos'.

On this exposed sector of the coast the relentless hammering of successive storms caused a breach in the original breakwater in 1944. A rampart of 37-ton concrete blocks was built, but by 1963 about 60 per cent of them had become useless – and replacement by yet larger units was not financially viable. A solution to the problem was offered by East London's harbour engineer, Eric Merrifield, who suggested utilizing irregularly shaped concrete 'armour units' of a kind which had already been developed overseas. The principle of these was not to resist the power of wave action directly with a fixed barrier, but to use randomly placed units of an irregular design which would break up the wave and dissipate its energy. Moreover, if shifted during a storm, they could easily be moved back into position.

In view of patent restrictions on the overseas models, Merrifield set out to produce a design of his own. The inspiration for his 'armour unit' came from close at hand. Over the years many ships' anchors had been lost between the leading piers of the East London harbour. A local businessman who set out to salvage these anchors by winching them onto his barge unfortunately overloaded the barge with his loot, and it promptly sank. So entangled had the anchors become that it was impossible now to raise them and they had to be left at the bottom of the harbour until they and the barge could be cleared with explosives.

The image of entangled anchors lodged in the engineer's mind. His design, in the form of an 'H' with one arm rotated through 90 degrees, was not difficult to manufacture and had a high void-to-solid ratio, increasing the absorption of wave energy and allowing for a lower wave run-up and less overtopping during storms. At the same time, its anchor configuration gave it strong interlocking powers and high stability.

Merrifield christened his invention 'dolos', after the knucklebone of a sheep which bears a resemblance to the shape of the structure, and had little difficulty in persuading the authorities to put his creation to practical use. He made some 18-ton dolosse, installed them on the East London breakwater and invited his superiors to watch them in action against the Indian Ocean. Soon they were being used on a wide scale, the first major project, completed in 1968, being the two kilometre-long shore protection at Port Elizabeth which took 25 000 dolosse. Now a familiar sight around the southern

coastline, some 150 000 units are currently in use in ten major coastal and breakwater structures. And in recent years they have found their way to a number of countries in Europe and Africa, as well as to America and Australia.

Among all the other shipping in the harbour at East London is a thriving fishing fleet, working the waters of the Agulhas stream. The catch is mostly endemic fish with a good few sharks thrown in, but on occasion a more exotic animal comes up in the net. In 1938 one such creature made scientific history. Its discovery could hardly have been more unexpected, or more casual.

On 22 December a trawler named *Aristea*, under Captain Goosen, was working the fishing grounds along the coast to the west of East London. On the way back to harbour that day the captain, on an impulse, turned aside to take a run off the mouth of the Chalumna River, an area which, though generally unreliable, sometimes gave good catches. On this occasion it yielded a good haul of edible fish, together with about two tons of sharks. Half concealed at the bottom of the net lay a fish which quickly caught the fishermen's attention. Nearly two metres long and heavily built with rough, hard scales, it was a striking, vivid blue colour when first taken from the water. It had an unusual arrangement of two dorsal, two pelvic, and two long stiff pectoral fins, and was also armed with a set of ferocious teeth. When pulled out of the net it fought viciously, and attempted to bite Goosen's arm when he touched it.

Intrigued, the captain ordered this strange creature to be put aside, and forthwith turned his boat for home. The curator of the small local museum, Marjorie Courtenay-Latimer, was immediately informed of the unusual find, and when she arrived at the wharf was shown a pile of fish. Almost immediately her eye was caught by the big, bluish, heavily armoured fish with its odd configuration of fins, and she asked for it to be pulled out. Never having seen anything like it before, Miss Latimer hazarded a private guess that it was a kind of lungfish. But whatever it was, she already had a presentiment that it was something important. After a number of hours out of the sea on a hot summer's day, the fish was beginning to show signs of decomposition by the time it reached the East London Museum. Miss Latimer handed the animal over to the museum's taxidermist, with instructions that he keep the soft inner parts separate from the stuffed specimen.

The following morning she wrote a

short note, both describing the fish and including a rough sketch of it, and addressed it to Dr James L. B. Smith, at Rhodes University in Grahamstown. No better person could have been found as a target for Miss Latimer's query. Smith taught chemistry at Grahamstown, but the main interest of his life was ichthyology, pursued with intense, obsessive passion. Perhaps as important for coming events was his interest in and knowledge of the palaeontology of fossil fishes, among which one of the most important was the coelacanth.

The name 'coelacanth', meaning 'hollow spine', refers to the backbone of cartilage in the form of a hollow tube (instead of the bony vertebrae characteristic of modern fishes) which was a feature of this particular fossil fish. Another unusual characteristic was the number of stiff pectoral and pelvic fins which gave the impression that the fish could 'walk', or at least manoeuvre itself along the sea-bed with their aid. It was also believed that these fins were precursors of the fin-limbs developed by

143

the lungfish in their migration from the sea to the land. In other words, at however great a remove, the coelacanth was an ancestor of land animals, among them man. The most impressive aspect of the coelacanth, however, was its longevity, for it had a palaeontological innings of an incredible 250 million years, longer than any other known vertebrate. It had lived through vast seismic and climatic

upheavals which spelled extinction for many other species, including the then rulers of the earth, the great reptiles. Equally notable was the fact that during its long span its anatomy had undergone few changes. The coelacanth was evidently one of nature's habitual survivors.

According to the fossil record, however, it had eventually died out. Coelacanth fossils, most abundant about 300 million years ago, gradually dwindle and appear to run out some 70 million years ago, about the time of the demise of the last of the great dinosaurians. When Smith opened Miss Latimer's note, he found himself looking at a drawing of a coelacanth, not a fossil, but a fish which had been caught alive a few days before. The effect of this stark information on a man who was an expert on both modern and ancient fishes is not hard to imagine. Smith was overwhelmed with excitement, and with fear – fear that a mistake had been made, that his immediate instinct for the identity of the fish might be wrong.

Owing to urgent university work he

reached East London only on 16 February 1939 and, in a torment of self-doubt and uncertainty, drove straight to the museum. Later he recorded the impact of his first meeting with a living fossil:

'Although I had come prepared, that first sight hit me like a white-hot blast and made me feel shaky and queer; my body tingled. I stood as if stricken to stone. Yes, there was not a shadow of doubt, scale by scale, bone by bone, fin by fin, it was a true Coelacanth.'

It was a moment of awe, a glimpse of the eternal. It was not only a true coelacanth, complete in every external detail, but was also one of impressive size. Dr Smith promptly named the fish *Latimeria chalumnae*, in honour of Miss Courtenay-Latimer, and the next day, roped off and vigilantly guarded, it was put on view at the museum. Overnight the coelacanth became famous, though response from the scientific establishment was guarded until Smith published a preliminary description of its external features in the British scientific journal *Nature*.

Amidst the excitement of discovery and the glare of publicity, he was aware that the find raised as many questions as it answered. The first priority was to locate more of these fishes, and their true place of origin. It was clear that this specimen was a stray in the well-fished waters of the south-east coast. Many scientists believed the coelacanth to be a deep-water fish, but Smith deduced that this slow-swimming, heavily armoured fish with a powerful array of teeth was ideally suited for life in a coastal reef where its scales would protect it from the rocks and where it could lie in wait to ambush its prey. He also argued that it was probably carried southward by the powerful Mozambique Current to South African waters from somewhere on the tropical east coast of Africa. With extraordinary intuition he pinpointed the animal's probable location as a small group of French-owned islands, the Comores. The inaccessibility of the islands and the intervention of the Second World War prevented further investigation, and it was fourteen years before 'Old Four-legs', as Smith had nicknamed the fish, turned up again. It did so in the area he had predicted, in the Comoro Islands, where several dozen

more have since been found by French scientists. From their work a detailed knowledge of the living coelacanth has been assembled.

In a number of spheres, geographically, climatically and culturally, this stretch of coast marks a turning point between the south and east coasts of southern Africa. From now on new kinds of marine and shore life, as well as new styles of human society, begin to appear as the temperate zone gives way to the subtropical.

143. *Flowers of the sour fig decorate the dunes at Aston Bay. The juice of the leaves is popularly used as an antidote for bluebottle stings.* **144.** *Anglers try their luck in the well-stocked waters south of Hood Point, near East London.* **145.** *Sedge and salt-marsh rim the banks of the Gamtoos River.* **146.** (Overleaf) *Prelude to the Wild Coast, south of Morgan's Bay.*

THE WILD COAST

'. . . INCREDIBLY POPULOUS AND FULL OF CATTLE'

Strewn around the small rocky bay of Lambasi, on the Pondoland coast, is a curious collection of relics. Dating mostly from the late Nineteenth Century, they are the remains of attempts to salvage the wreck of *Grosvenor*, an East Indiaman which went down in August 1782.

A century after the wreck a rumour circulated that the ship had been laden with treasure. The *Natal Mercantile Advertiser*, apparently on no authority but its own, published in 1880 an article claiming that over a million pounds in gold bullion had been listed in *Grosvenor*'s bill of lading. The mere thought of so much treasure going to waste on the sea-bed was enough to inspire a series of salvage operations, some of which were decidedly eccentric. Besides many individual attempts, at least four companies were set up. Divers searched for the wreck, cranes were erected to haul up anything that might be found, and cables were dragged across the floor of the bay. When these schemes failed more elaborate ideas were dreamed up, one of which involved digging a tunnel under the bay from the shore, with hope of coming up beneath the wreck. The minor problem of holding back the sea was to be solved with a system of air-locks in the tunnel. Even more grandiose was one company's plan to erect an enormous dyke cutting off the entire bay, which would then be pumped dry.

All this wonderful ingenuity came to nought. The rim of the bay is rocky and shelves steeply into deep water, while the wreck itself, besides being protected by heavy wave action, has long since been almost completely buried beneath the

sandy substratum. Despite this, many objects of great interest have been recovered, including, if not the fabled 'million pounds', several thousand gold coins, as well as many fragments of crockery and other small objects. The most impressive haul, though, was that of *Grosvenor*'s cannon, five of which were recovered and now grace the Umtata Museum, a park in Port St Johns, the Old Fort in Durban, and the Royal Hotel in Lusikisiki. To these the rusted carcasses

of the machinery at Lambasi make an ironic footnote.

Grosvenor was far from the only ship to come to grief on this aptly named 'Wild Coast' which extends 260 kilometres from the Kei River in the south to the Mtamvuna River in the north. It forms the seaboard of the Transkei, home of the Xhosa, Tembu and Pondo people, where rugged cliffs and lonely, wave-pounded beaches skirt a coastal terrace of rolling green hills which rise step-wise to the

147. *The early morning sun lights up the cliffs near Mapuzi Point, on the Wild Coast of the Transkei.*

ramparts of the Drakensberg range, 150 kilometres inland. From the mountain catchment many rivers flow down to mangrove-enclosed estuaries. The sea is warm and richly stocked with fish, notably large shoals of sardines which arrive in the autumn and are attended by predators such as barracuda, bonito and galjoen.

The relentless action of sea on rock has created some spectacular coastal landmarks, of which one of the best-known is the 'Hole in the Wall'. The locals call it 'esiKhaleni', the 'place of the sound', describing how the sea thunders through the hole it has bored in a detached cliff of stratified sandstone. Further to the east, between Port St Johns and Port Grosvenor, soars the Cathedral, a granite outcrop hollowed out from within by the waves. Equally impressive are the Mfihlelo Falls, plummeting 160 metres over a sandstone cliff directly into the ocean.

The local flora and fauna are protected in a number of reserves along the Wild Coast. These include the Hluleka, the Mount Thesiger, and the Mkambati nature reserves. A particularly varied and interesting sanctuary is that of Dwesa, at the mouth of the Bashee River. The first nature reserve to be declared by an independent homeland, it was officially opened in September 1976 and consists of about 600 hectares of grassland and 3 300 hectares of thick indigenous forest, intersected by a number of rivers. An additional area to the south of the Bashee River mouth has been fenced in and stocked with buffalo, blesbok, eland, red hartebeest and warthog, amongst others.

Another reserve has been mooted for the estuary of the Mngazana River, a small but exceptionally rich area supporting many species. Some 340 hectares of mangrove swamps include the black mangrove, which grows here at the southern limit of its distribution. The Mngazana estuary, however, is at the centre of a conflict of interests; it has also been proposed as a harbour on this coast which to date has no outlet for local produce.

Apart from these protected areas much of the land is given over to agriculture, including many maize and pineapple fields. Cattle are of great economic as well as symbolic importance, and although the coastal strip is generally sour veld, particularly in the eastern Pondoland region, inland the grazing is good. Over the generations the livestock have left their mark on the landscape, having grazed the hills to lawn-like smoothness.

It is not known precisely when the first Bantu-speaking peoples came to settle in this area. By the middle of the Sixteenth Century, however, they had displaced the indigenous Bushman hunters and Hottentot herders. A memory of this encounter is preserved in the clicks of the Khoikhoi tongue which have become a feature of the Xhosa language. Though they shared common traditions and culture, the Bantu-speaking tribes showed regional differences and identities. The dominant Xhosa people settled in the south, around the Kei River, with the Tembu and Bomvana to the north of them and, further to the north, the Pondo and Pondomise. These divisions were already clearly marked by the time the first Europeans set foot on the sands of the Wild Coast in the 1550s.

The earliest known account of a shipwreck on the southern African coast was that of *São João*, stranded here on 5 June 1552. It was after this vessel that Port St Johns was named. Two years later another Portuguese ship, *São Bento*, met a similar fate near the mouth of the Umtata River, not far from the Hole in the Wall. The survivors of both strandings left fragmentary descriptions of the people among whom they had fallen and with whom they had bartered copper and iron

for cattle. But the first detailed account of the Xhosa and their society came from the crew of the seventeenth-century Dutch ship *Stavenisse*.

Stavenisse was a third-class ship of the Dutch East India Company, under the command of Captain Willem Knyff. Returning from India to Holland with a cargo of pepper, she was wrecked in the Bay of Natal on 16 February 1686. Of the 71 men on board, 60 reached the shore, and there split into two groups. Forty-seven of them set out to walk along the coast to the Cape, while the rest, under the leadership of the captain, stayed in the region of the wreck and set about building a small ship from timbers washed up from *Stavenisse*. Soon they were joined by survivors from the wreck of two English ships, *Bonaventura* and *Good Hope*, the latter a slave-trading vessel. A large crowd of local tribesmen gathered to watch the sailors at work with their improvised tools, and to barter bread and millet for nails.

When the 25-ton ship was finished it was dubbed *Centauris*. On 17 February 1687, almost exactly a year after the wreck of *Stavenisse*, the party of sailors set off, and after a fair voyage arrived in Table Bay on 1 March 1687. There they found that none of the crew who had set out

overland had arrived. In November, therefore, *Centauris* was despatched back around the coast to search for survivors. Several weeks of sailing brought no results until, on 7 February 1688, 21 men were found near the mouth of the Kei River, dressed only in karosses and burned almost black by the sun. They had been taken in by the local Magobesi tribe and treated well, though other tribes on their journey down the Wild Coast had given them a less friendly reception. Two more survivors of *Stavenisse* were picked up at the Bay of Natal, and another expedition a few months later rescued two more.

From the deposition made by the survivors to Simon van der Stel, much was learnt about the people in the distant land between the Buffalo and the Tugela rivers. Some of the sailors, who had been living with the Xhosa for nearly three years and had learnt their language, were impressed by the hospitality shown them and by their hosts' rule of law. Unlike the Dutch and English, the Xhosa did not deal in slaves, and a traveller among them was looked after, provided he was careful not to offer too great a temptation for gain:

'One may travel 200 or 300 mylen through the country, without any cause of fear from men, provided you go naked,

and without any iron or copper, for these things give inducements to the murder of those who have them. Neither need one be in any apprehension about meat and drink, as they have in every village or kraal a house of entertainment for travellers, where these are not only lodged but also fed.'

The coastal area was reported to be 'exceedingly fertile, and incredibly populous, and full of cattle'. While the cattle provided the base of the economy, other main foodstuffs included kaffir corn, beans and pumpkins. Iron and copper were much valued, both for decoration and for weapons, and the smelting of the metals was attended with much magic and ritual.

At the centre of the social structure was the chief, whose degree of importance depended on the size of his tribe or clan. At the time of the wreck of *Stavenisse* the

148. *Marine animals such as the octopus being gathered here at Ntlonyane, form an important part of the Xhosa diet.* 149. *Underlying rock strata are revealed in the reefs projecting from the sand at Mpandi beach.* 150. *Breakfast of mealies waits on a blanket, while the womenfolk of Ntlonyane gather red-bait and brown mussels.* 151. (Overleaf) *Bored by the sea through a detached cliff of stratified sandstone, 'Hole in the Wall' is known locally as 'esiKhaleni', the 'place of sound'.*

150

152. *Besides its decorative quality, the colour scheme of these Xhosa huts near the Mngazi River has an important effect in heat regulation throughout the day.*

paramount chief of the Xhosa was Togu. Each man in the tribe was seen as a 'shield of the king', so an offence against an individual was interpreted as an attack on his chief, and the fine for a misdemeanour went not to the injured party but to his king. Booty and game were likewise the property of the head of the tribe, to be dispensed to his subjects at his pleasure. He was also the focus of the legal system. 'Revenge has little or no sway among them', the *Stavenisse* account records, 'as they are obliged to submit their disputes to the king, who, after hearing the parties, gives sentence on the spot, to which all parties submit without a murmer; but should the matter in dispute be of great importance, and when he cannot rely upon his own judgement, he refers the parties to an older king in his neighbourhood.'

Slow or reluctant evidence was hastened by the judicious application of witchcraft and torture. Despite his importance, however, the king was by no means above the law, and could be tried and fined by his own privy council.

With the spread of European settlement eastwards along the Cape coast during the Eighteenth Century, relations between the tribesmen and the newcomers became increasingly clouded with suspicion. The change in attitude is reflected in the fate of the people washed up at Lambasi, the survivors of the *Grosvenor* wreck.

In August 1782 this 729-ton East Indiaman was bound on her return journey from Madras to England. The ship's last planned voyage, it turned out to be more final than had been anticipated. There were 150 people on board, including 18 passengers with their servants and a number of children. After a fair voyage from India, the weather turned against them on the south-east coast of Africa. In storm and darkness, Captain Coxon lost track of his position, an error compounded by inaccurate charts. Late in the evening of 4 August the lookout caught sight of a strange light which appeared to float in the air. Before anyone had time to realize that it was shining from the shore there was a violent impact as *Grosvenor* was driven headlong onto the rocks. In spite of the gale, the ship did not sink immediately, and when dawn came was found to be within reach of the shore. All but 15 people managed to reach the beach alive before the ship broke up in the late afternoon.

The troubles of the survivors, however, were just beginning. To heat and thirst, hunger and exhaustion, were to be added the hostility of the local tribesmen, still smarting from an early border conflict with the Dutch three years before.

On 7 August the survivors set out to walk from Lambasi to the Cape along the coast. It was to be an epic and a terrible march. Given their numbers, it was impossible to keep the party as a coherent whole and prevent people either from pushing ahead or falling behind. At first they tried to keep to the coast, but were regularly driven inland by the river estuaries. Some they could ford near the river mouth, but often they were forced to make long detours to find passable places upstream. And their progress was further slowed by the women and children.

The men had guns, but no gunpowder. On 9 August they experienced their first taste of local hostility, when a group of tribesmen fell upon them. Several hours of inconclusive stone-throwing followed before the Englishmen could move on again. By the time they reached the Mntafufu River three days later, the party had broken up, the stronger among the sailors forming a group of about 50 under a Mr Shaw. They pushed ahead to cross the Mzimvubu and Mngazi rivers inland, then returned to the shore, where they met friendly tribesmen for the first time. Having traded a watch-chain for a bullock, they ate the meat and made improvised footwear out of the hide. Later they encountered a lone *strandloper*, a Hottentot who took pity on them, showed them where to find mussels, and even lent them a cooking pot.

By the end of August the first of the castaways had reached the Umtata River, with the rest strung out behind them along the Transkeian coast. At the river six of the men found a dead whale, which they ate almost raw before moving on again. They arrived at the Mendwana River on 6 September and there had the un-English experience of being chased by elephants. Another friendly *strandloper* helped them to gather shellfish, but by now they were in a weakened condition. The leader, Shaw, died on 18 September and was buried by his servant. With heat, exhaustion and starvation, the death toll among the stragglers mounted rapidly.

The first group of six seamen reached Algoa Bay, where they found a second stranded whale near the mouth of the Zwartkops River. While making ready to devour the corpse, they were found by two white men and taken to a nearby farm. Their journey of over 500 kilometres had taken them a harrowing 92 days. The news of the disaster was carried to Cape Town, from where the Governor, Baron van Plettenberg, sent instructions to the *landdrost* at Swellendam to organize a search party. Accompanied by two of the rescued sailors, a large expedition of over 200 people set out under Helbert Muller and reached the Bushmans River in the middle of January 1783. They continued to the Umtakatyi River before turning back. Only 12 more survivors were found, the greater part of the crew and passengers of *Grosvenor* having long since perished on the shore. Persisting rumours that many were still alive, captured and held in bondage by the Xhosa, led to a second expedition in 1790. Though it reached the site of the wreck, no sign of *Grosvenor* remained, nor were any more survivors discovered.

As European settlement continued to
expand towards the Kei River, the tension
mounted. By the beginning of the
Nineteenth Century the border country
had become a kind of 'Wild East'. Herding
and hunting, and trading in ivory and
hides alternated with raiding cattle on
both sides. A series of nine 'Frontier
wars', spread over a hundred years,
slowly broke the power of the Xhosa
chiefs, and the military ascendancy was
accompanied by religious penetration of
the territory, primarily by Scottish and
Wesleyan missionaries. In 1827 a
Wesleyan mission school was built at the
site of today's town of Butterworth, the
oldest European settlement in the
Transkei, though the mission itself was
later burnt down in a border skirmish.
Further pressure on the Xhosa came from
the north, with the expansion of the Zulu
empire of Shaka and his successors and
the influx of refugees which followed the
Zulu massacres. Gradually the British
imposed indirect rule through magistrates
who dealt with paid headmen rather than
hereditary chiefs.

By mid-century a mood of despair had
come over the Xhosa people as their
independence was removed from them
piecemeal. Many of them, deprived of
their land, sold their labour to the farmers
south of the Kei River, and were gradually
absorbed into the European economy.
There were several reactions to the
destruction of tribal hegemony, of which
perhaps the most bizarre and tragic was
that of the vision of a 14-year-old girl
named Nongqause.

She was a member of the Gcaleka
branch of the southern Xhosa, in the
region of the Qolora River. One day in
March 1856, while she was sitting on the
rocks at the edge of a river pool, she saw a
vision which appeared to rise from the
depths of the water. The tribal ancestors
appeared to her, accompanied by
'beautiful oxen' whose horns emerged
from among the rushes fringing the pool.
To Nongqause the ancestors gave a
message of great portent, a prophecy of
the deliverance of her people.

Such visions, particularly those of
young girls, were taken seriously by the
Xhosa people. Nongqause transmitted
the message to her uncle, Mhlakaza,
councillor to the Gcaleka chief, Sarili.
It produced an immediate reaction, a
ferment which spread far and wide. The

153. *Two youths display the traditional
regalia and ceremonial paint which
accompany the rites of initiation into
manhood, the turning point in the life of the
young Xhosa male.*

154

ancestors, speaking through Nongqause, promised many and wonderful things. The tribal heroes of old, they predicted, would rise from the dead to help the living, who would themselves be restored to youth. Grain pits would overflow with corn, the land would throng with cattle. Wagons loaded with beautiful clothes and ornaments, as well as guns and ammunition, would appear. Best of all, a great whirlwind would come and sweep all the white men into the sea.

All this, however, required a price. As a proof of faith, the Xhosa must first kill all their cattle and destroy all their crops. No grain must be sowed. Those who refused would be turned into frogs, mice and ants, and snatched away into the sky by the same mighty whirlwind. Only in this way could the promised millennium be assured.

It was a grim bargain, but the Xhosa kept their side of it. For 10 blood-stained months a mass slaughter of cattle took place, thousands upon thousands, until the earth was corrupted with rotting flesh. Grain pits were burned, and the crops destroyed. As the destructive frenzy

mounted white missionaries in the area tried desperately to intervene. One of them, John Brownlee, rode through the country buying up all the grain he could, despite warnings from the Gcaleka prophets. In October Nongqause warned that all remaining cattle must be killed within eight days. On the eighth day, she promised, the dead would rise to make good their promises.

The day came and went. When the ancestors failed to materialize, those who had not killed their cattle were blamed. Now they too were swept into the hysteria, and the slaughter continued even more relentlessly. By February 1857 more than 150 000 head of cattle had been killed and the country was in the grip of starvation. Again Nongqause fixed the day of deliverance. On 18 February, she predicted, a blood-red sun would rise, stand still above the horizon, then set again in the east. Thereafter, everything that had been promised at the pool would finally come to pass.

Across the rolling hills and valleys the dying nation waited through the long heat of a summer's day. As the sun slid below

the western horizon, hope crumbled into defeat and despair, and the ineluctable certainty of starvation. Many tried to escape. Relief was provided at a number of mission stations in the border towns. Some 30 000 people moved into the Cape Colony, while many others threw themselves on the mercy of neighbouring tribes. None of this, however, helped the estimated 25 000 people who died of starvation, about a fifth of the Xhosa nation.

Among those who survived was Nongqause herself. To escape the vengeance of her people she fled to King William's Town and later, for her own safety, was kept for a while on Robben Island, in Table Bay. She spent the rest of her life on a farm in the Alexandria district of the Eastern Province, finally joining her unreliable ancestors at the turn of the century.

Today many aspects of traditional tribal life are still preserved in the Transkei. Social and religious customs such as the ceremonies initiating boys into manhood are still performed, styles of dress and dance are maintained, as

155

156

is the design of the familiar mud-and-thatch huts.

These huts have evolved over many generations in response to the local conditions. Recent research has analysed their structure and colour scheme, generally of alternating areas of white and brown, to show the way in which they combine to maintain temperatures in the hut at a comfortable level throughout the day. This applies particularly in the inland areas, away from the cooling effects of the coastal winds. The side of the hut facing the sun during the hottest part of the day is painted white to reflect the heat, reducing the temperature through the hours of noon. The area on the west side of the hut, which receives the declining warmth of the late afternoon sun, is left unpainted, retaining its natural mud colour so that in the evening heat is absorbed to warm the hut for the impending night.

The experience of many generations lies behind this design. Recent years, though, have seen an increasing use of corrugated iron, favoured for its durability. Unfortunately, iron heats

154. *In the aloe-dotted surrounds of Mapuzi, goats forage for what they can find on the stony beach.* **155.** *Gathering mussels can be hazardous when a large wave crashes unannounced over the rocky shelf.* **156.** *A couple of cows serenely chew the cud while their young herders take time off to romp in the surf at Presley Bay.*

rapidly in the morning and cools equally quickly at night. The result for the occupant is alternating conditions of fire and ice.

The invasion of corrugated iron is a small symptom of larger changes taking place in this society. On 26 October 1976 the country was given independent status and the seat of the government was established at Umtata. The Xhosa people provide a large labour pool for South

African industry, and many thousands of men travel each year to major centres as contract workers. Local industry and agriculture, however, languish. Heavily over-populated, the country offers little local employment, and there is much poverty. Bad farming methods are exacerbated by soil erosion and frequent drought. As in so many other parts of Africa, the old and the new meet uneasily on the shores of the Transkei.

NATAL

GIFTS OF THE AGULHAS STREAM

The might of the Agulhas Current sweeps down the east coast of southern Africa, following the margin of the continental shelf. In Natal, where it flows close to the shore, it compresses an intermittent counter current returning northwards. One of the effects of this is seen in June every year – the famous 'sardine run'. These are young sardines and the northward journey up the east coast is part of their life cycle. North of Durban they are probably carried out to sea, from where the Agulhas returns them to their breeding grounds off the south-western Cape.

The sardines arrive on the south coast of Natal in enormous shoals, thousands upon thousands. Spotter planes lie in wait for them near Port St Johns, on the Wild Coast, while further up the coast the fishermen make ready boats and seine nets. Then, in the warm blue waters of the Indian Ocean, the pilots catch sight of the shoals – dark, fast-moving shadows which flash silver in the sun as the fish veer to avoid a reef or a predator.

From the lighthouse at Port St Johns the planes follow the sardines northwards, signalling ahead to the fishermen in Durban. For them this is a big day in the calendar, with the added spice that it may not happen every year. When it does, though, they are ready to gather a harvest which may amount to 300 tonnes of fish. And it is a harvest which almost reaps itself, for by the time the shoals arrive off Durban the compression of the counter current is such that many thousands of sardines are often thrown up onto the beach in writhing, glittering heaps.

The fishermen's livelihood may be at stake, but it is the reactions of the local

public to this phenomenon which give it a carnival flavour and raise it to the status of an event. For with the first intimation of the arrival of the fish, 'sardine fever' strikes. A joyful dementia seizes the populace, and they descend on the piles of stranded fish, wade in to catch those milling in the shallows, and even plunder the fishermen's nets. People from all walks of life throw dignity to the winds, filling every conceivable kind of container, from buckets to hats, skirts and even briefcases. Nuns have been observed calmly trotting out of the surf, their habits filled with wriggling fish!

The sardine run is only one aspect of the natural wealth of this part of the east coast. There is a subtropical abundance, both in the sea and on the land. Man-made and natural crops flourish side by side. Pineapples and sugar cane, lala palms and wild bananas, the vivid scarlet accents of hibiscus flowers – all complement the lush greens of the

157. *With the annual sardine run off the Natal coast in full swing, anglers' rods bristle on a jetty near Durban.*

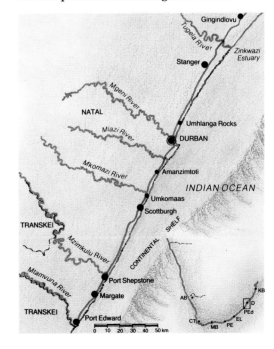

landscape, particularly in the summer season. For this is a summer-rainfall area, and the months from October to March are hot and steamy, heavy with an enervating humidity and with torrential rains which carry many tonnes of brown silt down the rivers to the sea. In contrast, the Natal winters provide a relief – warm by day, mild and cool in the evening.

Not surprisingly, this is a major tourist coast, and many of the villages strung out along the shore depend on the annual migration of visitors who come to relax and absorb the subtropical ease or stir themselves to walk, swim or fish. For whatever the season, the sea has many gifts for the angler, from barracuda and shad to bream and grunter, rock cod, kingfish, musselcracker, salmon and galjoen.

The capital of the coast is Durban. This large modern city, spread around a broad lagoon, has a long and often dramatic history. In 1497 the Portuguese navigator Vasco da Gama celebrated Christmas off a stretch of coast which came to be known as the Land of Natal. Three days later he rounded a bluff point and at the mouth of a lagoon he lowered his sails and began to fish. Such was his success that he named the bay 'Porto da Pescaria'. However, later European sailors confused the names and to them the lagoon became 'Rio de Natal'.

For those who inhabited its mangrove-girt fringes it had other names. When the first white settlers trickled into the vicinity towards the end of the Eighteenth Century they found a smattering of tribes of the Lala and Luthuli peoples. For them the lagoon was 'Thekwini', and the rivers feeding it were 'Mhlatuzana' and 'Mbilo'. These people lived simply, planting crops and catching fish in the lagoon in traps made from wattle fencing woven with reeds. The traders who encountered them quickly lost interest, since they had neither ivory nor slaves to sell.

Inland lived many more tribes, Nguni peoples who had lived for a number of generations in this land of rolling hills and valleys between the sea and the ramparts of the Drakensberg mountains. Their social structure consisted of many small, often family-sized clans which depended on cattle for their livelihood. The pleasant monotony of watching the herds chewing the cud was interspersed with border squabbles, during which much abuse, and occasionally assegais, were hurled. Theirs was the kind of society not often remembered.

Then, at the turn of the Nineteenth Century, it abruptly and violently entered history. In 1787 was born an illegitimate son to Senzangakhona, a young chief of

158. *Amanzimtoti, Shaka's place of the 'sweet waters', is a centre for local Zulu crafts, including the making of these traditionally designed pots.*

the minor Zulu clan, and Nandi, a girl from the neighbouring Langeni tribe. Attempts were made to persuade Nandi that she was merely suffering from the effects of an intestinal beetle, 'iShaka', and for a while after the birth of the 'beetle' the joke lingered. But not for long. An outcast from birth, mocked and tormented as a puny and underweight child, Shaka grew to be over two metres tall, and of animal strength and courage. He was also a man of high intelligence, ambition and a ruthless will, all of which were soon put to use.

In the days of Shaka's youth one of the two dominant groups in Natal was the Mthethwa tribe, led by Dingiswayo, who over the years had built up a powerful military machine based on conscription and a system of highly trained and disciplined regiments. At the age of 22 Shaka was conscripted into Dingiswayo's army, and he quickly rose to become a regimental commander. Senzangakhona died in 1816 and was succeeded by his son, Sigujana, who was promptly murdered by another son of Nandi. Shaka, with an escort from Dingiswayo, took over the leadership of the Zulu clan, then numbering no more than 2 000 people. Beginning on a small scale, he applied Dingiswayo's principles in his own army, and added some refinements of his own. He introduced a method of close fighting with a short stabbing assegai instead of the traditional throwing spear. On the larger field of battle he developed a new

formation, the famous 'chest and horns of the bull'. Neighbouring tribes were quickly conquered and assimilated, and when the Mthethwa power disintegrated after Dingiswayo's murder, its regiments were absorbed into the Zulu army.

It was this vastly enlarged army which Shaka now let loose on the surrounding tribes. He abandoned his predecessor's diplomatic style of warfare which allowed the defeated at least a marginal chance of survival, giving his soldiers instead the motto 'Victory or death!' In a series of shock waves, his barefoot armies swept north and south through Natal.

Almost two centuries later, his name still lingers. In 1828, the last year of his life, Shaka led an expedition down the coast in the course of which his impis massacred the Pondos and all but wiped out the Hlongwa tribe. On a river bank he stopped to drink the 'sweet waters', whence comes the name 'Amanzimtoti'. Umkomaas derives from a corruption of the Zulu 'Mkhomazi', meaning the 'Place of the Cow Whales', for it was here that the king watched cow whales giving birth in the shallows at the mouth of the river.

A more tangible relic of this raid survives in the form of 'Isivivane', the 'luck heap'. On a ridge overlooking the river Malkake, a tributary of the Mzumbe, Shaka took the precaution of propitiating the spirits in advance. Picking up a pebble with the toes of his left foot, he transferred it to his right hand, spat on it and then laid it on the ground. Thereafter, each member of the army followed suit until a small hill of stones had accumulated.

Shaka's life, darkened by increasing tyranny, came to an appropriately violent end. In 1826 he transferred his capital to Dukuza, on the site of today's seaside town of Stanger, with its nearby Shaka's Rock. Here, as the sun went down on the evening of 22 September 1828, the 41-year-old king, now a brooding recluse, was murdered by two of his half-brothers, Dingane and Mhlangana. His body was furtively buried in an empty corn pit.

The rise of the Zulu nation, with its power and wealth, had attracted a number of traders to Rio de Natal, 250 kilometres from the Zulu capital. In 1823 a merchant expedition sailed up from the Cape, under Lieutenants James King and George Farewell. Blown by a squall across the bar leading to the lagoon, they decided to make this place their base, and returned to organize a full-scale venture. In May the following year a party of settlers under Henry Fynn sailed up in the sloop *Julia* to set up a trading post on the banks of the lagoon. They hacked a clearing out of the bush, and built themselves a group of wattle-and-mud houses which they named Port Natal. The founding of this nucleus of today's Durban was watched from a distance by the wary Zulus. The activities of the 26 traders and ivory hunters spelled profit, but this did not prevent them from being spied on from 'uKangel' amankengane', the 'Watch on the Vagabonds'.

By the mid-1830s this small settlement on the fringes of the Zulu dominions, now ruled by Dingane, had grown large enough to establish an identity and a new name. On 23 June 1835, the settlers held a meeting to lay out the town in formal style, and to rename it after the Governor of the Cape, Sir Benjamin D'Urban. The next few years were hazardous. The

advance guard of the Voortrekkers had reached the southern borders of Zulu territory. In 1838 Piet Retief and many of his followers were murdered by Dingane, and in the bitter clashes which ensued, culminating in the Battle of Blood River, the men of Durban joined in alliance with the trekkers in the formation of the Natal Republic.

It was a short-lived state. In May 1842 the British reasserted control over this distant outpost, sending up a garrison under Captain Smith. They were promptly besieged by the Voortrekkers in what is now called the Old Fort. It became urgently necessary to get reinforcements, or the heavily outnumbered garrison would lose its hold on the colony. On board *Mazeppa*, a merchant ship lying in the bay, was a young man named Dick King. Born in England, King had arrived at what was then still called Port Natal in 1828. Having fought alongside the Voortrekkers against the Zulus, King now agreed to help his compatriots against his former allies. When Captain Smith sent a message to *Mazeppa* asking King to ride to Grahamstown for reinforcements, he assented immediately. At nightfall he went ashore where he was joined by his 16-year-old servant, Ndongeni. They took two horses and at midnight were ferried across the bay, the horses swimming behind them. Picking a route along a secret path through the mangrove swamps, they worked their way through the Voortrekker lines.

There followed an epic ride of over 950 kilometres to Grahamstown. There was no road, and 122 rivers and streams had to be forded. Ndongeni, lacking a saddle, dropped out halfway, leaving King to complete the ride alone. In spite of a two-day delay because of sickness, he rode into Grahamstown ten days later. A relief force was hastily assembled, and the soldiers, shipped from Port Elizabeth in *Conch*, arrived at Port Natal on 24 June. Two days later the siege was broken, and Natal remained firmly in British hands.

In spite of continuing upheavals, including the Anglo-Zulu War of 1879, the area rapidly gained in prosperity. In the fertile soil and well-watered climate almost every kind of crop grew in abundance. One in particular became important. Forty-eight kilometres from Durban is the farm 'Compensation' where,

159. *Basket weaving near Margate. Traditionally it was the task of the Zulu women to make the everyday eating and sleeping mats and baskets for domestic use, while the men wove the more decorative baskets.*

160. *Founded in 1863, the Royal Natal Yacht Club in Durban is the country's oldest yacht club.*

in 1851, the pioneer Edward Morewood crushed the first commercial sugar cane crop in Natal. As sugar cane farming spread, more labour was urgently needed, and this came by way of large numbers of indentured workers from India.

Mainly of Tamil, Hindi and Gujarati stock, the first labourers arrived in Natal in November 1860. Their starting wages were 10 shillings a month, and they were indentured for three years, later increased to five. Between 1860 and 1911, when the system was stopped by the Indian government, some 152 000 of these immigrants entered South Africa. During this time most of them lived in dire poverty and with negligible political rights.

Then, in 1893, a 24-year-old Indian lawyer named Mohandas Karamchand Gandhi arrived in Durban, *en route* for Johannesburg where he was to act as advocate in a dispute involving an Indian trading company. He remained in the country for the next 21 years, becoming increasingly concerned in the political welfare of the indentured workers. In 1894 he founded the Natal Indian Congress and in 1904 started a small self-help community called Phoenix, outside Durban, where he published the still extant newspaper, *Indian Opinion*. At the same time he crystallized the principles of his doctrine of *ahimsa*, or passive resistance. His resolute opposition to the immigration laws led to spells of imprisonment in 1908 and 1909, but

culminated with the Smuts-Gandhi agreement of June 1914, after which Gandhi returned to India and the greater struggle for Indian independence.

The flavour of Indian life and culture today permeates many areas of the Natal seaboard, particularly in Durban. Curios and jewellery, curry and spices, fruit and vegetables, are sold in the Indian market in Warwick Avenue, and many beautiful and exotic Hindu and Moslem temples grace the city. Annual religious celebrations include the Kavadi festival, where a procession of decorated and garlanded chariots is ritually thrown into the Mgeni River at the climax of the festivities.

Cosmopolitan and colourful, the life of the city at large is inevitably focussed on its modern harbour, spread around the lagoon. The ninth largest in the world, this harbour boasts over 15,5 kilometres of quays, providing mooring for some 55 vessels and accommodating well over 3 000 ships every year. Cargo handled annually at Durban amounts to 18 million tonnes, three times more than that of the country's second largest port, Cape Town. Among Durban's facilities are a graving dock, a grain elevator capable of storing 42 000 tonnes of grain, specialized ore-loading machinery and bulk oil storage.

If the land has become tamed, the sea remains another matter, for off the coast of Natal runs one of the world's most powerful currents. Up to 160 kilometres wide, flowing at a speed of about five knots and carrying 80 million tonnes of water a second, the Agulhas is a swift

and massive current, supplying a major component in the forces which generate some of the world's most turbulent seas. Its influence has long been recognized. An early guide from 1773 speaks of the 'Great Current', and laments the 'monstrous high seas' it creates in conjunction with powerful south-westerly gales. These winds, meeting the current head-on, have the effect of shortening the interval between the waves, pushing them higher and often superimposing them to create enormous isolated 'killer waves' which can reach a height of 20 metres.

The 'killer waves' have a stark record of destruction. A ship meeting one of them finds its bows dipping into the trough which precedes the wave, only to be crushed the next instant as thousands of tons of water disintegrate over it. A small vessel may be swallowed whole, but even the largest ships have no guarantee of immunity. The captain of the 93 000-tonne Swedish tanker, *Malmöhus*, recovering in Durban from the effects of one such wave, described it bitterly as 'Unbelievable!' The five-storey wave had effortlessly torn away *Malmöhus'* bows, and to the captain it was 'almost inconceivable that a sea dumping on the forecastle could split the bow open like that'. Another ship had even more conclusive proof of the fury of these waves. In October 1970 the 499-tonne German-built supply vessel *Stephaniturm* was on her maiden voyage from Europe to the Malagasy Republic. She was a model of her kind, and her skipper, Captain

161. *High-rise buildings crowd down to the waterfront at South Beach in Durban, a major focus for holiday-makers.*

Schröder, boldly sang her praises on arrival in Cape Town. 'My ship,' he said, 'can sail with absolute impunity in any of the seas between Alaska and Singapore.' Alas, *Stephaniturm* lasted exactly one week on the Agulhas seas. Though the wind was not exceptional, being about force nine, a series of 'killer waves' sent the ship to the bottom off Durban. A numbed Schröder, rescued with five members of his crew, said he had 'never seen such seas'.

One of the abiding mysteries of this part of the coast may have originated with such a freak wave. When *Waratah* left Durban on the evening of 26 July 1909, on the return leg of her second voyage, she was the newest and proudest of the splendid Blue Anchor Line. Similar to her predecessors in most respects, she had been given one structural difference, the addition of an extra upper deck. Under the command of Captain Ilbery, she carried about a hundred passengers and a cargo of meat and flour.

On the morning after her departure *Waratah* was sighted by *Clan MacIntyre*, and the two ships, neither of which carried wireless, exchanged signals by lamp. A little before 10 o'clock that night the Union-Castle liner *Guelph* signalled a distant vessel off the coast near East London. Visibility was poor, and only the last three letters of the ship's name could be made out. They were -TAH.

That was the last that was ever seen of *Waratah*. Seventeen months later, after a wide-ranging search for the missing vessel, an enquiry was held in London, at which a great number of theories of varying credibility were aired. No trace of wreckage had been found, which suggested that the liner had sunk rather than been wrecked. Much attention was paid to the extra deck, as it was believed that this may have made the ship top-heavy, dangerously raising her centre of gravity. The combination of a freak wave and the top-heaviness may well have

overturned *Waratah*. The findings of the enquiry concluded with the verdict that 'the Court has expressed itself as inclining to the view that the vessel capsized', and added that the 'particular chain of circumstances leading up to this matter is a matter of mere conjecture'. *Waratah* thus became immortalized as a perpetual question mark.

Contrasting with the more malevolent aspects of the Agulhas Current are areas of tranquillity on the shore itself. Among these are the mangrove forests which fringe many of the lagoons and estuaries of the Natal shore. The word 'mangrove' is of uncertain provenance, but may come from the Malay 'manggi-manggi'. Members of a unique group of plants, the halophytes, mangroves have worked out special adaptations which allow them to settle and grow in tidal salt waters. They are a particular feature of tropical shores,

and constitute some 12 genera commonly found worldwide, distributed across eight diverse plant families. On the Natal coast five mangrove genera from three distinct families are found. *Avicennia* is a member of the family Verbenaceae, *Lumnitzera* of the combretum family, while *Bruguiera*, *Rhizophora* and *Ceriops* all belong to the family Rhizophoraceae. Of these, *Avicennia* and *Bruguiera* are dominant in the local mangroves, and *Rhizophora* is an important genus both here and worldwide.

Mangroves have evolved complex and fascinating adaptations to the advantages and drawbacks of their intertidal environment. Among their characteristics is an ability to carry out progressive colonization of the mudbanks, in effect reclaiming land from the sea. Their elaborate root systems trap silt brought down by the rivers so that the mudbanks are not only stabilized by the trees, but also slowly consolidated with silt to form a new shoreline. In the course of this process the trees are faced with two main problems deriving from their choice of habitat. One of these is the presence of salt in the water. As with all the higher plants, mangroves rely on transpiration of water from their leaves to draw water and nutrients up from their root systems. If water is drawn up and evaporated from the leaves, how do the plants handle the salt which is thus concentrated in their tissues? Their second problem is the lack of an oxygen supply at root level. The soil which is washed down to form the mudbanks is rich in nutrients, but very fine in texture. It forms a deep, black and pungent mud. The surface of this is aerated by the action of the tide, but its deeper layers are almost entirely lacking in oxygen.

162. *The mosque in Grey Street is one of many serving Durban's large Moslem community.*
163. *The colour and bustle of the Indian market in Grey Street.*

168

167

164. (Previous page) *The rolling hills of the Natal coastal terrace, from Durban Bay to the snow-clad ramparts of the Drakensberg mountain range.* **165.** *A close-up of the jaws of the ragged-tooth shark clearly shows the rows of fearsome teeth. A lost or damaged tooth is replaced by the one behind it so that the shark's armoury is kept constantly razor sharp.* **166.** *The regular ritual of emptying shark nets off Durban. Laid in shallow water behind the breakers, the nets have resulted in a dramatic reduction of the shark hazard in the past two decades.* **167.** *The highly dangerous Zambezi shark, with an attendant remora or sucker fish 'hitching' a ride. This shark is unusual in that it is equally at home in salt and fresh water, and makes a speciality of hunting far up coastal rivers.*

An example of the ingenious ways in which mangroves have solved these difficulties is seen in the locally dominant *Avicennia*, the white mangrove, which acts as a pioneer, arriving ahead of other species to colonize the mudbanks. It is a large tree, growing up to 12 metres high, and has a whitish-grey trunk and easily recognizable small silvery-green leaves which grow to form a compact, evergreen crown.

Like those of all mangroves, the root system of *Avicennia* is adapted to cope with the instability of the mudbanks. Instead of a main tap root there is a shallow but extensive system of 'cable roots' which radiate from the trunk of the tree to anchor it in the mud, to a depth of about 50 centimetres. From these largely structural roots, other subsidiary roots develop, shooting straight upwards from the cable roots as unbranched 'pencil roots', or pneumatophores. Soft and corky in texture, these aerial roots can grow to a height of some 70 centimetres. When exposed at low tide, they absorb oxygen directly from the atmosphere and supply it to the main root system. The pneumatophores thus act as 'ventilating chimneys' for the mangrove, supplying the oxygen that is not available in the mud.

The problem of the disposal of salt concentrates is solved in different ways by the various kinds of mangroves. In the *Avicennia* species sodium and chloride ions are partly excluded at root level, but are also exuded through the leaves by special salt glands. These methods are less efficient than in some other species, but the white mangrove appears to compensate by having a very high tolerance to salt in its tissues, its sap being about a hundred times more salty than that of an average land plant.

Life on a mudbank requires particular ingenuity too in the matter of gestation. With the constant tidal action around their roots, the mangroves have seeds which are unique in that they germinate while still attached to the flower. In the case of the white mangrove, these seedlings are round. When they fall from the tree they land on the mud and are

usually washed away. This normally coincides with the advent of the highest spring tides, those of the equinox, with the result that the fruits are widely dispersed. It is this dispersal which gives the white mangrove its pioneer rôle in the development of a new mangrove forest.

The second most common mangrove on the Natal coast is *Bruguiera gymnorrhiza*. Though it sometimes grows to 18 metres, it is generally much smaller than the white mangrove. It is also something of a camp-follower, taking over the space left it by the pioneering white mangrove, and

often ousting it in the centre of the swamp where the substratum has already been stabilized. A reflection of their contrasting characters is found in the tendency of *Bruguiera* to prefer a shaded, more protected environment of the kind offered by the white mangrove's dense canopy, whereas the white mangrove itself prefers an unshaded location. The root systems of the two genera work on the same basic principle. The sturdy *Bruguiera* has radiating curved 'buttress roots' which give it a firm grip on the mudbank, since it too has no strong tap root. The buttress

168. *The major 'colonist' of the mangrove swamps is the white mangrove, growing here in the Mtumzini Reserve. Silt trapped by the mangroves' extensive root systems consolidates on the mudbanks and gradually forms a new shoreline. The problem of lack of oxygen for the roots is solved by means of vertical aerial roots, or pneumatophores. Clustering around the trunk, they supply the tree with oxygen when the main root system is submerged by the incoming tide.*

roots spread out below the surface and reappear above ground as aerial roots with a similar function to the white mangrove's pneumatophores. They differ in shape, however, having a characteristic fleshy protuberance where they loop, which has earned them the name 'knee roots'.

In the *Bruguiera* species, the mechanism for the exclusion of salt appears to be more efficient than in the case of *Avicennia*. Unlike the white mangrove, *Bruguiera* has no salt glands on its leaves, but relies instead on more rigorous exclusion at root level so that its tissues contain only a tenth of the salt concentration found in *Avicennia*. It is believed that the plant also has a mechanism for accumulating salt in its older leaves which then drop, ridding the tree of the unwanted chemicals. Like the white mangrove, this species is viviparous, producing seedlings already germinated on the tree. In *Bruguiera*, however, and in most mangrove species, these seedlings are not round, but are long, slender, cigar-shaped hypocotyls which, when they drop, stick in the mud and are not carried away by the tide. Even when taken by the tide, *Bruguiera* seedlings have remarkable powers of survival and can last in sea water for as long as a year, even crossing the ocean to colonize new shores.

Of the worldwide genus of *Rhizophora*, only *R. mucronata* is locally important. It resembles *Bruguiera* in that it prefers to settle in mud which has already been stabilized by other species, and is like the white mangrove in that it has special glands on its leaves which exude a salt concentrate. In spite of this mechanism, it, too, has a high salt level in its tissues. Strut-like roots protruding from high on its trunk act as both stabilizers and pneumatophores.

All these trees, once established as a swamp, make a very amenable habitat for a great many creatures. They provide ideal places of shelter, particularly for birds, which abound in the thick leaf canopies. The leaves contribute to the decaying detritus that is at the heart of the estuarine food web, and the mud is high in nutrients. At the same time, the animals face much the same problems as do the trees themselves, including the lack of oxygen in the mud and the effects of constant tidal action.

Variations on the theme of survival under these conditions are legion. Some animals live on the mud, others in the trees. Most, to one degree or another, are amphibious. All of them need to stay out of the way of the predators which are brought in on the tide.

169. *The mangrove snail,* Cerithidea decollata, *is adapted to life in the mangrove swamp, feeding on the mud surface at low tide and retiring up the mangrove tree as the tide advances.*
170. *Mangrove crabs,* Sesarma meinerti, *forage the mud surface for mangrove leaf detritus at Mtumzini.*

The mangrove snail, *Cerithidea decollata*, for example, feeds on the surface of the mud at low tide. When the tide comes in, bringing with it fish and crabs, the snail moves up the mangrove trunks to escape from them. How this creature is able to predict the arrival of a tide with such precision is a mystery, one deepened by the fact that the mechanism for prediction, the snail's inbuilt 'clock', works for the fortnightly spring tides as well. At these times, when the water rises considerably higher than normal, fewer of the snails descend to feed, and they retire earlier and climb higher.

Another mangrove mollusc, the winkle, *Littorina scabra*, also relates to the high spring tides, but in a slightly different way. It lives almost exclusively on the mangrove trunks where it forages for food, but returns to its marine origins when it comes to reproduce, for its larvae are free-swimming plankton. To save itself time and trouble, however, the winkle times its descent to the water to coincide with the spring tide, thus making its journey shorter. Other animals take their chances by staying on the mud during the tides. The tiny snail *Assiminea ovata* is one of these. It lives permanently on the surface, losing many of its numbers to predators with each incoming tide. In contrast to the 'wanderers' are the 'burrowers', creatures which forage on the organically rich surface of the mud and, as the tide rises, retreat not upwards but down into burrows.

One of the most versatile of mangrove animals is *Periophthalmus*, the mud-skipper. This amphibious fish moves freely from water to mud or onto the roots of the mangroves, its grey-brown mottled skin blending perfectly with its muddy background. It grows about seven centimetres long and in profile tapers

from a round, stumpy head to a flat tail. Large, bulbous eyes are mounted like miniature periscopes on top of its head, and its pectoral fins have a fleshy, muscular base and an elbow-like bend, giving them a passing resemblance to the forelimbs of a land animal. Behind these, the pelvic fins fan out radially on either side of the body.

The mud-skipper can swim, albeit somewhat ponderously, but its real medium is the surface of the water. Here it has evolved a rapid and effective way of getting about. It swims along with its eyes projecting above the surface, then uses its tail to launch itself into a miniature 'flight' lasting about one-twentieth of a second. During this, the pectoral fins are rigidly held out sideways as stabilizing 'wings'. As it lands, a further flick of the body sends it into flight again. The whole progress is seen as a series of quick, skeltering skips.

On land or on the branch of a mangrove, the pectorals are further adapted, this time to 'crutching'. Here the mud-skipper extends the fins forward together, then swings its weight over them. In the new position it anchors itself with its pelvic fins, then throws out the fore-fins again. Progress is slow, however, and when alarmed or in pursuit of its prey, the mud-skipper uses a variant of its skipping technique on the surface of the water. It bends its tail like a spring, forward and to one side. Thrusting against the mud with its tail and straightening its body, it shoots forward in a series of bounds, again using the pectoral fins as stabilizers.

The mud-skipper is insectivorous, feeding largely on land. In the water it breathes through gills as a fish, but when it moves out of the water onto land, it must carry its own air supplies. As it breaks the surface, it takes a large gulp of air into its gill chambers, which are then muscularly sealed, along with a quantity of water. Catching a fly usually means losing its supply of moisture, so feeding is almost always followed by a return to the water.

When the tide rises, *Periophthalmus* joins in the mass exodus from the mud surface, either hopping onto a mangrove root or moving for the duration onto the land. During the long sojourns out of the water, the animal is able to 'breathe' through its skin because of fine superficial blood vessels capable of absorbing oxygen directly from the air. When it comes to breed, however, it retires to a burrow in the mud, often on the edge of one of the water channels which run through the mangrove stands. During the breeding season it is believed that the burrow remains occupied even during high tide. This subterranean 'nest' is dug out by the male mud-skipper and has twin openings at the surface, with a little circular 'turret'

of excavated mud around each. The openings lead down to a common chamber, about 30 centimetres below the surface. This is normally at the water-table and thus permanently filled with water. After courtship (a highly aggressive affair, with much hopping and displaying of fins), the male mud-skipper mates with the female in the burrow and the eggs are laid on the chamber walls. When the young hatch they remain for a period in the chamber, for the hatchlings are aquatic larvae which become amphibious only after they metamorphose into adults.

Among other burrowers in the mud are a number of crabs. A familiar inhabitant of mangrove swamps, for example, is *Sesarma catenata*, which occurs in large colonies. It uses its burrow mostly as a bolt hole when alarmed. The larger *Sesarma meinerti*, which lives off leaves and detritus from the mangroves, is an accomplished excavator, and digs deep burrows down to the water-table. These

can reach down as much as two metres, allowing the crab to live much further inland than other species, sometimes hundreds of metres from open water.

Perhaps the best known and most colourful of the mangrove crabs are the *Uca* species, the fiddler crabs, of which there are five southern African species, *U. annulipes*, *U. urvillei*, *U. gaimardi*, *U. vocans* and *U. inversa*. Though they come in a variety of colours, from pink and red to blue and yellow, they share a common life-style. They belong to the family Ocypodidae, and like other members of the family have a wide carapace with a straight front edge, grooved to accommodate long-stalked eyes. Males have an outstanding feature in that one of their chelipeds, or 'nippers', is greatly enlarged. The claw itself, the chela, can be almost as large as the carapace, and is vividly coloured – it is this feature which has given the fiddler crab its name.

Like the mud-skipper, fiddler crabs are amphibious, and they too have evolved gills in which moisture is retained while they are out of the water. More agile on land than in the water, they run sideways at high speed on their eight walking legs. They are highly gregarious, but are shy of intruders and are particularly sensitive to ground vibrations. At the first hint of a tremor they scuttle for the cover of their burrows. Fiddler crabs also feed off organic detritus, eating voraciously during low tide. Their chelae, hollowed out like small shovels, collect the surface mud and transfer it to their mouths, in which organic matter is extracted from the mud. The residue is discarded as a trail of small round pellets, or 'pseudofaeces'.

Burrows are made independently by both male and female fiddler crabs. The depth varies, but is usually between about 12 and 18 centimetres, and at the bottom is a chamber in which the crab can rest and reorientate itself before returning to

the surface. This 'turning chamber' is at the water-table, so that, even at low tide, it retains some water.

As the tide comes in, the crabs take refuge in their burrows, plugging the entrance with mud behind them. This not only secures them against marine predators, but encloses a supply of air. When the tide recedes again, the crabs return to the surface, where they make much of cleaning themselves, lavishing special care on their enlarged chelipeds, before settling down for another spell of mud-swallowing.

With the approach of the mating season at the height of summer, changes in the hormones of the males trigger an intensification of their colour. Aggression rapidly increases, and there are frenzied contests between the males in which the single large cheliped is wielded like a medieval club. Later, when territory has been agreed upon, the males turn their attention to the females. In the courtship ritual the cheliped is used by the male to beckon to his potential mate. This amusingly human gesture is particularly pronounced in *Uca annulipes*, where the swing of the cheliped has a distinctly 'sailor-to-tart' air about it. Scuttling to and fro, beckoning and waving with manic vivacity, the ritual develops into a frenzied 'dance' in which the entire *Uca* population takes part. Copulation takes place on the mud, with the partners locked together 'face-to-face'. When the eggs are laid they are kept by the female on her body until they develop into free-swimming marine larvae, joining the plankton in the open sea.

The threat of predators is a constant in the life of many animals, on land or sea. The richly stocked waters of the coast of Natal have the dubious privilege of attracting one of the world's most efficient and unpredictable marine killers, the shark.

Sharks, like dogfishes, sawfishes and rays, belong to the class of cartilaginous fishes. Their ancestry reaches back more than 300 million years, during which surprisingly little change in their structure has taken place. The exact number of today's species is unknown, partly because they so often resemble each other. It is believed, however, that there are between 275 and 300 species worldwide, of which about 80 are found in southern African waters. Most of these are dangerous only to each other or to other fish, but a few also attack man.

171. *Aloes in the foreground add to the impression of lushness at Uvongo, on Natal's south coast.*

The tiger shark, growing to about five metres, is a solitary scavenger with a penchant for lurking in river mouths. Highly dangerous, it has been involved in many attacks. It is matched by the equally ferocious Zambezi shark, which can reach 3,2 metres. This latter species is almost unique among sharks in its tolerance of fresh water, and often frequents shallow, muddy waters in estuaries, lagoons and rivers, sometimes travelling hundreds of kilometres upstream – it has even been recorded in Lake Kariba, 2 000 kilometres from the mouth of the Zambezi River.

Dusky sharks are also abundant on the Natal coast; most are small, but they can grow to 3,5 metres and are potentially dangerous to man. Other species, while dangerous, are deep-water animals, rarely coming close inshore. The mako shark, for example, while fast and lethal, is more likely to attack boats than humans. The hammerhead shark, with eyes set at the ends of the 'hammer', has been known to attack in tropical waters, but is rarely aggressive on the Natal coast, and the enormous 15-metre whale shark does not normally attack unless provoked.

All, however, take second place to *Carcharodon carcharias*, the great white shark. Growing to over six metres in length, it has little trouble in biting a seal in half or in swallowing a man whole. Its sinister reputation, while well founded, has also been enhanced by fiction and film, and by the hysterical hyperbole which inevitably surrounds the unknown and the fearful. It constitutes only about two per cent of the shark population along the Natal coast, where many attacks probably have been ascribed to it without evidence.

Structurally, the different shark species have many features in common. Their skeletons, unlike those of the majority of fishes, are made not of bone but of cartilage. Their skin is covered in tiny, hard scales giving it the texture of sandpaper. There is no 'swim bladder' of air to control flotation as in most other fish, so to maintain buoyancy the shark must keep moving. Besides a highly developed sense of smell, it has sensitive lateral organs along the sides of the body which pick up vibrations in the water across a considerable distance, directing it towards its prey. Eyesight is acute at short range, and the attack is swift.

Like the rest of the skeleton, the shark's jaws are composed of cartilage, supported by powerful muscles. The teeth are not of bone, but are enlarged and modified scales, their structure varying from species to species. The jaws of the great white, for example, are armed with five

172. (Previous page) *The mouth of the Zinkwazi estuary is closed by a wave-driven sandbar, a common occurrence at east coast estuaries during the dry season.* **173.** *Cutting sugar cane near Port Shepstone on the Natal south coast. Introduced in the mid-Nineteenth Century, this crop is an important staple in the local economy.*

rows of usually triangular, serrated and razor-sharp teeth. Only the foremost rows are in use, however, as the others are kept in reserve, coming forward in 'conveyor belt' fashion to replace the working teeth as they are lost through wear and tear. With ageing, the teeth grow larger and stronger and the rate of production slows down, so that in the mature animal tooth replacement takes place about every two to three months. In the course of its lifetime, *Carcharodon carcharias* wears out about 20 000 teeth. In repose, little can be seen of the teeth. On attack, however, the upper jaw is disengaged and thrust forward to engulf the prey. The muscular power of this action is enormous. Experiments on sharks in captivity have shown that a force of up to 3 000 kilograms is exerted over one square centimetre.

Given the high worldwide population of sharks, reported attacks on humans are rare, averaging about 25 a year. Of these attacks, only some are fatal. Their psychological effect, though, heavily outweighs cool knowledge of the odds, as the history of shark attacks off Natal well demonstrates. The fine beaches and warm water have long attracted tourists to this area, and the revenues they bring are an

important part of Natal's economy. The high water temperatures, however, also attract sharks to the good feeding found here, particularly in the summer months. Relatively few attacks take place when the water temperature is below 20 degrees centigrade, whereas from 25 degrees centigrade and above attacks increase rapidly. They are compounded by the murkiness of the water at this time of the year, when the flooding of the rivers brings down silt which can spread three kilometres out to sea.

Until 1940 no consistent record of shark attacks was kept. They certainly took place, however, for as early as 1904 the Durban City Council voted to put up the first anti-shark barrier. This was a semi-circular enclosure, about 100 metres across, cutting off a segment of the beach. Finished in 1907, it worked well for over 20 years until pounding seas rendered it unsafe and it was pulled down. Until the Second World War few attacks appear to have taken place, but in the post-war years, with the increase in tourism, a new wave of attacks began. Between 1943 and 1951 a total of 21 shark attacks were recorded off the Durban beaches.

Many different solutions were put forward, most of them based on a

permanent barrier or fence. These were not only costly, but vulnerable to wave action. Then, in the early 1950s, an oblique but effective solution was found. It came from Australia, where a fisherman in New South Wales experimented with a large-mesh net in the hope of trapping larger fish. He laid the net in 25 metres of water, but returned the next day to find that it had disappeared. Two weeks later it floated to the surface, buoyed up by the bloated and decomposing bodies of over a hundred large sharks.

From this accidental discovery the principle of today's shark nets was developed. The object is not to erect a fixed barrier, but to reduce the inshore population of the larger sharks. At the same time the nets are simple to install and less costly than other methods. Each about 190 metres long, they are laid behind the surf line in about 12 metres of water and are arranged in a double row, with a gap between each net. Buoyed, they hang suspended in the water with their upper edge about three metres below the surface. A similar gap is left between the bottom of the net and the sea-bed where it is anchored.

When sharks come inshore they swim around the nets, but one may become entangled, usually catching its gills in the mesh. Because the shark must keep moving to circulate water over its gills, it 'drowns' in the net. Its death throes attract other sharks to the attack, and these, too, become enmeshed.

The first set of shark nets in South Africa was installed by the Durban City Engineer on 1 March 1952, and extended from Addington Beach to a little below the Mgeni River mouth, with further nets off Brighton Beach and Anstey's Beach. Their effectiveness was soon realized and appreciated, but it was some while before other municipal authorities up and down the coast followed suit. The events of December 1957, however, soon woke them up to the urgency of installing nets in all places where sea-bathing took place. In 'Black Christmas' of that year, five attacks took place along the Natal south coast. On 18 December at Karridene, a 16-year-old life-saver, Robert Wherley, while body-surfing in 1,2 metres of water about 50 metres from the shore, had his leg snatched away at the knee. He was lucky; expert medical care saved his life. But the attack was followed by four others, the last at Scottburgh on 9 January 1958. All occurred in about a metre of water and none further than 30 metres from the shore. Three of them were fatal.

Panic swept up the Natal coast. Almost overnight a good part of the tourist population melted away, to leave the R300 million tourist and hotel industry reeling. More extensive nets were obviously needed, as well as tighter controls and organization. In 1964 the Natal Anti-shark Measures Board was set up, with a brief to make the Natal coast safe for bathers. Since then 263 nets covering 39 bathing beaches have been installed along 275 kilometres of coastline, and they are serviced by a permanent field staff operating from ski-boats. Weather permitting, the nets are inspected every day, dead sharks are removed and the nets relaid. The dead sharks are brought back to the Board's headquarters for examination and recording. Since the nets were installed over 12 000 animals have been caught, enabling the Board's experts to build up a detailed picture of the shark species in the area.

Notwithstanding the success of the nets, other methods are still being tried. A theory that dolphins are antipathetic to sharks and can be trained to attack them has been tested with moderate success. The dolphins, however, understandably balk at taking on the larger species such as the great white. Curtains of bubbles have proved ineffectual, though another kind

of 'curtain' shows promise. An electric field generated from an insulated cable on the sea-bed can cause larger animals such as sharks to lose voluntary control of their muscles, while leaving smaller animals, including man, unaffected. The concept is still at the experimental stage, however, and to date shark nets remain the most effective form of control.

They may, perhaps, be too effective. In recent years marine scientists have noticed a drop in the population of the larger sharks, reflected in the demise of the famous '1 000 Club', membership of which was restricted to those who had caught a shark weighing over a thousand pounds. The long-term consequences of the removal of the larger sharks is difficult to assess. One effect to date has been a population explosion among the smaller dusky sharks. Big sharks tend to eat smaller sharks, whereas the latter prey mostly on fish, including the game fish

which are an important part of the coastal economy. Even as savage a predator as the great white shark plays its part in the balance between man and nature.

174. *Wild banana trees,* Strelitzia nicolai, *hang over the blue waters of the river at Uvongo.*
175. *The broad, silt-rimmed Tugela River forms a natural, and unofficial, boundary between Natal proper and Zululand. During the dry season the flow of water is impeded by heavy siltation, a situation exacerbated by the cultivation of sugar cane along the river banks.*

174

175

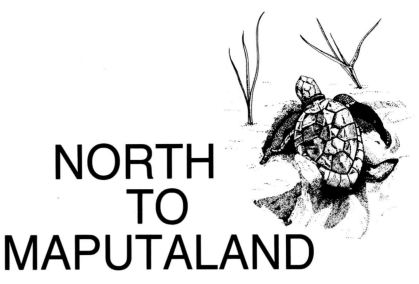

NORTH TO MAPUTALAND

ESTUARIES AND CORAL REEFS

The coastal strip of northern Natal just to the south of the Mozambique border is known as Maputaland. Though it is generally infertile and the land difficult to farm, the sea here offers a generous alternative. At Kosi Bay a channel links it with a complex network of lakes and estuaries comprising the so-called 'Kosi system', which provides nursery areas for many fishes. Juveniles of such marine fishes as grunter, perch and pouters, as well as different species of mullet, enter the system seeking food and shelter, and in so doing provide the local Thonga people with their main source of protein.

The Thonga have developed an ingenious method of harvesting the fish by way of communal traps, or fish kraals. Set up in the shallow, sandy channels which wind through the main entrance to the sea and through which the fish must pass, they are made of indigenous plants and creepers. A 'guide fence' of branches woven together is sunk in the water across the channel, in the middle of which the fence is shaped into a narrow funnel pointing upstream. At the end of the funnel a gap is left in which a basket is suspended. This is woven in the form of a valve, on the lobster-pot principle, so that the fish can enter but cannot escape. Tied in position with fronds of the Natal wild banana, the basket is left overnight. In the morning it is untied and carried to the shore, where the night's haul is tipped onto the bank. Depending on luck and the season, the catch may vary. Mullet

form the staple, but other species are sometimes caught in quantity. One recorded catch contained 62 large milkfish.

There are about 80 of these fish kraals at Kosi Bay, each bearing up to sixteen baskets. All are carefully maintained, and are handed down from father to son. Sometimes they are loaned out to relatives or friends. Almost every family has some connection with a kraal and access to its fish supply. A new kraal is carefully integrated into the existing system so that it does not reduce the fish flow through the other traps. When the new kraal is

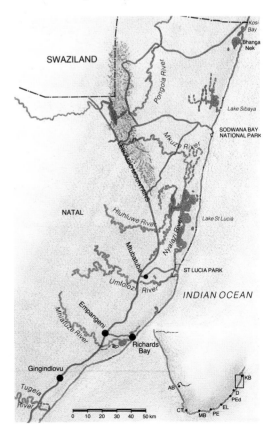

176. *Sunset over Richards Bay. The original lagoon area has been divided between a wildlife sanctuary and a large modern export harbour, part of which can be seen on the right of this view from the harbour control tower.*

installed, the local headman, or *induna*, is approached for his approval and official blessing. To prevent depletion of stocks, a channel about 30 metres across must be left clear in the centre of the main outlet to allow exit for a percentage of the fish.

Kosi Bay is only one of a series of important estuarine areas along this hot, subtropical coast. During the Cretaceous period some 100 million years ago, when the Indian Ocean reached to the foot of the Lebombo Mountains, this flat coastal plain lay beneath the sea, as is witnessed by coral deposits found far inland. When the coastal terrace was raised in later eras a ridge of coastal dunes developed along

its front, isolating a broad, low-lying plain between mountains and sea. Rivers ran down from the mountains and out across the plain, creating large, shallow lakes. From south to north, the most important of these are Richards Bay, Lake St Lucia, Lake Sibaya, and the complex of four interlinked lakes and the estuary at Kosi Bay. With the exception of Lake Sibaya, these lakes are connected with the sea to varying degrees and are influenced by its salinity and the rise and fall of the tide. Floods also have their effect when rivers such as the Pongola and Mkuze burst their banks, annually inundating the surrounding plains.

In this 7 000-square kilometre corner of southern Africa is found a vast variety of plants and animals. For example, in the Ndumu Game Reserve to the north-west is a dense wilderness of forest and water, inhabited by elephants and crocodiles. Here are found thick stands of the lala palm, while in the central floodplain region are communities of *Phragmites* reeds and papyrus. Reptiles are legion, from small skinks and burrowing snakes to the two-metre forest cobra and the ominous five-metre African python. A familiar scavenger in lakes and rivers is the water leguaan, which often eats crocodile eggs and hatchlings. In the

coastal lakes and estuaries there are over 200 species of birds and fishes, as well as eight species of snake and four kinds of terrapin.

Human history appears tenuous in the face of all this natural history. We do not know when local tribes such as the Thonga and the Tembe first came here, but they have long inhabited this region as well as what is today southern Mozambique. They lived a simple, somewhat slow existence in their fever-infested forests and swamps, their pace of life further decelerated by a passion for lala palm wine. Besides trapping fish in the estuaries and on the plains during the

178

floods, they practised a kind of 'shifting cultivation'. In this, an area of bush was burned and the relatively rich mixture of wood ash and humus left behind was sown with sorghum, millet, maize and groundnuts. When depleted, the area was abandoned and another patch of forest burned.

The smoke from these fires was noticed from a distance by early Portuguese mariners plying their long journey to the east, and it was they who dubbed this part of the coast 'Terra dos Fumos', the 'Land of Smoke'. The mouth of the Kosi Bay lakes they christened the 'Rio de la Medãos do Ouro', or the 'River of the Sands of Gold'. This romantic name has been scratched from the charts, but survives in abbreviated form eight kilometres to the north of Kosi Bay as the 'Ponto do Ouro', the headland which divides the coast of South Africa from that of Mozambique. A small lighthouse marks the spot where the sands, golden by day, glow with phosphorescence by night.

Observing the 'Land of Smoke' from the distance was one thing, but coming ashore was another. The area was not only home to many dangerous animals, but was infested with bilharzia, malaria, and the latter's extreme and fatal form, blackwater fever. European penetration of this fever-ridden, crocodile-rich swampland was thus understandably slow. Various intrepid explorers entered the area, and some even emerged alive. Then, in the mid-Nineteenth Century, one came to stay. A German trader named Bruheim arrived in the forest, which at the time was ruled by a chief called Noziyingili. Adopted by the tribe under the name of

177. *A Thonga fisherman services one of the 80 or so fish kraals in the mouth of the estuary at Kosi Bay.* **178.** *Weaving a 'guide fence' into which the basket of the fish trap will be set. Held in common by Thonga families, the fish kraals are carefully maintained.*

'Madevu', the European married one of the chief's daughters. After Noziyingili's death in 1877 'Madevu', recalling the ways of his own ancestors, coolly extracted from the chief's widow a concession giving him ownership of the Kosi lakes.

By this time the notion that a use might be found for this beautiful wilderness had occurred to a number of imperial spirits further south. In particular, the potential for a harbour at Kosi Bay had been recognized. The same idea had come to the Portuguese at Delagoa Bay, and with the increase of British influence in Natal a boundary squabble broke out. In 1875 the French President, Comte Edme de MacMahon, settled the dispute. In the rôle of final arbitrator he drew a line from the Usutu River in the west to the Ponto do Ouro in the east, a decision which, without their knowledge, divided the Thonga in half.

Today the area is divided into the magisterial districts of Ingwavuma in the north and Ubombo in the south. Some ambiguity exists over the name of the region as a whole. The name 'Thonga', strictly, is a misnomer, since it was originally used by the Zulu as a blanket term for those tribes, generally defeated, to the north of them. Such connotations have led to the replacement of the title 'Tongaland' by that of 'Maputaland', favoured by the KwaZulu authorities under whom the region falls.

If the 1875 decision blithely split the Thonga in half, the latest and even more procrustean move, this time on the part of the South African government, has been to give them away. On 14 June 1982 the Minister of Co-operation and Development, without prior consultation with the parties concerned, announced to the KwaZulu Legislative Assembly the government's intention of ceding the Ingwavuma District, including the Ndumu Game Reserve, the northern part of the Lebombo Mountains, the Sihangwana Forest, Lake Sibaya and Kosi Bay, as well as most of the Thonga population, to Swaziland.

The announcement of this 'land deal' came out of the blue and shook up a storm of protest. The result was a Supreme Court action and appeal leading to a ruling that the government had acted beyond its powers. The political future of the area, however, remains far from certain. Swaziland is landlocked. Inevitably, Kosi Bay would become its harbour and the outlet for its produce. But a commercial and political 'corridor' across the Ingwavuma District would cut through one of the subcontinent's most

179

179. *Unperturbed by the crash of waves, Thonga women explore the rocky shore for the gifts of the sea, fish, mussels and octopus. Like the Xhosa on the Transkei coast, the Thonga depend heavily on the sea as a source of food.*

180

181

180. *A local fisherwoman displays her catch, a distinctively patterned ladder wrasse. Grunter, mullet, bream and milkfish are also common catches in this area.* **181.** *Sifting through the day's gleanings.*

182. *Originally an estuary, Lake Sibaya has long been cut off from the sea, and now relies on a fresh-water source. A number of estuarine animals have shown remarkable tolerance of these unfamiliar conditions.*

valuable surviving wilderness areas and would, in effect, destroy it as an entity.

The problems of bringing the Twentieth Century into a region as yet unprepared for it have already been well exemplified in the past decade with the development of the harbour at Richards Bay. Named after the British naval commander during the Zulu War of 1879, the bay lies some 190 kilometres up the coast from Durban. In its original form, before the building of the harbour, it was dominated by a large lagoon, a sedimentary basin covering about 3 500 hectares and varying in depth from 0,25 to 1,25 metres, with a deeper channel around its margin. At its north-eastern edge it was linked by a channel to the sea. A number of rivers fed in fresh water, creating deltaic areas of silt. On the northern side, the Mzingazi River brought water down from Lake Mzingazi, while the catchment area to the south-west was dominated by the Mhlatuze River.

The banks of the lagoon were generally low-lying and marshy, overgrown with thick swamp vegetation, mangroves and reeds, particularly in the region of the swamp at the mouth of the Mhlatuze River. In the entrance channel linking the lagoon with the bay beyond were large beds of eelgrass, *Zostera.*

Richards Bay was a typical estuarine environment, showing a gradient of salinity ranging from the salt tidal area at the mouth to fresh water in the west. Some 180 species of marine fish had been recorded in the lagoon, a great number of which took advantage of the 'nursery'

conditions of food and shelter, especially in the *Zostera* beds. To the west were many fresh-water fishes, mangrove animals and reed-dwelling birds. Not all were small. The freshwater-tolerant Zambezi shark was a frequent predator, hippos were numerous and crocodiles flourished. The largest South African crocodile on record, a specimen over seven metres in length, was shot here.

The spectacular natural wealth of Richards Bay has long been recognized. In 1935 the lagoon was proclaimed a game reserve, and in 1945 an area on its northern shore became the Richards Bay Park. Although the needs of the animals received recognition, so did the ambitions of man. As early as 1826, two traders in ivory, King and Isaacs, had made abortive plans to develop the area. And in 1897 a detailed survey was carried out to examine its potential as a harbour. Twice the area of Durban Bay, the lagoon was sheltered and, although the mouth was only three metres deep, it could be dredged to accommodate large vessels. Another survey in 1902 confirmed these findings, and it became only a matter of time before economic and industrial expansion put theory into practice.

This process began in 1970, when the South African government announced the intention to develop Richards Bay as a harbour. There were a number of pressing reasons. An outlet was needed for coal mined in the Transvaal, as well as for other minerals. Export facilities were also needed for the increasing industry of

Zululand. Besides this, the projected harbour offered employment for many thousands of people.

The announcement caused immediate reaction, from the general public as well as from environmentalists, and led to a major debate on the issues involved. In August 1970, under the aegis of the Council for Scientific and Industrial Research, a number of organizations were brought together. They included, besides representatives of the CSIR itself, the South African Railways and Harbours, who would be responsible for the building of the harbour, the Richards Bay Town Board, the Town and Regional Planning Commission of Natal, the Zoology Department of the University of Cape Town, and the Oceanographic Research Institute of Durban.

The crucial questions to be thrashed out were those of the preservation of the ecology of the lagoon, and the effects of possible pollution. Inevitably, the harbour would alter the existing ecological balance. The gradient of salinity in the lagoon in particular would have to be preserved if the spectrum of animals was to be retained. It was also imperative that marine creatures should have continued access to the estuary as a nursery area.

A suggestion was put forward which appeared to satisfy all parties. The lagoon area would be divided between man and nature by a large earth barrier or 'berm', some four kilometres in length, erected from west to east across the lagoon and joining the shore below the mouth. To the north of this dyke the new harbour would be sited, while the remaining 1 200 hectares to the south would be a sanctuary for the animals.

For the harbour engineers this concept had solid advantages. It promised a reduction in the amount of silt reaching the harbour, especially from the Mhlatuze River. It would make the berthing of ships easier because of reduced wave action, and the berm would also provide road and rail access to the important coal-loading area. At the same time, from the ecological point of view, it had the advantage of sealing the animals off from the effects of harbour activity, including pollution.

It would, however, isolate the lagoon from its original opening to the sea, since this would now be the harbour mouth. It was therefore proposed that a new channel be cut through the dunes to the south of the eastern end of the berm so that tidal action, access for juvenile marine organisms, and the estuary's salinity gradient could be guaranteed. In effect, the original structure of the lagoon would be preserved, but on a smaller scale. As an additional aid to this balance, control gates were to be introduced at a point in the berm to regulate salinity and wave action between harbour and sanctuary.

On paper at least, all this looked good. One point, though, troubled ecologists at the meeting. The Mhlatuze River, the main fresh-water source to the south-west of the lagoon, fed its waters out through a delta swampland in which grew thick stands of reeds and mangroves. During the regular heavy flooding which occurs here large quantities of silt were carried down through these swamps. The reeds and trees acted as a barrier to the silting up of the lagoon, as well as breaking up the onslaught of the floodwaters. But, for a number of reasons, part of the plan proposed by the engineers involved draining the swamps and canalization of the lower reaches of the river. The main road and railway from the south had to cross the swamp. At the same time it was necessary to ensure that floodwaters debouched into the sanctuary rather than adding their burden of silt to the harbour itself. Moreover, the land reclaimed from the swamp could be put to good use by the local sugar farmers.

The ecologists foresaw that the removal of the buffering and filtering function of the Mhlatuze swamp might well have disastrous consequences, both for the plants and animals of the sanctuary and for the farmers. The plan as mooted, however, was accepted, and building of the harbour commenced.

Its construction was a model of speed and efficiency. The enormous earthen berm was thrown up, dividing the original lagoon. The Mhlatuze swamp was drained, the river canalized, and the land around it reclaimed. A new mouth was cut to link the sanctuary with the sea, while the original mouth of the lagoon was dredged deeply to create the harbour entrance. The channel thus formed was continued in a straight line across the lagoon, to end in a ships' turning circle of 500 metres radius. This design allows a loaded bulk carrier of 250 000 tonnes deadweight to enter the harbour under adverse sea and wind conditions at the seven knots needed to keep the vessel correctly on course. Two rubble headlands were built out into the sea north and south of the entrance, protecting it from heavy wave action and reducing turbulence within the harbour itself. Control gates under a 40 metre-span bridge were introduced into the berm, and a series of flood-control and water supply dams were built on the Mhlatuze River to supplement the supply to Richards Bay and to irrigate the cane fields planted on the reclaimed land.

Completed in 1976, the harbour has fulfilled its economic promise, and more. Collateral industries have sprung up around it, and job opportunities for thousands of people have been created. Each year a staggering 24 million tonnes of export coal are transported some 500 kilometres from the Transvaal coalfields in 4 000-tonne trainloads, each of which can be unloaded in less than an hour. Other bulk materials now being shipped from Richards Bay include pig iron, titanium slag, phosphoric acid, rutile and zircon. Besides berths for clean and dirty cargoes, others have been built to handle tanker and containerized loads. Three massive quays have been equipped with multi-purpose handling machinery, and the elaborate control system allows for continuous simultaneous truck-offloading, dumping and cargo-loading.

Both before and since the building of the harbour, South African Railways and Harbours engineers were co-operative and sensitive to ecological needs. Pollution, for example, has been kept to a minimum and has had little effect on the animals. Siltation, though, has been another matter, and ecologists' misgivings about the canalization of the Mhlatuze were soon borne out. In the summer of 1976 sugar farmers, well established on the land reclaimed from the river's swamps, were overwhelmed by sudden and violent floods. Without the restraining effect of the original marsh vegetation, a vast mass

of water and silt hurtled down, tearing down the banks of the canal and washing away many hectares of valuable sugar cane. The main road bridge over the Mhlatuze, linking Richards Bay with Durban, was swept away. And some 3,2 million tonnes of silt were dumped into the estuary, forming a huge delta.

This was an ecological shock of the first magnitude to both man and beast. While sugar farmers totted up the cost, ecologists also took stock. Silt had caused about half the sanctuary to be exposed at low tide, and the situation was made worse by further floods in 1977. Two-thirds of the sanctuary area is now exposed at low tide, while water covers the remainder to a depth of only a few centimetres. At the same time, the impact of the floodwaters has scoured away and enlarged the mouth of the sanctuary, allowing an increased tidal effect.

What was once a tidal estuary is now being turned into a salt marsh, with an accompanying change in the balance of the animal life. For the farmers there appears little long-term solution to their

183. *A Nile crocodile leaving the water at Lake St Lucia. Sole survivors of the age of the large reptiles, these animals, which grow to great size in this area, are rigorously protected.*

184

184. *A lone goliath heron, the largest of the heron family, ponderously wings its way over the St Lucia estuary, one of the richest areas of birdlife on the coast.* **185.** *A flock of yellow-billed storks, summer visitors to South Africa, work the muddy shallows for their prey of invertebrates and fish.* **186.** *A rarer species than the white pelican, a family of pink-backed pelicans gathers on a mudbank.*

185

186

dilemma, but there are hopeful signs that nature is adjusting to the changes. These adjustments are being watched and recorded with interest by scientists, who see the sanctuary as a large-scale laboratory for the study of ecological impact.

Whereas the initial effect of the floods was to drown most of the mangroves and many of the other swamp plants, the new delta created by siltation is rapidly being colonized by new mangroves, assisted by artificial transplantation of seedlings from other areas. With time, the reeds and mangroves will resume the filtering function once performed by the Mhlatuze swamps, allowing the river to make its way more leisurely to the sea. Many waders and water birds, from pelicans and flamingoes to goliath herons, have already been attracted to the area. And recent surveys have shown a recovery in the fish life, indicating that the sanctuary may regain its former strength as a nursery, if only in the channels and inlets in the swamp.

Even without man, these coastal lakes often come under stress. Fifty kilometres up the coast from Richards Bay is the famous Lake St Lucia, fed largely by the Mkuze River which rises on the slopes of the Hlobane Mountains and flows eastwards through the Lebombo range before veering southwards to join 'eCwebeni', the 'lagoon'. The complex here comprises two main lakes, False Bay to the west and Lake St Lucia proper to the east. These are linked by a channel popularly known as Hell's Gate, once the haunt of hippo and crocodile hunters.

The main lake is 40 kilometres from north to south, 10 kilometres across, and an average of 2 metres deep. Three islands dot its surface: Bird Island, Lane Island and Fanie's Island, named after a local Zulu chief. The southern end of the lake opens into an estuary which follows a winding course to the sea close to the mouth of the Umfolozi River.

The almost 37 000-hectare extent of the lake was declared an official game reserve as early as 1897, and in 1939 a kilometre-wide strip of land around the lake was also proclaimed, as the St Lucia Park. A further 2 247 hectares of False Bay were incorporated in 1944. Until recently the northern part of the lake was the site of a missile-testing installation. This is being progressively phased out, though the main area remains closed to the public.

St Lucia is positively heavy with wildlife. The reserves are the home of many animals, of reedbuck, nyala, suni, bushbuck, steenbok, duiker and bushpig. Over 25 species of aquatic birds are found here, with pelicans, flamingoes, fish eagles, geese, ducks, herons, cormorants and kingfishers being especially prolific. Crocodiles breed in large numbers, particularly near the mouths of the tributary rivers, and there is a 400-head population of hippo. Large game fish and the menacing Zambezi shark abound in the estuary area to the south.

The lake supports all these animals in style, but it exacts a price. The major problem faced by the plants and animals here is that of evaporation. The lake receives fresh water from its tributary rivers, from the run-off from the

187

surrounding land, and from rain. A number of man's activities have reduced this supply, river water having been diverted for irrigation, to plantations of timber, and into storage dams. All these diversions have exacerbated an already acute problem of high salinity. Immense evaporation takes place in this hot climate, and in periods of drought salt concentrations in the water may reach lethal levels for the shoals of mullet, bream, grunter and salmon. In the main lake complex a salinity of 120 parts per thousand has been recorded, almost four times that of sea water and over twice the 55 parts per thousand which is the limit of tolerance for most marine creatures. The situation may be further aggravated by the closing up of the estuary mouth, preventing access of sea water.

In the normal course, rainfall and floods eventually restore the balance, lowering the salinity of the lakes and flushing out the estuary, reconnecting it with the sea. With the increased demands of local agriculture, though, the incidence of lethal salinities has increased. Several practical solutions have been suggested, of which the most viable would be the release of water from storage dams in time of drought. The human demand being what it is, however, this scheme is likely to remain largely an ideal.

North of Lake St Lucia is the Sodwana Bay National Park. Its name comes from a small stream, the 'Sodwana', meaning 'the little one on its own'. Proclaimed in 1950, it is a 413-hectare coastal strip of forest-clad dunes where species such as the Natal wild banana and the coastal red

milkwood tree are interspersed with cycads, including *Encephalartos ferox*. Intensely hot and humid in the summer months, the area is home to a number of antelope, such as reedbuck, steenbok and suni. The small Lake Mgobezeleni at Sodwana also supports a remarkably rich fauna of fish and riverine animals.

Further north is Lake Sibaya, which is of particular interest to marine scientists. Originally an estuary, changes in sea-level cut it off from the sea and the lake is now fed only by fresh water. Despite this, a number of estuarine animals continue to inhabit it quite happily, including crabs, amphipods and planktonic copepods. The crab *Hymenosoma orbiculare*, for example, is an estuarine creature that has the ability to regulate the concentration of salt in its tissues, enabling it to live in Lake Sibaya.

The final stretch of the northern Zululand coast, the chain of lakes at Kosi Bay and the 'River of the Sands of Gold', also forms an appropriate climax to the 4 600 kilometre-long mosaic of sandy beaches and rocky shores, of islands, estuaries and headlands which make up the coast of southern Africa. The name 'Kosi' originated in a mistake by an early marine surveyor, who marked it on his charts as the mouth of the Mkuze or, as he had it, the 'omKosi', River. The whole system occupies 3 500 hectares of coastal plain and drains a catchment area of about 500 square kilometres. The soils here are mostly leached acid sands, with the result that Kosi Bay is almost entirely silt-free, in contrast to most of the other Natal estuaries.

The Kosi system comprises a series of four lakes running from south to north parallel to the coast for approximately 18 kilometres. Each lake has its own character and degree of salinity, and therefore its own specific mix of aquatic life. Southernmost is a peat-stained, fresh-water lake named 'Amanzimnyama', meaning 'dark water'. Next is 'Nhlange', the 'reedy lake', which is the largest, being about eight kilometres long and more than 30 metres deep. The lake closest to the sea, from which it is separated at Bhanga Nek by only 250 metres of sand dunes, it is also distinguished by having the 20-hectare Kosi Bay Nature Reserve on its shores. North of Nhlange two smaller lakes, joined by channels, lead to the estuary proper and the three-kilometre channel opening into the sea. The setting for the Thonga fish kraals, the Kosi mouth is known locally as 'EnKovugeni', the 'up and down action of the water'.

There are many distinct plant communities in the area. The swamp forests in particular are unique, and include the magnificent swamp fig and the umdoni, or water berry. Under these trees grow thick tangles of ferns and wild orchids, including rare species such as the climber *Tiliacora funifera* and the orchid

187. *A brilliant yellow weaver bird perches watchfully at its nest in the Sodwana Bay National Park, north of Lake St Lucia.*
188. *A group of hippos surface in the warm, shallow waters at the head of the estuary at Lake St Lucia.* **189.** (Overleaf) *The turtle nesting beaches at Bhanga Nek, where only 250 metres of sand dunes separate the Kosi lake system from the sea.*

Platylepsis australis. There is also a small but important stand of mangroves at Kosi, about 32 hectares in extent. Of the five species represented here, three are already familiar from the southern Natal coast: the dominant *Avicennia marina,* and the smaller *Bruguiera gymnorrhiza* and *Rhizophora mucronata.* Two others are of special interest since they occur here at the southern limit of their distribution and are found nowhere else in South Africa. These are the Indian mangrove, *Ceriops tagal,* and the Thonga mangrove, *Lumnitzera racemosa.*

One of the most important members of this swamp community is the Kosi palm, of which the largest concentration in southern Africa, covering 50 hectares, is at Lake Amanzimnyama. Until the 1960s this tree was identified with *Raphia vinifera,* a West African species whose sap is used in the fermenting of a particularly ferocious kind of palm wine. It was also speculated that it had been planted here centuries ago by Arab traders working down the east coast. In 1969, however, the Kosi palm was recognized as a distinct species indigenous to Mozambique and northern Zululand.

It is a striking and beautiful tree, soaring up to 15 metres and bearing enormous leaves up to 10 metres long and about 60 centimetres broad. Like the mangrove, it has special 'breathing roots' which grow upwards from water level and enable the palm to flourish in swamps. Other roots grow from the axils of lower leaves, penetrating the fibrous lower trunk of the tree to form a five centimetre-thick mat. Not only do the trees form dense waterside communities, but each comprises a vegetal society of its own, playing host to many other plants. Humus collects between the sheath at the base of the leaf and the trunk, and rain water runs down into it along a groove in the leaf, providing ideal conditions for the growth of a variety of ferns, including one of the world's most primitive land plants, *Psilotum nudum.*

The Kosi palm is monocarpic, that is, it bears fruit only once in its lifetime and then dies. Prior to this, it takes from 20 to 30 years to reach maturity and flower. Understandably, flowering is a serious business, and the Kosi palm performs it on a grand scale. Enormous inflorescences develop, from which up to 10 000 fruits, weighing about 270 kilograms in total, form on each fruiting plume. As the seeds ripen the tree dies, slowly collapsing before being brought down by the wind, its fall scattering seeds over a wide area.

Each fruit is about four centimetres long

190

and covered in scales, beneath which is a spongy yellow material enclosing the seed. This sweet, sticky substance has an enthusiastic adherent in a local swamp bird, the palmnut vulture, the rarest bird breeding in southern Africa. An aerial survey carried out in May 1982 revealed only ten adults. Sometimes classed as an eagle, it is more probably related to the Old World vulture and is a handsome creature, with a white abdomen, black back and a rounded black tail tipped with white. Its name is well earned, for though it eats crabs, molluscs and the general carrion washed up on the shore of the lake, the passion of its life is the oily husk

192

around the nut of the Kosi palm. It ensures itself a supply of these by building its nest at the top of the tree, close to one of the fruit-bearing plumes. Here it feeds its young exclusively on the husks, the whole family tearing and gobbling with gusto.

A few kilometres from the lakes and rivers of the Kosi system, across the dunes, lie the open sea and the 'golden sands' of the early navigators. Here, along a 50-kilometre stretch of beach, but particularly in the area of Bhanga Nek, takes place one of the mysteries of the sea, the nesting of the loggerhead and leatherback turtles.

Five sea turtles occur in southern African waters. Three of these, the hawksbill, green and olive ridley turtles, are occasional visitors only as, although they are sometimes stranded, they do not voluntarily come ashore. The loggerhead turtle and the leatherback, however, come ashore here to lay their eggs in the sand. By the standards of endangered species, the loggerhead is relatively common. The leatherback is more rare, and also has the distinction of being the world's largest turtle, and one of the largest living reptiles. Twice the length and about six times the weight of the loggerhead, the leatherback can reach an awesome size – the world record specimen, caught off California, was nearly three metres long and weighed 865 kilograms.

For many years these animals, helpless while on land, were remorselessly hunted for their flesh and shells. The result was a critical drop in their numbers. In the 1966 season, for example, only five female leatherbacks came ashore at Bhanga Nek to nest. By then, however, action had been taken to protect them. Game rangers from the nearby Kosi Bay Park patrol the beach during the nesting season, with the result that a dramatic increase in numbers has been observed. The leatherbacks have increased from five to over 80, while loggerhead numbers have risen from

about 200 to a healthy 400. Meanwhile, tagging of the animals has been carried out, giving scientists a record of their movements and a clearer idea of their life cycle.

These turtles travel far afield, ranging from Zanzibar in the north to Cape Agulhas in the south, a distance of some 4 700 kilometres along Africa's eastern seaboard. They have even been found in Madagascar, across the Mozambique Channel. But every year, after mating, the females return to their ancient nesting place on the Maputaland coast. They are drawn by instinct to the beaches where countless generations of their egg-shells have impregnated the sand with their scent. Carried down into the sea, this helps to guide the animals ashore. They arrive exhausted, and often torn and bleeding from the attacks of sharks and other predators. But they will leave the water only if conditions, particularly the sea temperature, are right. The nesting season is linked with the warming of the Agulhas Current, which takes place in early summer. This ensures that the young emerge when the sea temperature has reached its maximum, in about March, and also when the Agulhas is closest inshore. If the sea temperature is below normal, hatching is postponed, but if conditions are right several hundred female turtles make their way up the beach, lumbering clumsily away from their natural medium. In the warm sand they scrape holes in which they each lay upwards of 600 eggs in a season. Over a lifetime of about 18 years, averaging six laying seasons, this can total 3 600 eggs.

When the eggs are laid, the mother turtle covers them with sand before returning to the sea. An incubation period of four months follows, then the three centimetre-long hatchlings emerge, usually at night. They struggle out of the nesting hole and scramble down to the ocean, where they are swept away by the Agulhas Current into the great gyre of the

Indian Ocean. They have been found, still no more than six centimetres long, some 1 600 kilometres from the beaches at Bhanga Nek. Only as adults do they return to South African waters. At least, those which survive return, for of every thousand hatchlings, only two reach adulthood.

The turtles are a gift of the tropical seas, carried by the power of the Mozambique Current past the Tropic of Capricorn, the normal southern limit of tropical conditions. Another gift of these warm, clear waters is the offshore coral reefs, which create an exotic submarine environment inhabited by a colourful variety of animals.

Corals are tiny polyps belonging to the sub-class Zoantharia, of the phylum Cnidaria. Related to sea anemones and jelly fish, they share many features in common with them. Two characteristics of coral polyps, however, give them a unique importance. Firstly, while a few species are solitary, the majority are colonial, forming extensive and closely integrated communities. Secondly, these colonies are housed in a continuously growing structure created by the polyp itself. Absorbing calcium from the water around it, the polyp forms a calcium carbonate shell or cup which acts as an external skeleton inside which it retreats when threatened. It is these hermatypic corals, members of the order Madreporaria, which build some of the most spectacular underwater reefs.

Only a small percentage of a coral reef is composed of living animals. When the polyp dies, its shell remains as a base for the growth of further generations. The result is a graveyard of untold millions of limestone skeletons supporting a layer of living polyps. The scale on which this principle operates can be awe-inspiring. The Great Barrier Reef of Australia consists of more than three thousand coral islands. Equally impressive are the many coral islands and atolls of Oceania, for some of these have kept pace for millions of years with the subsidence of the sea-bed, rising hundreds of metres through a constantly renewed surface growth. The corals of the Maputaland coast, while no less dazzling in their variety, are more modest in scale. Moreover, they are

190. *Butterflyfish of the genus* Chaetodon *are characteristically exotic denizens of the richly stocked Maputaland coral reefs.* 191. *Despite being more agile in water than on land, loggerhead turtles come ashore annually in their hundreds to lay their eggs in the sand in the Bhanga Nek area.* 192. *The brilliant colours of this* Pseudochromis *species vie with the softer shades of the coral.*

193

195

194

196

193. The sharp spines of the spectacular firefish, Pterois antennata, bear a poison that, although rarely fatal to humans, can cause painful wounds. **194.** A shoal of fishes finds food and shelter among the branches of the staghorn coral, Acropora. A remarkable 1 200 species of fish, over 80 per cent of those found in southern African waters, live in this coral habitat.
195. The gorgeously coloured clownfish, Amphiprion, lives among the stinging tentacles of an anemone and aggressively defends it against other intruding clownfish.
196. Wall-to-wall zoanthids, Zoanthus natalensis. These polyps, relatives of the anemones, are linked together to form large colonies. **197.** Zoanthids are a particular feature of the rocky shore in Natal, where they form continuous sheets low in the intertidal zone.

anchored not to the sea floor, but to underwater offshore sandstone reefs which provide them with physical support and a buffer against wave action.

Despite its warmth, the tropical current in this area is not rich in nutrients, and competition for food is intense. The life of a coral colony is a long, slow scramble for space, food and light, against the demands of other species. Territorial aggression can take the form of the overgrowing and smothering of one colony by another, or of stinging campaigns between rival communities. Competition has also led to structural differentiation among the species. *Acropora* species, for example, escape from the pressures lower down by rising on a 'stem' to the shape of a flat-topped thorn tree near the surface of the water. Other branched corals include the aptly named staghorn corals which are branched in a number of ways, depending

on the genus. *Stylophora*, for example, has flat branches, while a common genus in this region, *Pocillopora*, features branches with projecting knobs. *Pavana* forms scroll-like plates, while *Galaxia* develops small turrets, crowned with spine-like septa. The branched design aids exposure to sunlight, but makes the corals more vulnerable to wave action. Staghorn corals thus tend to grow in more sheltered areas. The brain corals, on the other hand, form tightly packed clusters resembling a human brain, giving them a strong resistance to wave action.

Equipped with tentacles around a mouth which also doubles as an anus, the polyp is a simple animal, with modest nutritional needs. Some are filter-feeders, dependent on the flow of zooplankton brought by the tropical current. The brain coral is a nocturnal carnivorous filter-feeder which emerges at night to feed as

the plankton rises to the surface. In almost all the polyps, however, up to half the animal's energy needs is supplied from an unusual source, from microscopic unicellular algae called zooxanthellae which live in its tissues. Besides food, the algae provide a number of other useful services to the polyp. They dispose of nitrogenous waste products and carbon dioxide given off in respiration. They also release compounds such as glucose, alanine and glycerol, which can be used by the polyps and indirectly assist in the formation of the calcium carbonate shell — for this reason corals grow in warm, shallow waters where photosynthesis of the algae can take place sufficiently fast to supply the needs of the reef-building corals.

Within the framework provided by the coral reefs lives a kaleidoscopic variety of other forms of marine life. In no other comparable area is there such a profusion of animals, from sea anemones to sea urchins, sea stars to serpent stars, from shrimps to rock lobsters to octopuses, from tiny boxfishes to rays and sharks. At least 1 200 species of fishes, representing over 80 per cent of all known southern African species, live here, an abundance rivalling the 1 500 species on the Great Barrier Reef.

In varying ways and degrees, these animals all make use of the coral in their strategy for survival. Some live directly on the polyps. Angelfish, triggerfish and butterflyfish, for example, devour the soft corals, while the hard corals are the speciality of the parrotfish, with its powerful 'beak'. Others rely on the reefs for shelter or as places of concealment from which to ambush their prey. One small crab, for example, has developed a commensal relationship with *Pocillopora*. Settled on the end of one of the branches, it is eventually surrounded by the living coral until only a narrow opening is left. The flute-mouthed butterflyfish has an elongated beak with which it probes the crevices for the small crustaceans which are its prey. Larger carnivores include the rockcod and the moray eel, their sharp teeth capable of being folded inwards to help their victims on their way. Stonefish and scorpion fish are equipped with 'hypodermic' spines which inject a powerful, and sometimes lethal, poison. Many of the fishes, such as snappers and soldierfish, are nocturnal hunters, spending the day resting in shoals in caves in the coral and emerging to hunt at night.

In the struggle for survival, nothing is wasted. Anything that falls from the table of the larger fishes is quickly snapped up

198

198. *Ghost crabs, normally nocturnal creatures, hunt for food at low tide on the sandy Zululand shore. They feed on almost any animal life and even scavenge.*

199

199. *The gaunt, wave-cut outline of a rock dominates an empty beach near Mission Rock, an area named after an erstwhile local mission station.* **200.** (Overleaf) *Painted surgeonfish, Acanthurus leucosternon, are equipped with sharp spines on either side of the tail. These can be erected to lacerate predators or unwary captors.*

by the smaller species. Specialists such as the cleaner shrimps *Stenopus hispidus* and *Periclimenes* form a symbiotic relationship with some larger animals, *Stenopus* removing dead scales and parasites from the fish, and *Periclimenes* forming a similar partnership with the giant anemone *Stoichactis*, gaining protection within its tentacles in return for its cleaning services. Cleaner fish, such as the cleaner wrasse, perform a similar function for their larger brethren, often swimming inside their open mouths to retrieve food particles or remove parasites. Both the cleaner shrimps and the cleaner fish are brightly coloured as a reminder to carnivores of their protected status. This beautiful relationship, however, can sometimes be marred by a third party. The sabre-toothed blenny, *Aspidontus taeviatus*, both resembles the cleaner wrasse and mimics its behaviour. Having gained the trust of a larger fish, instead of performing the expected cleaning operation, it takes a quick bite

out of its benefactor before darting away.

If forms of attack are varied, so are those of defence. An interesting example is the boxer crab, *Lybia plumosa*, which carries two small anemones in its front nippers, using them to ward off predators. Others use their colours to remind possible aggressors of the stings in their tails. Among these are the nudibranchs, the sea slugs. A great variety of these molluscs lives in the waters of the coral reefs, and they are among the most beautiful of all sea creatures. Having long dispensed with the protection of a shell or mantle, they rely instead on a toxic armoury. The sea hare, *Notarchus*, for example, when threatened emits an obnoxious purple fluid, guaranteed to repel the most determined attacker. The tough-skinned *Phyllidia varicosa* can kill a fish with its toxic flesh. Others, while not in themselves poisonous, borrow their venom from other creatures. Several nudibranch species, such as *Godiva quadricolor* and the elegant *Glaucus*

atlanticus, eat anemones and Portuguese men-o'-war respectively, and extract the stinging cells of their prey, storing them in their bodies for future use.

These are a few of the fascinating creatures which inhabit the underwater coral cities. Much remains to be learned about such communities, with their many hundreds of 'niches' in the food web. In time, many of these questions will doubtless be answered. Other questions, however, are likely to abide. Many areas of the coast of southern Africa have long felt the ambiguous hand of man, as his influence has spread, exploring, settling, exploiting, and sometimes destroying. True, he has learned to protect as well, but too often protection has followed tardily upon destruction. Perhaps here, though, on the coast of Maputaland, the sequence of the past will be reversed. Perhaps protection will precede exploitation and set a permanent limit upon it. In that happy event, natural history will indeed have been made.

REFERENCES

Allen, G. and Allen, D., *Clive's Lost Treasure*. Robin Garton and Co., London. 1978.

Bannister, A. and Gordon, R., *The National Parks of South Africa*. C. Struik, Cape Town. 1983.

Berjak, P., Campbell, G.K., Huckett, B.I., and Pammenter, N.W., *In the Mangroves of Southern Africa*. Natal Branch of the Wildlife Society of Southern Africa, Durban. 1977.

Blakey, G.G., *The Diamond*. Paddington Press, New York and London. 1977.

Branch, G. and Branch, M., *The Living Shores of Southern Africa*. C. Struik, Cape Town. Revised edition. 1984.

Bulpin, T.V., *Discovering Southern Africa*. T.V. Bulpin Publications, Cape Town. 1970. Revised and enlarged 1980.

Burman, J., *The False Bay Story*. Human and Rousseau, Cape Town and Pretoria. 1977.

Burman, J., *Strange Shipwrecks of the Southern Seas*. C. Struik, Cape Town. 1968.

Burman, J., *Great Shipwrecks off the Coast of Southern Africa*. C. Struik, Cape Town. 1967.

Burman, J. and Levin, S., *The Saldanha Bay Story*. Human and Rousseau, Cape Town and Pretoria. 1974.

Butler, G. Ed., *The 1820 Settlers. An illustrated commentary*. Human and Rousseau, Cape Town. 1974.

Cubitt, G. and Richter, J., *South West*. C. Struik, Cape Town. 1976.

Greenland, C., *The Story of Peers Cave*. Published by the author. Fish Hoek. 1978.

Grindley, J., *Riches of the Sea*. Caltex, Cape Town. 1969.

Hendey, Q.B., *Langebaanweg. A Record of Past Life*. Published by the South African Museum. 1982.

Henshilwood, N.G. Ill. Higgs, C., *Kelp Coast*. David Philip, Cape Town. 1976.

Inskeep, R.R., *The Peopling of Southern Africa*. David Philip, Cape Town. 1978.

Lees, R., *Fishing for Fortunes*. Purnell, Cape Town. 1969.

Life at the Cape a Hundred Years Ago. By a Lady. Centaur, Cape Town. 1983.

Louw, G. and Seeley, M., *The Ecology of Desert Organisms*. Longmans, London. 1982.

Richards, D., *South African Shells. A Collector's Guide*. C. Struik, Cape Town. 1981.

Ritter, E.A., *Shaka Zulu*. Longmans, London. 1955.

Smith, J.L.B., *The Sea Fishes of Southern Africa*. Central News Agency. 1953.

Smith, J.L.B., *Old Fourlegs. The Story of the Coelacanth*. Longmans Green, London. 1956.

Storrar, P., *Portrait of Plettenberg Bay*. Centaur, Cape Town. 1978.

Tietz, R.M. and Robinson, G.A., *Tsitsikamma Shore*. National Parks Board, Pretoria. 1974.

Van der Elst, R., *A Guide to the Common Sea Fishes of Southern Africa*. C. Struik, Cape Town. 1981.

Vogts, M., *South Africa's Proteaceae. Know them and grow them*. C. Struik, Cape Town. 1982.

Wallett, T., *Shark Attack in Southern African Waters and Treatment of Victims*. C. Struik, Cape Town. 1983.

Wilson, M. and Thompson, L., Ed., *The Oxford History of South Africa*. Oxford University Press, London. 1979.

MAGAZINES

African Wildlife. Published by the Wildlife Society of Southern Africa. Reference was made to the following issues for specific topics covered:
The fauna and flora of Maputaland. Vol. 36, Nos. 4/5. Jul/Aug – Sept/Oct, 1982.
The Knysna elephants. Vol. 36, No. 6. Nov/Dec, 1982.
De Hoop Vlei. Vol. 37, No. 1. Jan/Feb, 1983.

General and scientific consultant: George Branch, Associate Professor of Zoology, University of Cape Town
History consultant: Eric Axelson, Emeritus Professor of History

C. Struik (Pty) Ltd
Struik House, Oswald Pirow Street, Foreshore,
Cape Town 8000

First edition 1984

Copyright (text) © John Kench
Copyright (photographs) © Ken Gerhardt, except for the following which were provided from the files of: Gerald Allen (190, 192); Art Publishers, Durban (164); Audio Image, Durban (166); Anthony Bannister (10, 19, 25, 26, 28, 40, 48, 109, 119, 131, 175, 180, 181, 182, 189, 195, 196, 197, 198, 200, 201); George Branch (47, 86, 96, 123, 124, 126, 127); Pamela Newby (104); Oceanographic Research Institute, Durban (165, 167, 172, 177, 191); Colin Paterson-Jones (97, 98, 99, 100); Jack Randall (193, 194); Sea Fisheries Research Institute (50, 84); Maureen Smith (178); Rudy van der Elst (157, 179). Copyright for these photographs remains with the owners.

House editor: Leni Martin
Design by Walther Votteler, Cape Town
Maps and drawings by Anne Westoby, Cape Town
Typeset by McManus Bros (Pty) Ltd, Cape Town
Lithographic reproduction by Unifoto (Pty) Ltd, Cape Town
Printed and bound by Tien Wah Press (Pte) Ltd, Singapore

ISBN 086977 205 8

201. *A sunset envoi to subtropical shores, with the sea wind gently stirring the palm trees.*

INDEX

Scientific names of plants and animals are given in italic after the common names. Page numbers in italic refer to photographs.